T0305997

Decoding Organization

How was Bletchley Park made as an organization? How was signals intelligence constructed as a field? What was Bletchley Park's culture and how was its work co-ordinated? Bletchley Park was not just the home of geniuses such as Alan Turing, it was also the workplace of thousands of other people, mostly women, and their organization was a key component in the cracking of Enigma. Challenging many popular perceptions, this book examines the hitherto unexamined complexities of how 10,000 people were brought together in complete secrecy during World War II to work on ciphers. Unlike most organizational studies, this book decodes, rather than encodes, the processes of organization and examines the structures, cultures and the work itself of Bletchley Park using archive and oral history sources. Organization theorists, intelligence historians and general readers alike will find in this book a challenge to their preconceptions of both Bletchley Park and organizational analysis.

CHRISTOPHER GREY is Professor of Organizational Behaviour at the University of Warwick. He was previously Professor of Organizational Theory at the University of Cambridge and Fellow of Wolfson College. Professor Grey has published numerous academic articles on the sociology and history of management and organizations, on management education and learning, on critical management studies and on professional services organizations. He is the author of the bestselling student primer *A Very Short, Fairly Interesting and Reasonably Cheap Book about Studying Organizations* (2009, second edition).

Decoding Organization
Bletchley Park, Codebreaking and
Organization Studies

CHRISTOPHER GREY

CAMBRIDGE
UNIVERSITY PRESS

CAMBRIDGE
UNIVERSITY PRESS

University Printing House, Cambridge CB2 8BS, United Kingdom

One Liberty Plaza, 20th Floor, New York, NY 10006, USA

477 Williamstown Road, Port Melbourne, VIC 3207, Australia

314-321, 3rd Floor, Plot 3, Splendor Forum, Jasola District Centre, New Delhi - 110025, India

79 Anson Road, #06-04/06, Singapore 079906

Cambridge University Press is part of the University of Cambridge.

It furthers the University's mission by disseminating knowledge in the pursuit of education, learning and research at the highest international levels of excellence.

www.cambridge.org
Information on this title: www.cambridge.org/9781107005457

First published 2012
First paperback edition 2014

A catalogue record for this publication is available from the British Library

Library of Congress Cataloging in Publication data
Grey, Christopher, 1964–
Decoding organization : Bletchley Park, codebreaking and organization studies /
Christopher Grey.
pages cm
Includes bibliographical references and index.
ISBN 978-1-107-00545-7 (hardback)
1. Great Britain. Government Communications Headquarters – History.
2. World War, 1939–1945 – Cryptography. 3. World War, 1939–1945 – Secret
service – Great Britain. 4. World War, 1939–1945 – Electronic intelligence – Great
Britain. 5. Intelligence service – Social aspects – Great Britain – History – 20th
century. 6. World War, 1939–1945 – England – Bletchley
(Buckinghamshire) 7. Bletchley (Buckinghamshire, England) – History – 20th
century. 8. Corporate culture – England – Bletchley (Buckinghamshire) – History –
20th century. 9. Organization – Case studies. 10. Corporate culture – Case
studies. I. Title.
D810.C88G74 2012
940.5408641–dc23
2012000127

ISBN 978-1-107-00545-7 Hardback
ISBN 978-1-107-67675-6 Paperback

Dedicated to my mother, Madeleine Grey

The fact is that the process of 'cryptography' would perhaps better be described as interpretation.

Josh Cooper, Head of Air Section at Bletchley Park, 24 June 1941

Inherent in all good interpretations is the casting of new light on something that earlier has either escaped serious attention or been understood in a conventional and thus partly conservative way.

Alvesson and Deetz (2000: 152)

Contents

Acknowledgements

In the writing of this book I have incurred many debts. Before acknowledging these I should make it clear that any errors of fact or inadequacies of analysis are entirely my responsibility and in no way those of the individuals or organizations named below.

The first debt is to my friend and sometime colleague, Professor Andrew Sturdy of Bristol University. It was with him that I first visited Bletchley Park, leading to our joint research on its organization; with him that I worked in the (then) freezing cold Bletchley Park Trust Archives; with him that I published the initial studies that inform this book. When I had the opportunity to take the work forward on my own, he generously – and that is perhaps too weak a word – allowed me to make use of our earlier joint publications and he has been unstintingly supportive, both personally and intellectually, throughout the preparation of this book. I also thank him for commenting in detail and with great acuity on the drafts of the text; but most of all for his loyalty and friendship, which have not only contributed to the writing of this book but also immeasurably enriched my life.

I am also very grateful to Professor Glenn Morgan of Cardiff University and Dr Jana Costas of the Free University Berlin for having read drafts of the text. Having known Glenn since the far-off days when I wrote my Ph.D., I have long been aware of his immense intellectual breadth and insight, and his helpful and supportive comments on this book are greatly appreciated. Jana was at one time my Ph.D. student, but has long since out-grown my capacity to teach her anything, and to have the brightest star in the new generation of organization theorists comment extensively on my work has been a privilege and an education. She has also been unfailing in encouraging me during my periodic doubts and anxieties as I wrote this book.

The eminent historian of Second World War signals intelligence, Ralph Erskine, not only commented in great detail on much of the draft text but was also quite extraordinarily generous in answering my many queries and identifying or providing me with a great many documents and references, which aided me very considerably. His kindness in this is all the more remarkable for being based on a very slight acquaintance, and I am in awe of the profundity of his knowledge of the topic. This type of work is time-consuming, immensely valuable but all too often invisible, and it is appropriate to record here the considerable contribution he has made to this book; and indeed to Bletchley Park scholarship more generally.

Some detailed comments were also made on some of the early work on which this book is based by the late Peter Freeman, then the GCHQ Historian, and another person of profound knowledge about Bletchley Park, and I am grateful for these.

Dr Todd Bridgman, then of the University of Cambridge and now of Victoria University Wellington, New Zealand, and Dr Ruth Halperin, then of the London School of Economics, undertook with great diligence some literature review work which has been useful in the preparation of this text.

General support and encouragement, as well as some specific pieces of information, have been provided by Professor Richard Aldrich (Department of Politics and International Studies, University of Warwick), Tony Campbell (Campbell Intelligence Services, Canada and formerly, amongst many other things, Executive Director of Intelligence Assessment to the Canadian government) and Michael Herman (Nuffield College, Oxford and formerly GCHQ); these three distinguished people generously welcomed an interloper in the intelligence studies field into their midst, for which I am grateful.

I also appreciate the assistance of Tim Robinson, the grandson of Alan Bradshaw, head of administration at Bletchley Park; Jonathan Byrne, the Bletchley Park Trust Roll of Honour administrator; and

Eunan O'Halpin (Department of History, Trinity College, Dublin) in providing some specific pieces of information. I am particularly grateful to Mrs Mimi Gallilee, formerly of Bletchley Park, for donating to me some rare texts and a collection of obituaries, and whose commitment to keeping the memory of the work of Bletchley Park alive is profound. I am also very grateful to Dr Edward and Mrs Rebecca Simpson for explaining to me their work on Italian and Japanese ciphers at Bletchley Park.

Christine Large, formerly Director of the Bletchley Park Trust, assisted with securing access to Bletchley Park veterans and to the Bletchley Park Trust Archives, where archivist Steve Ovens was helpful and welcoming.

I am extremely grateful to the veterans of Bletchley Park who were interviewed for or otherwise contributed information to this study. They are not identified by their real names in the book, but they exemplify all the extraordinary qualities of their peers.

The early period of data collection was funded by the Nuffield Foundation via its Social Science Small Grants Scheme. That seed corn money proved invaluable. The later phases of the work were undertaken under the award of a Major Research Fellowship from the Leverhulme Trust. I cannot express strongly enough my appreciation of this award, without which this book would certainly not have been written. At a time when research funding is so heavily circumscribed by bureaucratic regulation, the willingness of the Leverhulme Trust to support projects such as this is beyond praise.

My colleagues at the start of this project at the University of Cambridge and in its latter phases at the University of Warwick have been a constant source of support, and in particular I would like to express my thanks to Sandra Dawson, Peter Fleming, Philip Stiles, John Roberts and Hugh Willmott (all then, and some still, at Cambridge); and to the Industrial Relations and Organizational Behaviour Group at Warwick and in particular to its Group Secretary, Joanna Sheehan.

I am grateful to my editor at Cambridge University Press, Paula Parish, for commissioning this book and for her trust and support throughout its writing, and to Caroline Mowatt for overseeing the exemplary production process.

I appreciate beyond words the boundless support and encouragement of my wife, Nathalie Mitev Grey. Her intellectual and emotional contribution, not just to this book but to everything that I do, can never be properly acknowledged nor repaid and is all the more valued for that. Last, but by no means least, I owe a great debt to my mother, Madeleine Grey, for a lifetime of unstinting support. This book, which she so enthusiastically encouraged me to write, is dedicated, with love, to her.

Abbreviations and Acronyms

AD:	Assistant Director (at BP)
AI:	Air Intelligence
AM:	Air Ministry
ATS:	Auxiliary Territorial Service (female branch of the army)
BP:	Bletchley Park
BPT:	Bletchley Park Trust
BPTA:	Bletchley Park Trust Archive
BTMC:	British Tabulating Machine Company
C:	Chief (i.e. Chief of SIS, correlating to the Director of GC & CS or, from 1944, the Director-General)
CBME:	Combined Bureau Middle East
CCAC:	Churchill College Archive Cambridge
CCR:	Cryptographic Co-ordination and Records (at BP)
CR:	Crib Room(s) (of Hut 6 at BP)
CSC:	Civil Service Commission
DD:	Deputy Director (at BP)
DD (C):	DD (Civil)
DD (S):	DD (Service)
DF or D/F:	Direction finding
DMI:	Director of Military Intelligence (at the War Office)
DNB:	(Oxford) Dictionary of National Biography
DNI:	Director of Naval Intelligence (at the Admiralty)
D & R:	Distribution and Reference Section (at BP)
E:	Enigma
FECB:	Far East Combined Bureau
FO:	Foreign Office
GAF:	German Air Force

GC & CS (sometimes GCCS):	Government Code and Cypher (sometimes Cipher) School
GCHQ:	Government Communications Headquarters
GPO:	General Post Office
HUMINT (sometimes Humint or humint):	Human intelligence
ID8G:	Intelligence Division 8G (also known as NID 8G)
IE:	Intelligence Exchange (at BP)
ISK:	Intelligence (or Illicit) Services, Knox
ISOS:	Intelligence (or Illicit) Services, Oliver Strachey
IWM:	Imperial War Museum
JCC:	Joint Committee of Control (at BP)
JIC:	Joint Intelligence Committee
JN-25:	Japanese Navy code assigned the number 25 by the US Navy
KCAC:	King's College Archive Cambridge
KIO:	Knowledge-intensive organization
MI:	Military Intelligence
MI1b:	Military Intelligence 1b (WO cryptanalytic branch in WW1)
MI5:	Military Intelligence 5 (also known as the Security Service)
MI6:	Military Intelligence 6 (also known as SIS)
MI8:	Military Intelligence 8 (signals intelligence service of the WO)
MI14:	Military Intelligence 14 (Germany desk)
MOI (sometimes MoI):	Ministry of Information
MOS:	Mass Observation Society

MOW (sometimes MoW):	Ministry of Works
MW:	Military Wing (i.e. army section at BP)
MR:	Machine Room(s) (of Hut 6 at BP)
NAAFI:	Naval, Army and Air Force Institutes
NID:	Naval Intelligence Division (at the Admiralty)
NID 8G:	Naval Intelligence Division 8G. Section set up to liaise between NS and OIC (also known as ID8G)
NID 25:	Naval Intelligence Division 25 (formal name for Room 40, the WW1 cryptanalytic section of the Admiralty)
NS:	Naval Section (at BP)
OIC:	Operational Intelligence Centre (at the Admiralty)
OSA:	Official Secrets Acts (of 1911 and 1920)
PRO:	Public Record Office (part of TNA)
RAF:	Royal Air Force
RN:	Royal Navy
RR:	Registration Room(s) (of Hut 6 at BP)
SIGINT (sometimes Sigint or sigint):	Signals intelligence
SIS:	Secret Intelligence Service (also known as MI6)
SIXTA:	Traffic Analysis Section (formerly No. 6 Intelligence School, hence 'six')
SCU:	Special Communications Unit
SLU:	Special Liaison Unit
TA:	Traffic analysis
TNA:	The National Archives of the United Kingdom
UKB:	*Umkehrwalze* B
UKD:	*Umkehrwalze* D
UPW:	Union of Postal Workers
WAAF:	Women's Auxiliary Air Force; or a member thereof

WO:	War Office
Wren (sometimes WREN):	A member of the WRNS
WRNS:	Women's Royal Navy Service
W/T:	Wireless telegraphy
WTI:	Wireless telegraphy intelligence
WW1:	World War One
WW2:	World War Two

Introduction: Organization Studies, History and Bletchley Park

> I suppose that if you were to put forward a scheme of organization for any service which laid down as its basis that it would take a lot of men and women from civil life and dress some of them in one kind of clothes and some of them in another, and told all those dressed in black that they came under one set of rules and all those dressed in white under another and so on, and then told them that they had a double allegiance, firstly to the ruler of their black or white or motley party and secondly to another man who would partly rule over all of them, but only partly, any ordinary tribunal would order you to take a rest cure in an asylum. But suppose that the tribunal were somehow foolish enough to adopt your idea and in order that you might begin your work said 'We will now lend you some tools – they may not be quite what you want but you must make do with them, and tell us when they get blunt and we'll see if we can sharpen them for you', some higher power would presumably lock up the tribunal as a public menace – or, if it were in Russia or Germany, shoot them out of hand. Yet that is in fact the precise organization of Bletchley Park. Now it happens that Bletchley Park has been successful – so successful that it has supplied information on every conceivable subject from the movement of a single mine sweeper to the strategy of a campaign and the Christian name of a wireless operator to the introduction of a secret weapon.
>
> *Nigel de Grey, Deputy Head of Bletchley Park, Memorandum of 28 March 1943*[1]

As its title implies, this book has two purposes. One is to explicate the 'decoding organization' at Bletchley Park, the place most famous for the breaking of Enigma ciphers in conditions of complete secrecy during the Second World War. The other is, in the process, to develop a certain approach to the analysis of organizations; a way of making sense of, or 'decoding', organization which points to a way of reviving organization studies as currently commonly conducted. In this sense it is a contribution to the social science of organizations and will primarily be of interest to academics working in that field. However, it should also have a value to those working in the area of intelligence studies and history, and an appeal to general readers with an interest in Bletchley Park[2].

The overall intention is to provide an interpretative analysis which draws on a broad range of concepts in organization studies whilst engaging in considerable historical detail in order to illuminate how 'organization' is achieved or accomplished over time. This is a 'decoding' of organization in that, like the codebreakers of Bletchley Park, an interpretive analysis seeks an answer to the question 'what does this mean?'. It entails considerable complexity; a complexity which is analytical, methodological and empirical. This lengthy opening chapter introduces this complexity by first introducing Bletchley Park, then indicating the problems and possibilities of organization studies. This is followed by a discussion of organization studies and history, and what the linkage of the two has to offer. This serves as a prelude to indicating the approach to historical analysis which I will adopt and the methods and sources of that analysis. There follows a brief overview of the organization of Bletchley Park and, finally, an outline of the contents of the rest of the book.

BLETCHLEY PARK AS A RESEARCH SITE

One reason for choosing Bletchley Park (BP[3]) as the focus for this analysis is the widespread public interest its activities command. This is both a blessing and a curse. The blessing is that the BP story is, in a dramatic sense, an extremely exciting one, filled with human interest and historical significance. George Steiner may have been hyperbolic in claiming that 'it looks as if Bletchley Park is the single greatest achievement of Britain during 1939–45, perhaps during [the twentieth] century as a whole' (Steiner, 1983: 42), but that such a claim could even be made is telling. The official historian of British intelligence in World War Two (WW2), Professor Sir Harry Hinsley, himself an important figure at BP, suggested that its work may have shortened the course of the war by two to four years (Hinsley, 1993a, 1993b), whilst noting the difficult and dubious nature of such counterfactual claims (Hinsley, 1993a: 2).

The dramatic qualities of BP have provided the inspiration for a successful novel, *Enigma* (Harris, 1995), which became in turn a major film of the same title in 2001, whilst another film, *U-571* (2000), fictionalized the capture at sea of an Enigma machine. Bletchley Park was satirized in the BBC radio comedy show *Hut 33*, first broadcast in 2007, and was the subject of a 1999 Channel Four TV documentary, *Station X*. The BP site is now a major museum attracting many thousands of visitors each year and is regularly in the news because of the enduring interest in its codebreaking achievements and contribution to the conduct of WW2, its role in the development of computing and not least because of public interest in its best known luminary, Alan Turing (Hodges, 1982). There is a stream of popular literature explaining what happened at BP (e.g. Smith, 1998; McKay, 2010) and a growing number of reminiscences of those who worked there (e.g. Welchman, 1982; Hinsley and Stripp, 1993; Calvocoressi, 2001; Page, 2002, 2003; Hill, 2004; Luke, 2005; Watkins, 2006; Paterson, 2007; Hogarth, 2008; Thirsk, 2008; Briggs, 2011; Pearson, 2011)[4].

The 'curse' is that out of all of this has grown a degree of mythologization and perhaps even sentimentalization of BP. One reason for the mythologization is the very peculiar circumstances of the secrecy that surrounded it. The work of BP was not publicly known until the mid 1970s (Winterbotham, 1974), with fuller details only emerging slowly over the following decades. Indeed, although most of the papers relating to BP are now declassified, some of what happened there remains secret and much which lies in the declassified papers remains unexamined. One consequence of this is that there are many contradictory accounts of particular details, not least because no reminiscences were published for so long after the event. Moreover, the complexity of its operations and the way that these operations were very rigorously compartmentalized for security reasons make grasping the totality of the BP story difficult and perhaps impossible: 'there is probably no one alive today who could do that, given the organizational structure of the Park at the time' (Enever, 1999: 2) The sentimentalization of BP is a more complex matter, and relates, I will suggest, to the dominant narrative of WW2 in British – in particular – society and its place in contemporary cultural apprehensions of British nationhood. At all events, there is a kind of fuzzy, generalized popular knowledge of BP, one aspect of which is captured by this humorous description in a spoof history book:

> At Bitchily and Tetchily Park, highly strung men and women in thick spectacles sat stooped over crossword puzzles and chessboards in chilly, poorly lit rooms throughout the night attempting to catch the famous Enigma cold (Brown, 2005: 46).

So this background presents both opportunities and problems for a book of this sort which seeks to approach BP from a very particular angle. Given that so much has been written about it, one might wonder whether anything new remains to be said. For, apart from the more popular accounts I have alluded to, there has also been a considerable amount of scholarship devoted to BP. These include studies of its significance for intelligence and military history (e.g. Hinsley, 1993c; Bennett, 1994; Budiansky, 2000; Freedman, 2000; Lewin, 2008), for diplomatic and strategic history more widely (e.g. Ferris, 2005) and for the development of cryptographic and cryptanalytic techniques (e.g. Kahn, 1996; Smith and Erskine, 2001) and of computing (e.g. Goldstine, 1993; Copeland, 2001; 2004; 2006). These and a host of other historical studies of BP have some relevance to this book, but none is a social-scientific account of BP. Moreover, none has my focus here, which is specifically concerned with BP's *organization*, which has had very little academic attention. Apart from my own work with Andrew Sturdy (Grey and Sturdy, 2008, 2009, 2010), from which this book has grown, the main exceptions are some brief but important remarks by Herman (1996), some passages in Andrew (1985a, 2001), a book chapter by Davies (2001) and, most significantly, several parts of Ratcliff's (2006) book. The latter compares British and German signals intelligence organization and also analyses why Germany did not realize that Enigma ciphers had been broken by the British.

However, as I have already indicated, the provision of an account of BP's organization is only one of my aims. My other is to use this as a kind of 'experiment' to develop a way of conducting organization studies. For, whilst this book deals with historical material, I am not an historian but an organizational theorist, and it is to those working in this field that this study is primarily addressed. Of course, this distinction between history and organizational theory is itself an issue which needs to be considered, and one of my arguments in this book is that there is much value in, and much more that can be done by, studying organization historically. I will turn to this shortly, but for now I want to elaborate upon what I mean by developing a way of conducting organization studies. It makes sense for me to do this before, later in this chapter, giving an introductory presentation of the organization of BP because, of course, to give any such presentation entails a set of assumptions about, or at least predispositions towards, what 'organization' means and how one might give a 'presentation' of organization.

PROBLEMS AND POSSIBILITIES IN ORGANIZATION
STUDIES

My starting point is that something has gone badly wrong with the field of organization studies[5] (see also Mone and McKinlay, 1993; Weick, 1996; Greenwood and Hinings, 2002; Starbuck, 2003; Czarniawska, 2008; Gabriel, 2010; Grey, 2010; Suddaby, Hardy and Huy, 2011). What I mean by this is that it has in recent years moved further and further from providing incisive, plausible and readable accounts of organizational life which disclose more of, and explain more of, the nature of that life than would be possible without academic inquiry; but which do so in ways which are recognizably connected to the practice of organizational life. Let me unpack that rather convoluted sentence. As is basic to all social science, organization studies is concerned with human beings who themselves already have all kinds of explanations, understandings and theories of the lives they live. These may be under-examined or unexplored alto-gether, or they may be highly sophisticated. Yet, as Bauman (1990: 9–16), amongst many others, points out, these essentially common-sensical understandings of human life differ from those offered by social scientists in several key respects, including attempts to marshal evidence and provide reflective interpretations which in some way serve to 'de-familiarize' lived experience and commonsense. This is clearly not the same as saying that social science provides an objective or disinterested account of the social world; but it does need to provide one which goes beyond the self-accounts and self-understandings of individuals and collectivities, albeit perhaps (and probably) being con-cerned to give an account of those very self-accounts and self-understandings. This is what I mean by disclosing and explaining more of organizational life than would be possible without academic inquiry. So far, so basic, since some version of what I have said here would feature in any opening undergraduate lecture on a social science course.

What is problematic, at least in organization studies, is that this process of de-familiarizing lived experience has gone to extreme lengths. I have discussed this elsewhere (e.g. Grey, 2009) but, in brief, on the one hand, much academic work in the field has become highly quantified and abstracted, seeking to identify statistical relationships between different, artificially isolated, variables. Certainly, qualitative research in organizations studies has become much more common in recent years and this potentially speaks more directly of and to expe-rience. But whilst the best of it does just that, qualitative research has gained acceptability in large part by adopting technicist norms derived from positivism, being pre-occupied with methodological 'rigour' rather than narrative richness. On the other hand, some parts of the field, especially the more 'critically' orientated, are concerned with extremely arcane debates in social theory and scarcely refer to concrete human experiences at all. The consequence of this is that much of organization studies does not de-familiarize commonsense under-standings of experience but is almost entirely detached from them.

Thus, their immediate colleagues aside, hardly anyone is in a position to understand or to gain from most of what academics who study organizations write. One consequence of this is to create a vacuum which has been filled by the proliferation of 'airport lounge' business books providing, certainly, understandable accounts of organizational life but not ones which have the qualities of evidential and interpretative fidelity or of de-familiarization of commonsense that social science can and should provide.

It does not have to be like this, and indeed it is not uniformly like this. Greenwood and Hinings (2002) point to a kind of 'golden age' in organization studies in the 1950s when scholars such as Blau, Etzioni, Gouldner and Selznick wrote theoretically informed (mainly neo-Weberian) and empirically grounded studies of organization, written on a broad canvas, addressing 'big questions' and intelligible beyond the discipline itself. Whilst there are many reasons why such writing flourished in the 1950s and has rather withered now[6], it should not be thought that it has since died. On the contrary, from, for example, Kanter's (1977) neo-Weberian study of corporate life and gender at 'Indsco', through Pettigrew's (1985) contextualist analysis of strategy at ICI and Jackall's (1988) constructivist account of the moral entanglements of managers in various unnamed organizations to Kunda's (1992) ethnographic study of organizational culture at 'Tech' and beyond there have been many books written from numerous perspectives which share the basic quality of what I am claiming to be needed for organization studies.

Part of the issue here is stylistic. As one later exemplar of such work, Tony Watson's study of 'ZTC Ryland', expresses it:

I hope to appeal at the same time to a managerial and an academic readership, as well as to the general reader interested in a social science analysis of an important modern activity. I have therefore carefully crafted this book to avoid what Charles Wright Mills in his discussion of intellectual craft work, criticised as the 'dense and turgid' style of much academic writing. This does not mean I have

> suspended normal standards of academic rigour. It seems to me that
> good sociology which is meaningful and enlightening to the non-
> academic reader is a realistic possibility.   *(Watson, 1994: 2)*

There is more at stake here than writing style, of course, important
though that is (Grey and Sinclair, 2006). One of the many things which
has changed in organization studies since the 1950s, say, is the remarkable proliferation of different approaches, both theoretical and methodological, within the field. This fragmentation mirrors that which has
occurred in the social sciences more generally and reflects a changing
intellectual landscape but also, perhaps, the changing conditions of
academic life which tend to encourage ever narrower specialization. In
a detailed overview of the organization studies field, Reed (1992) identifies the manifold schisms which characterize it – and which have
certainly not decreased, and have probably increased, since then – and
makes an important proposal for regeneration. This consists of 'the
construction of, and dialogue between, intellectual narratives and
constituting *the* vital intellectual process sustaining the collective
search for a better understanding of modern organizations' (Reed,
1992: 280, emphasis in original). At least one aspect of the kind of
dialogue Reed envisages involves engaging

> with older narratives, which are in need of substantial overhaul but
> continue to relate to present problems and projected futures [if]
> retrieved from the collective amnesia or forgetfulness which is
> encouraged by recently fashionable modes of discourse and analysis.
>   *(Reed, 1992: 281)*

To put this last point into sharper focus and indicate what it means in
terms of the analysis contained in this book, one of the organizational
developments at BP which I will discuss in detail in Chapter 2 was a
series of transitions which occurred in the period 1940–42, during
which a far more factory-like form of organization emerged. When I
became aware of this, I realized immediately (for reasons which will be
explained at the relevant point) that it conformed in some ways to

some of the classic patterns identified by structural contingency theory (see Donaldson, 2001). Yet for a long time I resisted this realization. Why? Because, to an organizational theorist brought up, as I was, in a largely post-structuralist tradition, approaches such as structural contingency theory are regarded as, at best, outdated and, at worst, wrongheaded. I gradually came to the view that there was something peculiar, and perhaps intellectually dishonest, about my reluctance to consider contingency theory, and this realization very much informs the approach I will adopt throughout this book. Namely, I will deploy a range of organizational theories (not contingency theory in particular) regardless of what camp or perspective they come from and regardless of their current fashionability (cf. Oswick, Fleming and Hanlon, 2011). This does not, of course, imply an acceptance of any of them wholesale (contingency theory included), rather it means recognizing that in relation to particular questions or ranges of problem one kind of organizational theory may have purchase, whilst for another it may be quite irrelevant, or simply wrong.

Such an approach is likely to prove offensive to many organizational theorists and there is probably little which can be done to assuage that offence. But it is perhaps worth pointing out that I am not promoting a kind of vapid pluralism in which there is 'something in' each and every approach. Nor am I proposing any sort of unified field theory for organization studies, which I would regard as a doomed enterprise: the fragmentation and schism in social sciences has occurred for good reasons, and is not going to be mended. Rather, my concern is a more pragmatic one. As Tsoukas and Knudsen (2003: 5) have argued, 'paradigmatic' conflict is not susceptible to resolution in the abstract but may become less formidably 'incommensurable' through being reworked in specific sites:

> Like any other kind of work, empirical research is not a matter of mere 'application' of a given set of paradigmatic assumptions, but of active determination of those assumptions *in practice* . . .
> Researchers do not so much 'apply' or 'follow' paradigms in their

work as they explore particular topics, in particular sites and, having
to cope coherently with all the puzzles and tensions stemming from
the complexity of the phenomena they investigate, they extend,
synthesize, and/or invent concepts.

(Tsoukas and Knudsen, 2003: 13, emphasis in original)

This is very much the spirit in which I approach the study of BP in this
book. However, this does not mean that the utilization of various
theories arises simply or solely from the 'facts' of what happened at,
in this case, BP: I am not advocating naïve empiricism. Clearly the way
in which I select and identify those facts, questions and puzzles which
seem interesting or important is itself something arising from the
kinds of theories and ideas which I bring to bear in my selection and
interpretation of the evidence available to me. There is an iterative
process in play between theory and empirics, mediated, of course, by
own concerns, pre-occupations and predispositions, which is irreducible. So in saying that my approach is one of 'pragmatism' I do not seek
to deny the 'theory-ladenness' of empirical knowledge, I just endeavour not to become hamstrung by theoretical purism or tribalism. It
seems to me that this is the only way in which it is possible, given the
evaporation of broad consensus within the organization studies field,
to provide the kind of broad, intelligible, engaged study which I have
argued has become too rare within that field.

Drawing together what I have said in this section, I am suggesting that part of what this book attempts to achieve is the provision of a
form of organizational analysis which offers insights which would not
be possible without such an analysis, but to do so in ways which are
reasonably readily understandable to a range of readers and which
overcome at least some of the fragmentations within organizational
theory, and to do so not via an abstract discussion of that theory but
through a situated analysis of a particular organizational setting. It is
this kind of analysis which I am denoting as a 'decoding' of organization. It is important to clarify what I mean by this term. It should not be
taken to imply discovering the 'hidden truth' but, rather, providing an

interpretation of that which might otherwise be hidden. It is an important distinction and, in fact, much closer to the literal practice of
decoding than might be thought. For the work of BP did not simply
consist of deciphering messages to discover their content but of using
the multiple snippets of information from these messages to yield an
analysis of their intelligence. This analysis was necessarily a matter of
interpretation and judgment. Indeed, the head of the Air Section at BP,
Josh Cooper, explicitly stated just this in a memorandum of 24 June
1941: 'the fact is, that the process called "cryptography" [sic] would
perhaps better be described as interpretation'[7].

It is this interpretive sense of the term that I intend when speaking of 'decoding' organization, and I contrast it with the ways in which
organization is often 'encoded', for example when underlying organizational processes are reified into organizational charts, or when the
dynamics and complexities of organizational culture are encoded
into typologies of homogeneous cultural blocks. Thus what I am aim-
ing to do in 'decoding organization' is to make new interpretations[8] so
as to tell, in a way which I hope will be both illuminating and persuasive, a story of the organization of BP.

ORGANIZATION STUDIES AND HISTORY

But what kind of story is this? Many of the examples I gave of studies
which have the illuminating and persuasive character I am seeking are
studies of a particular sort, namely organizational ethnographies (e.g.
Kunda, 1992; Watson, 1994) in which the researcher lives among, and
to an extent as, a member of the organization being researched. This
makes it not easy but at least in principle possible to transmit something
of the lived reality of an organization whilst also standing somewhat
detached from it and analytically drawing attention to aspects of that
reality not normally obvious to those living it. In this way, such studies
speak both of and to organizational life. In the absence of time travel,
this is not an option as regards BP. Pursuing an historical case study
entails a somewhat – although, I will suggest, not entirely – different set

of issues from those presented by ethnographies or other forms of inquiry into contemporary organizations.

The relationship between organization studies and history has been somewhat limited and not always very satisfactory. Of course, there are exceptions to this, Whipp and Clark's (1986) study of innovation in the car industry being a good example. Nevertheless, the very legitimacy of such an engagement has been questioned (Golden, 1992) and, until Alfred Kieser's (1994) seminal paper, there was little discussion within the recent literature regarding the role and relationship of history to organization studies, unlike that which had occurred, for example and in particular, in sociology (e.g. Abrams, 1982). In that regard Kieser notes that Weber, in many ways the 'founding father' of organization studies, was as much historian as sociologist, believing contemporary institutions could be understood only by knowing how they developed in history. Indeed, this Weberian understanding was alive and well in organizational sociology in the 1950s, as in Bendix's (1956) classic work. However, over time, as organization studies separated itself from organizational sociology, interest in history dissipated 'and nowadays, excursions of organization researchers into history have become extremely rare' (Kieser, 1994: 609; cf. Zald, 1993), with the exception of labour-process analysis, which in his view was isolated from, and largely ignored by, the mainstream of organization studies and therefore did little to restore the status of historical analysis. The latter remark is significant because, just as organization studies separated itself from organizational sociology, so too did it move away from industrial sociology, of which labour-process analysis is one outgrowth. This had, and continues to have, a tradition of historically grounded analyses of work organizations (e.g. Edwards, 1979; Littler, 1982), as has the work of political economists with an interest in industrial relations and work organizations (e.g. Crouch, 1994; Streeck, 2009), but both of these literatures have developed rather separately from that of organization studies.

Almost contemporaneously with Kieser, Rowlinson and Hassard (1993) discussed the relationships amongst sociology, organization studies and history. They identify two issues – one methodological and the other epistemological – which they explore by reference to the literature on, specifically, organizational culture. The first issue refers to a heightened sensitivity towards meaning and understanding as explanations of behaviour, which privileges in-depth, qualitative interviewing and makes history relatively inaccessible, at least if potential respondents are dead. Within such approaches, culture is researched at the inter-personal level, with documents and other archival material rarely considered. The second reason for the failure of organization studies, or at least contemporary organization studies of culture, to engage with history is epistemological. Rowlinson and Hassard believe that much culture writing has succumbed to postmodernism, which is sceptical about the epistemological status of historical events. If taken to its logical conclusion this means that all history is subjective – history is what the historian makes it. By contrast, whilst recognizing that organizations and their cultures are socially constructed, they argue that

> the reality of a past need not be abandoned because it has undergone a process of social construction, to do so would result in abandoning historical research. Instead the production of history itself, the process of social construction, can be incorporated into the historian's account. *(Rowlinson and Hassard, 1993: 302)*

Of course, as regards the epistemological issue, these very debates were also (and still are) raging within the discipline of history itself (e.g. White, 1987; Appleby, Hunt and Jacob, 1995; Marwick, 1995; Evans, 2000), but clearly the modalities of that debate were very different from those within organization studies, where history of any sort had played little part, or only a marginal part, anyway. Indeed, the debates within organization studies about history in the 1990s were peculiar in that they coincided with, and became part of, more general debates about postmodernism in organization studies (e.g. Hassard and Parker, 1993) as well as the equivalent discussion of postmodernism within history. This perhaps accounts for the rather tortuous nature of some of the conversations that occurred:

how should organization studies engage with history when the very fundaments of each were being called into question?

Whilst such controversies continue, they have not prevented the emergence of a degree of acceptance of historical research in organization studies and the call for an historical turn (Clarke and Rowlinson, 2004; Booth and Rowlinson, 2006) has not gone unheeded[9]. One important aspect of this is the growing overlap between the discipline of business history and that of organization studies. Having in the past had some common points of reference – especially in the work of Alfred Chandler – they developed largely in isolation of each other, and they have also tended to be suspicious of each other. One reason for this was the way that traditional business history was sometimes associated with the production of official company histories and in this way open to the accusation of lacking a critical distance and, more generally, a sense within the organization studies community that business history was overly empiricist and lacked a serious engagement with social scientific theory (Hassard and Rowlinson, 1993; Clarke and Rowlinson, 2004)[10]. Whatever merit there may have been in these charges, the nature of business history has itself changed in recent years and these charges look increasingly outdated. Certainly there are many vigorous debates about how organization studies and business history relate to each other (e.g. Taylor, Bell and Cooke, 2009; Toms and Wilson, 2010), but this very debate is indicative of their reduced isolation, and the dominant sense emerging is one of considerable overlap, if not *rapprochement* (Booth and Rowlinson, 2006; Kipping and Usdiken, 2008; Popp, 2008; O'Sullivan and Graham, 2010; Usdiken, Kipping and Engwall, 2011)[11]. Indeed, in one respect, at least, this book is an example of such a *rapprochement* in that, as I will discuss shortly, it is to some extent based upon archival research, one of the staple methods of business history but relatively rare within organization studies.

THE POSSIBILITIES OF HISTORICAL DISTANCE

Given the greater acceptance of historical research within organization studies, it is not my intention here to advance general arguments for

conducting such research. However, I do want to highlight some particular reasons for providing the analysis of BP with which this book is
concerned. The first and perhaps most important of these is the way
that historical analysis can flesh out one of the most significant
insights of recent organization theory. This is the recognition that
'organization' is both a noun and a verb (Weick, 1979; Bakken and
Hernes, 2006). That is, on the one hand, it is a 'thing' – the organization – and on the other hand, it is a process – organization.
Commonsensically we speak of 'the organization', imagining it to be
in some way a solid, bounded entity. Certainly we may be aware that 'it
used to be different' or that 'it is changing' but that leaves untouched
the more fundamental sense that there is an 'it' which is the organization. This apprehension of the organization is by no means confined to
commonsense, however. Most academic case studies of organizations
adopt precisely the same ontology. Yet the apparent solidity of 'the
organization' is an accomplishment of a process – organizing – which
occurs in time and requires a day by day, indeed minute by minute,
enactment: the organization of the organization, so to speak.

Within organization studies, such an understanding can be
traced back at least as far as Melville Dalton's (1959) classic *Men
Who Manage* and has more recently been widely explored from a
variety of perspectives (e.g. Weick, 1979, 2001; Tsoukas and Chia,
2002; Czarniawska, 2008, 2009); for an overview of literature of this
type see Hernes and Weik (2007). This clearly opens up the significance
of temporality[12] in organization studies. Yet grasping temporality is
not easy when research is conducted in a contemporary organization,
whereas viewed from a historical distance it becomes easier to see how
a process operates or, as one might perhaps better say, *proceeds*.
Certainly the way that such a process is reconstructed is fraught with
difficulty – it is hardly a matter of simply discovering 'what happened' –
which I will discuss later. But historical distance at least opens up an
easier terrain in which to glimpse, if not reconstruct, temporality. To
put it another way, if, as I suggested earlier, a key aim of the social
scientific analysis of organizations is their de-familiarization, then the

simple fact of the relative unfamiliarity of the past gives a head start in this endeavour. The issue, then, is not so much that a historical case is in the past but that, by virtue of its being in the past, the relationship between researcher and organization is shifted: some unexamined assumptions drop away (although it may be that others come into play). In a sense, I am suggesting that an historical study can achieve something not dissimilar to an ethnographic study. An ethnography typically involves a member of one culture living amongst members of another culture and thus being both an insider and outsider. The possibility of insight resides in *both* closeness and distance (cf. Merton, 1972). An historical study of organization achieves something similar but via a different route: a closeness derived from careful study of (as it might be) documents and artifacts; a distance derived from elapsed time.

What I am offering here is clearly a particular version of what it means to do history – how could it be anything else? – and that begs enormous, longstanding and heavily contested questions, canonical discussions of which include Carr (1987) and Elton (1969); see also Evans (2000). These are well beyond the scope of this book and my own competence. Yet it is a version which finds strong support in a now standard introduction to the discipline of history:

> Historical *difference* lies at the heart of the discipline's claim to be socially relevant. As a memory bank of what is unfamiliar or alien, history constitutes our most important cultural resource. It offers a means – imperfect but indispensable – of entering into the kind of experience that is simply not possible in our own lives.
>
> *(Tosh, 2006: 32, emphasis in original)*

This closely matches the approach I have been mapping out in the previous pages. Firstly, it is concerned with the intersection of history with the concerns of social science. Secondly, it places the issue of de-familiarization centre stage. Thirdly, it points to the significance of distance, or difference, within such an endeavour. Of course 'contemporary history' provides relatively less in the way of distance, and this applies to the study of BP, with consequences I will discuss later. In this sense, as with the ethnographer, what is at stake is a blend of closeness and distance which brings some things, like organizational process, into focus whilst necessarily occluding others.

Returning to the issue of organization as process, I want actually to suggest something rather more than I have done so far. Firstly, in the way I have presented it, it might be inferred that I see history as a means of accessing organizational process rather than as studying an organization that existed in the past. In fact, whilst it is certainly inadequate to view organization as an entity or noun, so too is it inadequate to view organization solely as process or verb. The fact that it is possible, and indeed commonplace, to experience organizations as 'things' also has to be taken into account, for this experience represents, so to speak, the crystallization of organizational process. In this respect, I depart from the often-quoted passage from Weick (1979: 44) stating that 'in the interests of better organizational understanding we should urge people to stamp out nouns'. Rather, it is not a matter of organization as noun *or* verb, entity *or* process, being *or* becoming – it is that organization is always both at the same time. Thus my intention is to show (aspects of) organization in both of these senses through a lens of historical distance and via a case study of organization over several years.

However, I also want to indicate something rather more complicated about organization (in both senses). One might think that an attention to entity and process is to do with a consideration of the various kinds of actions and practices – organization – which collectively reproduce *an* organization over time. That is so, but it gives a perhaps overly mechanical picture of what process consists of. Instead, I want to show how organization involves a mish-mash of borrowings, adaptations and abandoned and modified initiatives, each leaving a greater or smaller trace of itself so that organization becomes a multi-layered and messy affair rather than a coherent whole – a *bricolage* (Weick, 1993; Gabriel, 2002), as I will discuss in Chapter 6.

The image here might be of a gigantic cityscape with streets and buildings in various stages of completion, built over other older structures, with patches of wasteland coming and going, main thoroughfares becoming back alleys, skyscrapers going up, coming down – a flux of adoption, adaptation and abandonment. Again, to represent organization in this way is greatly aided by historical distance and a temporal study in the same way that one might trace a city by reference to photos, maps, archeological digs and so on. Perhaps the language here seems slightly fanciful, but I hope it captures the stronger and richer sense of organizational process I will be concerned with and of which I believe BP offers a particularly vivid illustration. The main reason I make this claim is that BP provides a historical case of the agglomeration of a wide range of different organizations and organizational processes which develop and change not just over time but over a relatively short space of time – six years – and which are relatively well-documented. That seems to provide me with an ideal site to test out the ideas I have put forward: it is long enough ago to give historical distance; the time frame is short enough to make the processes visible; there is sufficient material to provide a rich and detailed picture.

This, then, is the first and most important reason for the kind of analysis I will provide in this book: the possibility of grasping organization as both entity and process by virtue of historical distance. But that might be achieved through a wide variety of different cases and, although I have just claimed, and hope I will show, that the BP case offers some particularly vivid illustrations of it, it is not the only reason why BP is worthy of the attention of organizational theorists. A second reason is that BP exemplifies one of the most profound developments in organizational life, in developed societies at least, during the twentieth century and beyond: the very close enmeshment of the institutions of the state, business and civil society (Middlemas, 1979; Cronin, 1991; Edgerton, 2011). Of course, these are always necessarily intertwined to a degree, but as a result, in particular, of wars (both 'hot' and 'cold') the twentieth century saw the emergence not just of a 'military–industrial complex' but, more generally, an orchestration of civilian populations by and through the state. The most literal instantiation of this orchestration might be the mobilization of civilians within the context of total war, and BP is one of many illustrations of this. However, in less direct ways, the manner in which welfare becomes a matter of state concern, leading to the development of an array of state and non-state organizations to promote this welfare, also shows a similar process at work. Welfare in this context is not confined to 'the welfare state', although that is a highly significant aspect of it, but includes also the more general ways in which the 'security' of populations is managed across a variety of domains (Hough, 2004; Miller and Rose, 2008). This is not simply about the size of the state, for example as a percentage of GDP, which can and does vary across countries and times: rather, it is about the thoroughgoing intermingling of state, market and 'associative' or civil spheres. Clearly this intermingling can take a variety of political forms – authoritarian, technocratic, corporatist, neo-liberal etc – discussion of which is well beyond the scope of this book, but it is difficult to think of any modern, industrialized society in which it has not occurred in some form or another.

As I have already indicated, BP is an example of this intermingling, occurring at one of the pivotal moments in its development, namely WW2 – perhaps an extreme example, certainly a particular example and in these senses should be regarded as *illustrative*, rather than *representative*. This is of interest not just for the empirical reason I have alluded to; it is also of theoretical interest. One of the most longstanding and influential distinctions in organization theory has been that between 'organization' and 'environment' (e.g. Aldrich, 1979), a distinction which is also commonplace within everyday parlance about organizations. Yet it is a precarious distinction, as many have noted (e.g. Pfeffer and Salancik, 1978; Perrow, 1986; Weick, 2001), because the interchanges between the two are so many and the boundary between the two is so fuzzy. Again, one of the ways that an historical analysis can help is by de-familiarizing this distinction. At any particular moment in time, the distinction between organization and environment can appear self-evidently 'natural' – who the 'we' of an organization are and who the 'they' are, where the structural boundaries of the organization lie and so on. Historical analysis is by no means the only way of identifying the limitations of such a distinction, but it is one powerful means by which it can be interrogated. Thus, in the analysis which follows, I will, for example, make much of the enmeshment of BP with wider cultural contexts of war and with the machinery of government, and of the interplay between different agencies and institutions. In these and other ways, then, the BP case can serve as an illustration of both the empirical nature of modern organizations as located within a heterogeneous institutional and ideational network and the theoretical deficiencies of conceptualizing organization and environment as distinct spheres.

So, to summarise what I see as the possibilities of the kind of historical analysis pursued in this book, my central claim is that, in ways analogous to ethnography, historical distance enables us to see organization in a particular light. That light illuminates certain things we perhaps take for granted, and I have suggested that these things might include the way that organizations are simultaneously entity and process, and the messiness and complexity of what 'process' means; the interconnectedness in modern societies of state and non-state institutions; and more generically the indeterminacy of what lies 'inside' and 'outside' organization. To the extent that 'the past is another country', an historical approach is revealing because it deals with the alien – in just the way that ethnographers encounter other cultures as alien. Yet, and this is also true of ethnography, an historical approach is a blend of the alien and the familiar. That is to say, neither the past nor other cultures are completely ungraspable. They do not represent entirely separate 'forms of life' to our own and, were they to do so, then we would not be able to understand them at all. Indeed, so far as the particular case of BP is concerned, whilst historical, it is by no means so far in the past as to be completely unrecognizable. It existed in living memory – and, as I will shortly discuss, this enables oral history methods to be used as part of the analysis – and in a world which is not so absolutely different to our own. So what historical analysis can do for the study of organizations is to provide a particular blend of closeness and distance which brings certain things into focus. Of course, the corollary of that is that other things fall out of focus: the historical gaze is not an all-knowing one; it has its own particularities, its own blind spots, its own occlusions.

It will be apparent that I have avoided claiming for this historical analysis of BP any suggestion that it enables us to 'learn from the past'. In relation to BP in particular, attempts have sometimes been made to do just this. For example, Page (2007) uses it as a central example for the value of diversity in the effective functioning of creative teams. In a more diffuse way I have myself suggested that there are allegorical lessons from BP in terms of how we understand organizational efficiency (Grey and Sturdy, 2010), so I am not altogether resistant to thinking about BP in this way. Nevertheless, it is not a claim which I want to make in a strong way and is certainly not the intention of this book. The possibility of learning from history in general is a subject of much dispute amongst historians. So far as organization studies is concerned, there is a similar question about whether 'what works' within one organization can ever be replicated within another, given the range and complexity of situational variables (this does not, of course, prevent continual attempts to do so). So any claim that organizations today can learn from organizations in the past would face a double hurdle. It seems to me that, in a general way, to the extent that an historical analysis (or any other kind of analysis) aids 'understanding' of organizations then it may indeed help to inform the actions of those who participate in organizations. But that is very far from raiding such analyses for 'how to' tips of the type often sought by managers. Indeed, one of the reasons for the demise of the 'golden age' of organization studies was, according to Greenwood and Hinings (2002), the shift of the discipline into the institution of the business school, which tended to conceptualize the subject in terms of its contribution to managerial and organizational efficiency. Thus, for all that managers and others may find in the story of BP's organization some insights of interest for practice, these are incidental to my main concern here.

APPROACH, METHODS AND SOURCES

I have made several claims for the value of an historical analysis and of the rich possibilities for such an analysis which the BP case presents. In this section, I will explain in detail the kinds of historical materials and methods upon which the analysis in this book is based. As a prelude to that, though, I want to make some brief comments about my general orientation towards these materials and methods. Simply stated, this is that they provide a partial and particular picture, mediated by own interpretations, cultural and historical location, and limited by my own cognitions and abilities, of what is nevertheless an organizational and historical reality. That reality is never completely knowable, never unmediated and always open to new knowledge and alternative interpretations. Nevertheless, there was (and indeed is) a place called Bletchley Park, there was a codebreaking operation there, the people who worked there existed and so on.

I have already stated, and will do so again here, that I am not an historian and historians have of course debated these kinds of issues at length; but I take it to be at least a defensible position within history to, in the words of one of its most distinguished present-day exponents,

> steer a middle course between the extremes of postmodernist hyperrelativism on the one hand, and traditional historicist empiricism on the other. *(Evans, 2000: 254–5)*

In any case, as mentioned earlier, very similar debates about epistemology and ontology to those in history have occurred within organization studies. Questions about the nature of organizational reality and the ways in which this might be apprehended (whether in historical or other methodologies) are now longstanding. It is not the purpose of this book to engage in such debates but it is reasonable that I should indicate that, within them, I take a position of what might be called 'soft constructivism'; that is, to recognize that organizational realities are in part constructed discursively (including through organization studies itself) and that this construction entails exercises of power.

Organizational reality does not exist objectively as 'a thing' independent of social constructions; but neither does it exist solely through those constructions. Similarly, organizational (and historical) reality does not exist independently of interpretations; but not all interpretations are equally valid, or even possible, given the evidence available.

It is from this very general set of commitments that I approach the study of BP. That study has as its main source of primary data archival material. With the near-complete declassification of the papers relating to BP, these are available at the United Kingdom's National Archives (TNA) in Kew, London, and copies of some, although by no means all, of the same documents are held at the Bletchley Park Trust Archive (BPTA)[13]. The documents relevant to BP mainly bear the catalogue identifier HW[14], and cover an enormous range of matters, many of which are not directly relevant to this book. For example, there are compendious records of decrypted intelligence material, which are of great interest to military historians but are not, except perhaps for what they reveal about the scale and complexity of its operations, particularly relevant for an analysis of BP's organization.

Even considering the papers most directly relevant to this study, it is important to understand that these comprise a massive number of documents, running to several tens of thousands of pages of text. It is doubtful whether any one person could read and absorb them in a lifetime and, although I will refer to a very wide selection of the documents, even this is only a small sub-set of the total. Moreover, these documents are enormously varied in character and interest, encompassing routine memoranda, minutes of meetings, detailed reports on operational and strategic matters and much else besides. Of particular importance are a number of internal histories compiled towards the end of and just after the war. These were not intended for public consumption, although they have now mostly been declassified[15], and are lengthy volumes (in some cases multiple volumes) containing a wealth of material. They also require careful handling since they were written by people involved in the events they describe and in the immediate aftermath of those events. These *internal* histories should not be confused with the *official* history of British Intelligence in the Second World War, including BP, which was written, primarily by Professor Sir Harry Hinsley, many years later and always intended for public consumption. For ease of reference, the archive documents I refer to the most frequently are summarised in Table 1.

Apart from the HW sequence, considerable use is made of some War Office papers (the WO sequence, also held at the TNA). In addition to TNA documents, various other archives have been consulted, albeit to a much lesser degree. These are Churchill College Archives Centre (CCAC) at Churchill College, Cambridge, the King's College Archives Centre (KCAC) at King's College, Cambridge and the Imperial War Museum (IWM) Archive. The College archives contain personal papers of various BP staff members, most notably those of its first head, Alastair Denniston at CCAC. The IWM Archive contains, amongst other things, audio recordings of interviews with people who worked at BP.

So much for the mechanics of the archival sources, but what of their standing? Here, the general points I made about an analytical approach take on a particular significance. It is emphatically not the case that the organization of BP can be reconstructed from the archive, for several reasons. Firstly, it is in principle impossible to think of organizations solely in terms of their written record: it is absolutely basic to organization studies that organization comprises a huge range of informal, uncodified social actions and interactions which could never be, and would never be, written down. At the very most, written records can give a partial glimpse of organization. That is not to say that such records are negligible, though. Clearly written records do comprise one important aspect of the way that organization is conducted and, so long as they are treated with regard to their limitations, then they have a use. But, secondly, or perhaps relatedly, as historians who use archival sources have long realized, the question of what kinds of things are committed to paper and, perhaps crucially, which of those papers are kept and archived – the social construction of the archive, so to speak – is something which makes such research a complex matter. Archival research by definition can access only that which is both

Table 1. *Summary of frequently cited documents*

Document	Author	Reference	Flagged in text as
Internal 'History of Hut 3'	Unknown[16]	TNA HW 3/119 and 3/120	The internal history of Hut 3
Introduction to internal 'History of Hut 6'	Stuart Milner-Barry	TNA HW 43/70	Milner-Barry's (or the) introduction to the internal history of Hut 6. When referring instead to the (multi-authored) main text of this history that is made clear.
Internal 'History of Hut 8' (one of two)	Hugh Alexander	TNA HW 25/1	Alexander's internal history of Hut 8
Internal 'History of British Signals Intelligence 1914–1945'	Frank Birch	TNA HW 43/1 and 43/2	Birch's (or the) internal history of sigint
1942 'Report on Military Intelligence at GC & CS'	Brigadier W. E. van Cutsem	TNA WO 208/5070	The van Cutsem report
1949 Internal post-war review of GC & CS (no formal title)	Nigel de Grey	TNA HW 14/145	De Grey's (or the) post-war review

recorded and kept. Again, this is not a reason to eschew such data but a very strong reason for treating it with circumspection, attentive to what it reveals but mindful of what it conceals or marginalizes. Thirdly, beyond what is recorded and kept, there lies the matter of the *meaning* of documents. In this sense, as in other forms of organizational research such as ethnographic observations or interviews, interpretation is key. Issues here might include the political purposes for which particular documents were drawn up or events recorded, and understanding this will necessarily be problematic and partial. To give an example, I mentioned above the post-war review of BP[17], which contains a wealth of information and evaluative comments about organizational issues. Yet it has to be understood, at least in part, within the context of the post-war development of what by then was the Government Communication Headquarters[18] (GCHQ) and machinations about how that agency should be organized and resourced[19]. Thus, valuable as it is, it cannot be taken as a simple or unproblematic representation of 'what happened'.

There has perhaps been a tendency amongst some historians, including some business historians, to ignore these complexities and to understand their craft primarily in terms of enumerating the facts discovered within archives. More than this is needed if one is to avoid an empiricism which is at once naïve and bland, in which 'unremitting primary research, with its necessary but obsessive attention to detail, can lead to a certain intellectual blinkering: "the dust of archives blots out ideas", as Acton rather unkindly put it' (Tosh, 2006: 160). One way of avoiding this fate, perhaps the most important way, is to seek to interweave archival material with broader theoretical concerns and in this way always keep in focus the meaning which the archive material might bear. Another way is to both leaven and supplement archival material with other forms of data. In this study of BP this is precisely what I seek to do. The other form of primary data I will use is material gathered from a limited number of interviews and other interchanges with surviving members of BP staff. Such oral history also presents complexities and dilemmas.

The interviews were conducted during the period 2004–2008 by myself and on some occasions with my colleague Andrew Sturdy. The intention was to supplement the many published reminiscences of BP (see below) with recollections of specifically organizational and administrative issues, with which those reminiscences are only indirectly concerned. To this end, via personal contacts, but also with the assistance of the Bletchley Park Trust (BPT), which put out a call to veterans for interviewees, I identified six respondents who represented a range of roles at BP. They were, almost by definition, drawn from those who at the time had been amongst the youngest of those working there. Written agreement to the interviews was secured in advance, primarily in recognition of the fact that these were very elderly – ranging from late seventies to nearly ninety – and perhaps therefore in some senses vulnerable people, and clear consent was an important ethical principle. Interviews were, in all but one case, held in the homes of the interviewees and typically lasted for several hours. They were, with one exception, tape recorded. For reasons which will be mentioned later, I will refer to the interviewees by pseudonyms. One of the interviewees, who had worked in the office of the BP Directorate, accompanied me on a tour of the BP site as a means of explaining the layout and aspects of the functioning of the offices of the directorate. Outline details of the interviewees are summarised in Appendix B.

In addition to these interviews, about ten other BP veterans contacted me by writing, either in response to the BPT appeal or as a result of having heard in other ways about my work. This led to correspondence of greater or lesser length. Additionally, I attended a reunion of BP veterans, at Bletchley Park in 2005, which had a drop-in session scheduled for those who wished to talk about their experiences with me, and about twenty did so. These various sources cannot really even be called oral history in the normal sense of the word, and I will make little use of them, yet they did serve to provide me with a certain sense of what life at BP was like.

Whilst the benefits of such oral testimony are obvious – they have the potential to capture something of the lived experience of past events – the limitations are equally obvious and have been widely discussed by historians (Lummis, 1987; Thompson, 2000). These limitations include the distortions of memory; the possibility of nostalgia and of having been unwittingly affected by subsequent knowledge of and reflection upon what is being recalled; the particularities of individual experience; and, as with all interview methodologies, the impact of the interviewer and the interviewer's agenda upon the testimony offered. These general limitations are particularly acute in relation to the BP case because, as will become clear, the requirements of secrecy meant that those working there never spoke of their experiences for at least 30 years after the event and these experiences were very rigorously compartmentalized. This means that the possibilities of mis-recollection and of recollection being overlaid by subsequent knowledge are especially profound. Moreover, the very stern instruction given at the time never to reveal anything about their work might be expected to create a degree of reticence even after the prohibition was lifted. Despite these caveats, the interview material is a useful way of filling out that collected in the archives and, in any case, I use it fairly sparingly to illustrate, in the main, relatively minor points, and that illustrative function is perhaps the main benefit: to bring a more personalized and embodied sense than the 'dust of the archives' can provide. Indeed, for this reason oral history has been used quite widely, in particular in relation to WW2 (e.g. Summerfield, 1998; Summerfield and Peniston-Bird, 2007).

I will make rather more extensive use of secondary data in the form of, in particular, reminiscences of BP veterans. This too is a form of oral history, albeit of a kind which perhaps entails even greater problems than are associated with that which is formally collected as such. As I indicated earlier in this chapter, there is now a very large number of published reminiscences of BP. They vary enormously in quality, but the best of them are extremely revealing. It should be borne in mind that many members of BP staff were not just highly intelligent but also intellectually gifted to an extraordinary degree. This has given rise to some very insightful accounts of many aspects of BP's work, in particular those of Welchman (1982) and Calvocoressi (2001) and the contributions to Hinsley and Stripp (1993). Such accounts are routinely cited within the academic histories of BP and of intelligence more generally and whilst, of course, they are subject to the same caveats as oral history itself – and in many cases themselves identify their limitations in similar terms to those indicated above – they do provide a rich source of material which, when taken in conjunction with other sources, has a considerable degree of credibility.

The reminiscences just cited do have a particular character, though. They are almost exclusively those of the 'elite' at BP, the cryptanalysts in particular. But, more recently, accounts of the 'rank and file' have begun to appear (e.g. Page, 2002, 2003; Hill, 2004; Luke, 2005; Watkins, 2006; Paterson, 2007; Thirsk, 2008). One of the guiding themes of some uses of oral history has been the intention to bring into history the voices of the marginal or neglected (Samuel, 1981), and these collections do serve that function. It is no coincidence in this regard that these are very largely the reminiscences of *women*, for, as I will make clear later, there was a profound gendered division of labour at BP. Perhaps, too, it is no coincidence that they are published by small, private publishers: for it is still the case that the dominant narrative of BP is one which foregrounds the work of the largely male, cryptanalytic elite. An important part of what I want to analyse in this book is how partial that narrative is. In that regard, this secondary literature, whilst variable in nature, is extremely informative.

Many of these published reminiscences, as well as some primary interview material, have been gathered together in a recent study of daily life at BP (McKay, 2010). This is a useful resource precisely because of its synthetic quality, and I will refer to it at various points. It is very much a journalistic treatment of BP[20], which I say not in a 'sniffy' academic sense but to draw attention again to the particular issues entailed in seeking to provide an academic account of something which has commanded so much public interest. Such treatments do not need to consider issues of theoretical analysis or of methodological complexity – and are all the more readable as a result – but they do nevertheless provide academic analysts with a valuable resource, in particular for grasping the cultural aspects of BP.

So, in summary, this study of the organization of BP is built upon a *smörgåsbord* of primary and secondary sources: a large amount of archival data, some oral and related history collected specifically for this study and a great deal of secondary material. In addition, as noted at the outset, there exists a variety of histories of intelligence in general and signals intelligence in particular and those having both a general remit and a particular focus on WW2 which are relevant (e.g. Hinsley *et al.*, 1979; Andrew, 1985a; Hinsley, 1993c; Kahn, 1996; Herman, 1996, 2001; Budiansky, 2000; Davies, 2001; Erskine and Smith, 2001; Aldrich, 2002; Ratcliff, 2006). I have also drawn upon some of the more technical papers about cryptanalysis (e.g. Erskine and Weierud, 1987; Hamer, Sullivan and Weierud, 1998; Marks, 2001). It is out of this heterogeneous assembly that I will seek to build my account which is emphatically *a* history rather than *the* history of BP's organization. The kind of material drawn upon will vary according to the topic at hand. Thus, for example, more use is made of oral history material when writing about cultural issues; much less when considering structural and political issues which are mainly based on the archives, since the interviewees knew very little about such matters at the time they were at BP.

It has rightly become standard practice within organization studies to offer some form of 'reflexive' account of one's own relationship to the subject of study (Alvesson and Skoldberg, 2009). In relation to BP, this has some complexity. There is a very slight family connection: during WW2 my mother lived in Stony Stratford, not far from BP, and her family had members of BP staff billeted with them. But my initial interest in BP came when I visited its museum with my friend and colleague Andrew Sturdy in 2003. In the course of that visit we discussed the question of how the work there had been organized and found, at that time, little in the museum displays to enlighten us. It was that which led to the initial research project which has now grown into this book. But there is more to it than that. Why did we visit the site at all? The answer, I think, lies in the role that WW2 played in the lives of those of my generation in Britain and in that sense is part of the wider issue of the social meaning of the war in British society (cf. Sandbrook, 2010: 174).

During my childhood, references to the war were ubiquitous. It framed my parents' childhood experience – my father, being in a reserved occupation, was a very youthful member of the Home Guard; my mother, then a schoolgirl, recalls seeing the skyline lit up by flames from the bombing of Coventry in 1940. Many of my school teachers had fought in 'the war' – what war it was needed no elaboration, it was a term in general currency. We were still living, in the 1960s and 1970s, in the 'post-war consensus', whilst the politics of the 1980s was often conceived of in terms of a breaking with that consensus and so was still defined by it. Culturally, war films, television dramas set in the war, Airfix models of Spitfires and Lancasters and so on all formed the background to my childhood. Indeed, this has hardly diminished, and perhaps in some ways has increased: turn on the television today in Britain and at almost any time you will find films and documentaries about the war; and commemorations of anniversaries of key events abound. So my interest in BP is surely in some way a part of the multiple ways in which memories of WW2 configured the culture in which I grew up and in which I still live.

One consequence of this is that I am by no means immune to the mythologization and sentimentalization of the war and of BP to which I alluded earlier and will discuss in Chapter 3. Thus, whilst in the analysis which follows I strive to set aside such feelings, it would be idle to deny that they are there. Indeed, in many respects I would not wish to deny them. It does seem to me that the war years exemplified a certain sort of commitment to social solidarity which is highly desirable; and I do not just respect but admire the sacrifices and hardships which the wartime generation made and endured. And I also have a huge admiration for what was done at BP, an admiration which has grown rather than diminished the more I have learnt of the work there. In particular, the experience of meeting and interviewing BP veterans has been extremely affecting.

Has all that led me to give a sanitized or sentimental account of BP? I hope not. If anything, my concern would be that in seeking to be analytical I may even appear to be insufficiently respectful to its memory and whilst that is certainly not my intention it is for that reason that I have used pseudonyms for those veterans I interviewed for this book. It is certainly the case that this study is a labour of love beyond that which attends any substantial academic endeavour. It is, in a way, also a tribute to the generation of my parents and teachers, of whom George Orwell spoke when he said that 'men sleep peacefully in their beds at night because rough men stand ready to do violence on their behalf'. The men and women of Bletchley Park were far from rough, but they were in their own way warriors and their role in defending civilization from barbarism was profound. But it is precisely because of my respect for them that I have sought to avoid sanitization and sentimentality: I suspect that most of them would have regarded an attempt at analytical rigour as a more fitting tribute.

Having indicated both the broad intentions of this book and the kinds of empirical materials and orientation that will inform it, I will now provide a brief explanation of what BP was, and the kind of work which occurred there, in order to orient those readers who may be completely unfamiliar with it, and possibly even to correct some misapprehensions amongst those who do have some familiarity. Of course, this account will be highly simplified and many aspects will be developed in much greater detail in subsequent chapters.

A BRIEF OVERVIEW OF BLETCHLEY PARK

Although I have referred thus far to Bletchley Park as if it were an organization, this is inaccurate. It was (and is) a place, and the organization[21] in question was the Government Code and Cypher School[22] (GC & CS or, occasionally, GCCS) which had its main home at BP during WW2. The site consisted of a medium-sized nineteenth-century manor house, outbuildings and grounds in Buckinghamshire, about 50 miles north of London (see Morrison, undated, for a history of the building). It was purchased on the initiative of Admiral Sir Hugh

Sinclair in 1938 for use as a Secret Intelligence Service (SIS, commonly known as MI6) war station[23]. Sinclair was the Chief of SIS, known, as were his successors, simply as 'C'. The main intended purpose of the site was to house GC & CS in the event of war breaking out, although at various times it housed other elements of SIS[24]. The choice of this site is often attributed to its location on the now-defunct Oxford to Cambridge railway line, being thus convenient for the many BP staff drawn from the universities in those cities. This is probably inaccurate, or at any rate secondary – as I will explain, at the outset it was not expected that BP would grow to the size it did and, in any case, whilst staff may have come from those universities, it was not the case that they were routinely travelling to and from them. A more plausible explanation is the proximity of BP to the main north–south telephone lines, allowing ready teleprinter access from listening stations and to government ministries in London[25].

The Government Code and Cypher School had been formed in 1919 (see Davies, 2001 for details) to bring together what had hitherto been the separate cryptanalytical endeavours of various agencies, principally the Admiralty's Room 40 and section MI1b of the War Office (in other words, roughly speaking, naval and army cryptanalysis). As will later become clear, some of the key organizational dynamics at BP were those between the various different agencies and interests that GC & CS brought together. Whilst Sinclair, and subsequently his successor Stewart Menzies, was the notional Director of GC & CS by virtue of his heading SIS, in real terms it was run by the Deputy Director, Commander Alastair Denniston, a Room 40 veteran who led British cryptanalytic operations in the early years of BP. To understand what cryptanalysis means, it is necessary first to consider the broader notion of what became known as signals intelligence (sigint). Sigint[26] is intelligence derived from the interception of communications. At its simplest, it means intercepting and reading messages passed by whatever means but primarily, in the modern era, by wireless transmission. In practice, in order to secure these communications, various codes and ciphers are used. Communications thus written are cryptograms; the practice of reading such communications is cryptanalysis or codebreaking; the information thus derived is sigint. Even from this brief account it can be seen that there are at least three key processes at work: interception, decoding and intelligence analysis. Given that very often the messages involved will be in a foreign language (and in highly technical form, at that), we can immediately add a fourth process, between decoding and intelligence analysis, namely translation. Finally, since the intelligence derived has to be passed to those who can make use of it, a fifth process, distribution, should be added.

By the time of WW2 ciphers had become extremely sophisticated, principally because of the development of machine (rather than 'hand') ciphers. The principal such machine in widespread use within Nazi Germany was 'Enigma', a device using a series of rotors and electrical connections to encrypt messages to be sent and to decrypt messages received (for excellent outline accounts, see Stripp, 1993; Erskine, 2000; Calvocoressi, 2001: 31–54; Carter, 2010). It is important to understand that, at different times and in different places, different versions of the Enigma machine were used. Enigma presented a challenge of enormous complexity for cryptanalysis since, although varying according to which version of the machine was in use, it had on one estimate approximately 1.59×10^{20} settings (Stripp, 1993: 86). This challenge was compounded by the fact that the settings for such machines were typically changed daily.

Even apart from machine modifications, Enigma existed in multiple variants according to the service deploying it, for example army (*Heer* or Army Enigma), air force (*Luftwaffe* or GAF Enigma), navy (*Kriegsmarine* or Naval Enigma), intelligence (*Abwehr* Enigma) and railways (*Reichsbahn* Enigma). Within each of these services were various user groups employing different 'keys'. There were many dozens, possibly hundreds, of different Enigma keys and by and large their BP cover names ran in series. Thus, for GAF Enigma, colours, e.g. Red, Blue, Light Blue; for Army Enigma, birds, e.g. Sparrow, Falcon, Vulture; for Naval Enigma, sea creatures, e.g. Dolphin, Shark, Porpoise[27]. The daily setting for each of these keys was also, confusingly, called a key at BP. So Enigma is an over-arching term covering different machines, each with a number of different keys (Hamer, Sullivan and Weierud, 1998). It is therefore a misnomer to speak of 'Enigma' having being broken: there were multiple Enigmas, and even when a key was broken the daily setting still had to be found. Moreover, modifications of that variant could and did lead to 'blackouts' of what had previously been readable transmissions. Thus not only were there multiple Enigmas but also an ongoing process of breaking them: it was not a one-off event.

Whilst BP is now inextricably linked with the breaking of Enigma ciphers, it should always be recalled that many other ciphers, including 'low-grade' and 'hand' ciphers, were being dealt with, as well as an even more complex machine cipher than Enigma, known at BP as Fish (the cipher for which the Colossus computer was developed), itself having three machine variants, Tunny, Sturgeon and Thrasher[28]. Moreover, it was not just German ciphers which were being 'attacked' and in many cases read: it was also those of other countries, in particular Italy and Japan[29], where, respectively, the high-grade cipher machine Hagelin C-38m and the super-enciphered code JN-25 were amongst the targets. Indeed, at the outbreak of war it was widely considered that the plugboard version of Enigma used by the German armed services was unbreakable[30], and initially there were only four people working on it at BP. Nevertheless, partly as a consequence of pre-war breakthroughs by Polish cryptanalysts (Smith, 1998: 17–19), partly because of the capture of machines and codebooks from the Germans, partly because of the genius of the BP codebreakers and partly as a result of mistakes made by operators of the Enigma machines, a wartime key was indeed broken, when some messages in the Army Enigma Green key[31] were read in January 1940 (Hinsley, 1993c: 14). Gradually, with many difficulties and periodic interruptions, many Enigma keys were regularly read, giving rise to many thousands of decrypts each day. The intelligence product thus derived (as well as that from other high-grade ciphers such as Fish) came to be called Ultra or ULTRA. The details of this extraordinary story have now been told many times (see, for example, Hinsley and Stripp, 1993; Smith, 1998; Budiansky, 2000; Sebag-Montefiore, 2000; Erskine and Smith, 2001).

Apart from the technical complexities of breaking Enigma and other ciphers, there are at least three other aspects of BP's operations which should be highlighted. Firstly, and lying outside of the BP site, there was an enormous network of intercept stations (i.e. listening posts to intercept the encrypted transmissions), the product of which had to be transported securely to BP. These intercept or 'Y stations' were geographically dispersed around Britain and the world, and were run by a variety of bodies including the army, navy, RAF, GPO and police[32]. Secondly, at BP itself, apart from cryptanalytic work there was an enormous amount of both translation and intelligence analysis work. The messages decoded, apart from being in German (or Italian, Japanese etc.), were typically of a highly technical character, requiring particularly skilled translation. Moreover, they typically consisted of multiple 'snippets' of information, the intelligence value of which could be identified only by careful analysis, comparison and cross-reference with other decrypts. This required, in turn, sophisticated information-management systems, principally in the form of indexes, in order to create useable intelligence outputs. These outputs then needed to be securely distributed to users or 'customers' such as government ministries or military commands. Thirdly, apart from crypt-analysis, a considerable amount of intelligence was derived from traffic analysis (TA), meaning the analysis of transmissions which, whilst not necessarily decoded, revealed information about, for example, the location and concentration of enemy activity.

Organizationally, the ongoing breaking of Enigma was of key significance, leading to a rapid and considerable growth in personnel. The original GC & CS staff who moved to BP in 1939 numbered about 200. By 1944 almost 10,000 people worked there[33], about three-quarters of whom were women, mainly working in a three-shift system across the 24 hours of the day. Much of the pattern of this organization was crystallized via a major and pivotal reorganization of BP in January 1942, which is examined in detail in Chapter 2. The work of BP as it grew was of an extremely varied sort, encompassing not just the functions of cryptanalysis, translation, indexing and intelligence analysis but also a huge range of other tasks, including the operation of an array of machine systems of which the 'bombes' (electromechanical devices for testing possible solutions to an Enigma cipher setting) are perhaps the best known. I will discuss the nature and meaning of these developments in great detail throughout this book, but the immediate point to note is that what is perhaps the received image of BP as consisting of a small number of male mathematical geniuses is very wide of the mark. Rather, it entailed a complex of processes. It is very important to understand that the drawing together of these processes so as to constitute sigint was by no means automatic, but rather developed through the organizational arrangements at BP, as will also be explained in Chapter 2. With that important caveat, for present purposes the overall process can be summarised as follows.

- Interception of signals at numerous listening (Y) stations, run by a variety of agencies and services, located around the country and the world.
- Transport or transmission of intercepts (often 'corrupt' i.e. with missing or incorrect segments) to BP.
- Decryption of intercepts (running to thousands a day) in different ciphers (e.g. Enigma and Fish) which themselves had numerous variants or 'keys' (e.g. Enigma Army Vulture), each one of which, in the case of Enigma, changed settings daily. Decryption was achieved though highly complex manual, electromechanical (e.g. 'bombes' for Enigma) and electronic means (e.g. 'Colossus' for 'Fish').
- Emendation (i.e. 'de-corruption') and translation of decrypts (including highly technical terms and abbreviations) into English.
- Intelligence assessment of decrypted material and traffic analysis (indexing and cross-referencing being crucial to this process).
- Secure distribution of intelligence product to customers (e.g. ministries, field commanders).
- Use in field or strategy (or not – since sometimes to have used the intelligence would have revealed its existence and thus led to the cipher being changed or abandoned).

The growth in personnel (even before the Enigma breaks) as these processes developed in turn meant that the mansion house at BP almost immediately became too small, and this led to a rapid growth of buildings across the site, many of which took the form of wooden huts (and, later, concrete blocks) in a process documented by Evans (2003); see also Watson (1993). It is this which gave rise to the well-known designation of 'huts' to describe aspects of BPs work, since these also grouped together particular functions (thus, sometimes, even when these functions had been moved from their original premises they continued to be referred to by their erstwhile hut number). The key huts mentioned most frequently in this book, because these were the ones primarily concerned with Enigma and also because their work is best documented, were

- Hut 3 (translation, evaluation and distribution of army and air force Enigma decrypts)
- Hut 4 (translation, evaluation and distribution of naval Enigma decrypts; and decryption, translation, evaluation and distribution of all non-Enigma naval ciphers)
- Hut 6 (decryption of army and air force Enigma)
- Hut 8 (decryption of naval Enigma)[34]

These huts were partitioned into various sections housing different types of work group, and the ways in which this happened are themselves of organizational interest. In addition to the provision of workspaces, the growth of personnel also entailed a wider set of operations to house, feed and transport BP staff.

As a final point in this very general overview of BP, it is important to note that all of these operations took place in conditions of extreme and complete secrecy, both internal and external. All staff were bound by the two Official Secrets Acts (OSA) in force at the time and were given very forcible warnings to tell no one, family included, any detail of their work, either at the time or afterwards. Their work was very tightly compartmentalized and they were not allowed to discuss their work outside those compartments. Their access to information was on a strict 'need to know' basis and, indeed, the majority of those working there knew very little about the work they were doing and in most cases did not know that, for example, Enigma ciphers had been broken. Many died never knowing what they had been involved with or, if they knew, never having spoken of it. Those who were still alive when the secret of BP was revealed in the 1970s in many cases learned of it only then, and only afterwards were freed to tell of it.

Even from the little that has been said here, I hope it is already possible to see the great interest that the BP story holds from an organizational point of view. The multiplicity of agencies, functions and work types involved in addition to the rapid growth of the operation and the secrecy that surrounded it all conspire to make this a complex and fascinating site within which to conduct an organizational analysis. In the remainder of this book, at least some of that complexity will be elucidated. I will now briefly outline what will follow.

BRIEF OUTLINE OF CONTENTS

This book contains some extremely detailed empirical material, which entails for those unfamiliar with it what may be a confusing swirl of acronyms, specialist terms, events and people. Such readers may well find it useful to make use of the list of abbreviations and acronyms at the beginning of this book, alongside the Timeline in Appendix A, which shows major events at BP and in WW2 itself, Appendix B, which tabulates interviewees, Appendix C, which lists the roles of recurrent personalities and Appendix D, which contains a series of simplified organizational charts, and the glossary of terms. Additionally, as the text proceeds, I will provide many reminders as to the meaning of terms or relevant facts, and numerous forward and backward linkages to inter-related discussions.

The book is divided into three parts, each containing two chapters. This enables me to deal with closely related material whilst keeping the chapters to a reasonable length. Each part has its own introductory overview, and thus the introductions to each chapter are simply brief summaries of the content; the conclusion to the first chapter of each part is similarly a brief summary of the main points, whilst the conclusion to the second chapter of each part also serves as a conclusion to that part of the book as a whole.

The book is not a chronological account of BP's organization, being instead orchestrated around a series of interlocking themes. Thus the three parts of the book are entitled 'Decoding Structures', 'Decoding Cultures' and 'Decoding Work', with decoding bearing the interpretative meaning I indicated earlier. I do not mean to imply that structures, cultures and work are separate entities, and I will point to the many interconnections between the three throughout the book and in the concluding chapter. Nevertheless, this tripartite structure allows me to manage a complex mass of material in a reasonably coherent way.

Within Part I, 'Decoding Structures', Chapter 1 is concerned with 'the making of Bletchley Park'. Here I am concerned primarily with the ways in which BP was constructed out of a complex of organizations going back (at least) to the foundation of GC & CS in 1919, and the conflicts and problems this created at BP. The accent is on how BP was 'made' in the face of and through these conflicts between different agencies such as SIS, government ministries and services. Chapter 2 continues this theme, but with a more specific focus on how the breaking of Enigma, in particular, was enmeshed within the 'making of sigint' at BP – that is, the bringing together of interception, cryptanalysis and intelligence analysis. This, together with the material in Chapter 1, is then used to analyse the main re-structuring that occurred at BP in 1942 and in particular the process which led to its first operational head, Alastair Denniston, being replaced by Edward Travis as part of that re-structuring.

Part II is concerned with 'Decoding Cultures' and it is argued that BP contained a range of cultural elements which were both integrative and differentiating. Integrative elements are described in Chapter 3 as 'pillars' of culture and encompass the wider context of British society during WW2, the very extreme secrecy which was a defining feature of BP, and the mode of recruiting, at least in the early years, a socially homogeneous workforce. Each of these elements is examined in detail. Chapter 4 is concerned with the differentiating elements of culture, which are referred to as 'splinters' of culture. Here a wide array of cultural distinctions are examined, relating to gender, hierarchy, educational background and access to different types of secret as well as affiliation to the variety of organizations outlined in Part I.

Part III builds on the previous chapters to provide an account of 'Decoding Work'. This refers to the kinds of work done at BP and the way that BP was made to work, especially in the face of the extreme compartmentalization associated with secrecy. In Chapter 5, I discuss three broad forms of co-ordinating work at BP: those based on informal networks, those based upon management and those based upon various formal mechanisms such as meetings and committees. Chapter 6 continues the theme of how BP worked, but now in terms of the relationship between ways of working and different ways of organizing. In particular, there is an assessment of BP in terms of the standardization of work, knowledge work and the centralization of work.

Across all three parts of the book the emphasis is on capturing organization as both entity and process; social relations as both action and structure; the fluidity of the notional boundary of 'organization' and 'environment'; and the interweaving of theoretical and empirical concerns. It is thus a kind of 'experiment' in providing a rather different kind of organizational analysis from that which is familiar in the field. The concluding chapter reviews the analysis offered, drawing out key claims both as regards BP's organization and concerning the 'style' of this analysis, and suggesting how these relate to the wider attempt to provide a revived form of organization studies.

NOTES

1. TNA HW 14/71. Bletchley Park rendered as 'BP' in the original text. See note 13 below for explanation of document citation protocol.

2. The many people with a specialized interest in BP may also find something of interest in this book, because of its organizational focus. To them I would make the point that, for ease of exposition, I have simplified many details, especially those relating to the technical details of cryptanalysis and in particular those relating to Enigma machines. I have also tended to confine very detailed empirical points to endnotes.

3. The abbreviation BP, which was in use there during WW2, will for many present-day readers connote 'British Petroleum', but it is hoped that in the course of reading the book its usage here will become familiar. Those working there also often used the term 'the Park' to refer to BP.

4. I have adopted the 'Harvard system' of referencing in this book, as is usual within many social science disciplines, including organization studies, although less common amongst historians, who tend to prefer the 'Vancouver system'. However, references to archive document catalogue numbers are placed in endnotes to avoid cluttering the text.

5. I use the terms organization studies, organizational analysis and organizational theory largely interchangeably for the purposes of this book to denote the broad sweep of the social-scientific study of organizations. My use on any particular occasion is guided by the particular context, so that I tend to use 'studies' to refer to the field in general, 'analysis' to refer to empirically informed studies and 'theory' to refer to conceptual work. When referring to practitioners of the subject I use organizational analysts or theorists in preference to the perhaps confusing term 'organizational students'. But I do not intend any substantive argument in my use of the terms.

6. Undoubtedly one reason is that in contemporary academia it is rare to have the time and institutional space to write such works (cf. Suddaby, Hardy and Huy, 2011: 245).

7. TNA HW 208/5125. During WW2 the term cryptography was usually, although incorrectly, used rather than cryptanalysis (incorrectly because cryptography is the *writing* of codes and ciphers). In this book I have used the term cryptanalysis throughout, except when quoting from archive documents, where I have left the original usage intact.

8. In this way my usage is quite different from that of Beer and Nohria's (2000) attempt to 'break the code of change', which is geared towards discovering (managerial) answers rather than providing an interpretative understanding.

9. Also there are flourishing sections both in the American Academy of Management and in the European Group for Organization Studies which

cater for historical analysis of management and organizations. However, that these are groups is perhaps indicative of how history remains in some ways apart from rather than fully integrated with organization studies.

10. Conversely, it may be the case that some business historians have regarded organization studies as overly pre-occupied with theoretical debates and insufficiently attentive to empirical detail.

11. A different kind of engagement should also be noted here, that between organization studies and the particular version(s) of history found in Foucauldian analysis (e.g. Jacques, 1996; Shenhav, 1999), but here again the impact on the wider domain of organization studies has been fairly limited.

12. I use the term temporal rather than 'longitudinal' here even though I am gesturing towards something similar to that term as used by Pettigrew (1985). My reason is that to me (although this was not Pettigrew's usage) longitudinal tends to denote the kind of study that returns to its site (e.g. an organization) to take, as it were, snapshots over time, rather than looking at processes as they unfold in time.

13. The TNA papers I will refer to used to be described as Public Record Office (PRO) papers and formally the PRO still exists as a part of TNA so that one should properly refer to them as TNA PRO holdings. However, in line with what has emerged as common practice amongst historians, at least in the intelligence area, I will simply use the abbreviation TNA when referring to them. Catalogue references are to the file containing the relevant paper (e.g. TNA HW 14/1). In many cases I also provide a date for the document to assist finding it within the file (the files being chronologically arranged). Where a quotation has no page number, this means that the document in question comprises a single page. For multi-paged documents (e.g. internal histories) page numbers for quotations are given.

14. Some catalogue identifiers at TNA are meaningful (e.g. WO for War Office papers) but others, such as HW, are randomly assigned and bear no substantive meaning.

15. One exception is the five-volume internal history of 'GC & CS and Naval Sigint', assigned the anticipatory catalogue reference of TNA HW 43/10–15.

16. F. L. Lucas is listed as the 'Responsible Authority' for the history but the actual author or authors are not recorded.

17. TNA HW 14/145.

18. The term Government Communication Headquarters was in use as a cover name for BP from early in the war and, indeed, a sign at the gates proclaimed it as such. However (although there are conflicting accounts of this), it was probably not adopted as the official name until after the war (Aldrich, 2010: 67). Note that whilst to the current-day reader such signage would seem to give away the codebreaking function of BP, that is only because we know the functions of GCHQ. At the time, it would have had no such connotation. For a detailed history of GCHQ *per se*, see Aldrich (2010).

19. I am grateful to the late Peter Freeman, the then GCHQ Historian, for explaining this context to me.

20. For example, oral history accounts are treated as eye-witness accounts without regard for their methodological problems, and archive sources are not referenced in a way which allows their retrieval.

21. A further inaccuracy since, as will become clear, it was not a unitary organization even in the commonsense usage of that term. But, for ease of exposition, I leave that aside for now.

22. Cypher is rendered as Cipher in some accounts, but the former spelling was what was used in official documents at the time. Subsequent usage favours the spelling 'cipher', which is adopted in this text except when quoting documents.

23. It is commonly said that Sinclair used his own money for this purchase. However, recent historical work – specifically the authorized history of SIS – has called this into question (Jeffery, 2010: 319).

24. The term 'Station X' to denote BP refers to one of these elements, namely a wireless room which was briefly situated there (Watson, 1993: 307). The 'X' indicates not, as is sometimes supposed, a secret or unknown quantity, but rather that it was SIS's tenth such station.

25. Aldrich (2010: 22) is of a similar view, although Ratcliff (2006: 77) and Welchman (1982: 9) emphasise the university aspect of the location. It is worth noting that there were many other WW2 secret establishments in the area (Taylor, 2005), again suggesting that the Oxbridge explanation is questionable.

26. Sigint is a broad term, normally used to distinguish it from human intelligence, or humint, the latter being that gathered by agents. Sigint itself nowadays breaks down into multiple forms, including electronic,

photography, radar intelligence (Elint, Photint, Radint) and many others. See Taylor (2007: 254).

27. Note also that ciphers other than Enigma also had keys e.g. Weather cipher keys were denoted by vegetables, e.g. Leek, Garlic, Beetroot.

28. Of these, only Tunny, the product of the Lorenz SZ 40/42 machine, was regularly broken at BP. A few Sturgeon messages were broken and no Thrasher messages.

29. Additional targets included the military ciphers of France and Spain, Portuguese Navy ciphers, some Persian (Iranian) ciphers and those of Axis allies e.g. Bulgaria. At some times and to varying extents, some Soviet Union signals were being read. Beyond military targets, GC & CS also dealt with diplomatic codes, but this work moved from BP to London in 1942. Moreover, apart from its role in codebreaking, BP was also centrally concerned with the *protection* of the ciphers being used by the British, i.e. cipher security. This area was neglected by comparison with the codebreaking effort (see e.g. Ratcliff, 2006: 159–179), with disastrous results at times in the Battle of the Atlantic. Many British codes and ciphers were read by the Germans, although the British Typex machine cipher was never broken. For reasons of space I do not consider the organization of cipher security in this book.

30. Other versions of Enigma were known to be breakable, and Italian Naval Enigma, based on the commercial machine, had been broken by Dilly Knox in 1937. The plugboard version used by the German military modified the cable connections in ways which made the cipher vastly more difficult to break than the commercial version.

31. Note that at this point the codename protocol of colours for GAF Enigma keys and birds for Army Enigma keys had not emerged. When it did, Army Green was re-named Greenshank.

32. Major locations of Y stations included Chatham (Army), Scarborough (Navy) and Cheadle (RAF), but there were dozens of others.

33. Depending on how counted, as discussed in Chapter 1. The post-war review gives 10,000 as the rough 'all-in' figure, TNA HW 14/145: 14.

34. This is not to say that other huts are unimportant, and some of them will also be referred to. Accounts of their functions are sometimes hazy and contradictory, but, from Evans (2003), would seem to have been thus (giving only the main function, because the actual use changed over time in many cases): Hut 1, originally a wireless room, later used for bombes; Hut

2, recreation room; Hut 5, military section; Hut 7, Hollerith card-punching and other machinery; Hut 9, administration; Hut 10, Typex room; Hut 10a, overflow of air section; Huts 11 and 11a, bombes; Hut 12, annexe to Hut 3, also IE; Hut 14, teleprinters; and Hut 15, planned to rehouse Hut 4 but never built. The function of Hut 13 is not known. There were numerous other huts and sub-huts, some shortlived, and numbering went up to at least 23 (photographic room), plus concrete blocks from Block A to Block H (mostly overspills of Huts 3, 4, 6 and 8), as well as the Newmanry and Testery, concerned with Fish and housing, in the former case, Colossus. There were also sites at some distance from BP itself, including Elmers School (diplomatic sections, until 1942) and various bombe outstations (Adstock, Eastcote, Gayhurst, Stanmore, Wavendon), as well as many other locations for disparate functions or overspills (I am excluding here the widely dispersed Y station network, mentioned above). Again, Evans (2003) is the key source here, being a painstaking documentation of the development of the BP fabric, as well as containing many pertinent points about organizational processes associated with the buildings.

Part I Decoding Structures

This part of the book is concerned with the inter-related issues of how BP and signals intelligence were made over the course of WW2. The focus is primarily upon various forms of organizational structuring, broadly conceived, and the emphasis on 'making' indicates that, in line with the general approach outlined in the introduction to the book, I will seek to explore some of the processes of 'organizing' which lie beneath the production of 'organization'. Such an exploration derives in a broad way from processual understandings of structure which emphasise multiple interactions and connections which weave and interweave to continually re-create structure (Strati, 2000; 2008). It is an approach which stands in contrast to more traditional contingency-theory accounts (e.g. Burns and Stalker, 1961; Pugh and Hickson, 1976), which remain widely used within organization theory (Donaldson, 2001). These, in general terms, regard structures as the rationally chosen most effective fit to various contingencies, such as organizational size or technology (Donaldson, 2003: 46). I will touch on such explanations at various points, but inflect them through the rather different approach adopted here.

In order to do this, I will go into some considerable detail (whilst also simplifying and, indeed, ignoring a great deal of complexity) about the empirics of the BP case in order to explicate selected aspects of how its structure changed over time. In Chapter 1 attention will be given primarily to the interplay between GC & CS and various other institutions and agencies, namely the army, navy and air force and their corresponding government ministries, the War Office, Admiralty and Air Ministry. This is further developed in Chapter 2, where the focus shifts to the way that signals intelligence – that is, the entirety of the process of interception, cryptanalysis and intelligence analysis – came to be substantially brought together, and the impact of this on, in particular, the large-scale re-structuring of BP in 1942. These are clearly inter-related issues, and thus some of the conflicts discussed in Chapter 1 are re-visited and their meaning amplified in Chapter 2. In order to orient the reader to these events, it may be helpful to summarise in skeleton form the chronology of their main elements:

- November 1939: establishment of 'dual control' of BP between GC & CS and SIS
- January 1940: first break of a wartime Enigma cipher
- 1941: conflicts within Hut 3, primarily over the relationship between cryptanalysis and intelligence analysis
- 1941: conflicts between GC & CS and government ministries, primarily over the relationship between cryptanalysis and traffic analysis, and interception priorities
- July 1941: Y sub-committee states the principle of inseparability of cryptanalysis and traffic analysis
- October 1941: leading cryptanalysts appeal to Churchill for more resources and implicitly criticize Alistair Denniston's leadership of BP
- December 1941: Brigadier van Cutsem, Deputy Director of Military Intelligence at the War Office, appointed to conduct an inquiry into organization of GC & CS
- January 1942: van Cutsem report completed
- February 1942: major reorganization of GC & CS, initiating, *inter alia*, establishment of a single administrative authority for the BP site; reorganization of Hut 3; placing of service personnel into BP lines of command; replacement of Alistair Denniston by Edward Travis as operational head of BP; separation of commercial and diplomatic section from BP
- February 1943: Travis' annual report for 1942 states the central credo of the unity of interception, cryptanalysis and intelligence analysis
- March 1944: second wartime reorganization of GC & CS, retitling Travis as 'Director'

In both chapters, the analysis touches upon the changing organizational charts at BP, which are reproduced in simplified form in Appendix D as Figures 1 to 4. Such charts are the most conventional way of thinking about organizational structure, indicating sub-divisions and the chains of command and communication between and within them. Yet such representations can be regarded as a particular form of 'encodement', which both conceals yet also expresses an underlying social and political process. The organizational chart is an end product of this process, or perhaps rather a snapshot of that process at a particular moment, but to understand such a chart requires an examination of what underlies it. Its meaning must be 'decoded' in the sense identified in the previous chapter. In any case, I am concerned to explicate structure not simply in terms of formal charts but in the much broader sense of the overall 'shaping' of organization.

This explication makes some reference to individual personalities and it is worth saying something about this. To explain organizational developments simply in terms of personalities or 'personality clashes' is generally highly discreditable within organization studies, and with some reason. Yet no less discreditable is an organization studies which proceeds as if individuals are irrelevant. The point is that organization entails issues of structures and interests that render personality partially irrelevant and yet these issues are themselves inflected through individual actors. In the same way, the actions of those individuals are inflected through the prism of structures and interests, and so organizations (and social relations more generally) cannot be explained simply in terms of 'personalities'. This point has been made in just about every significant discussion in social theory for the last thirty years or more, and it is now often recognized within organization theory that there is a structure–agency duality, rather than a dualism – that is to say, social relations are not a matter of *either* individual action *or* social structure but rather a matter of both/and action and structure (Giddens, 1984). I believe that the actual practice of organization studies has rarely been sufficiently attentive to what this means, so that there is a bifurcation of bloodless accounts of organization as if there were no real, recognizable people in them and highly individualized accounts of, especially, leadership as if there were no structural context to their actions. So one thing I attempt to do is to provide the kind of 'both/and' analysis mandated by a recognition of the inseparability of action/agency and social/organizational structure (cf. Willmott, 2011).

This, indeed, is one of the main characteristics of processual approaches to organizational structure, but so too is its challenge to another entrenched dualism within organization theory, namely that of organization and environment. Within a processual approach 'there is no environment of which the organization is part; rather there is a structure of processes leading simultaneously to the outside and to the inside of the organization' (Strati, 2008: 1187). This leads to the challenge set by one of the world's leading organization theorists, Steve Barley, to take what he regards as 'the path not taken', by which he means the widespread failure within organization studies to examine 'how organizations alter their environments' (Barley, 2010: 778). In terms of the approach adopted here, this means understanding how the 'line' between organization and environment was constructed in the particular case of BP and sigint.

It is not, of course, an easy matter to present an account which eschews dualisms of structure and agency and of organization and environment since these are so embedded not just within organization studies but in the wider ways of making sense of the social world. It is one thing to speak in the abstract about overcoming such dualisms, another to render it intelligible in relation to particular cases. To do so involves making what looks neat and comprehensible (as, for example, in an organization chart) appear messy and confused. But, if this is so, it perhaps reflects that mess and confusion are the stuff of organizational – and social – life and the purpose of organization studies should perhaps be to lay this bare rather than to encode it within the neater frames of its traditional forms of analysis.

I   The Making of Bletchley Park

INTRODUCTION

In this chapter I will begin the exploration of the organization of BP, first of all by showing the complexity of this organization. It might perhaps be imagined that a wartime intelligence organization would be characterized by rigid order and hierarchy, clear lines of command and control and strict rationality. If so, the organization of BP will come as a surprise. The manner of GC & CS's creation after WW1, the way that it brought together an array of different agencies and institutions and then grew very rapidly once on the BP site, has led to it being described both at the time and subsequently by historians as, amongst other things, anarchic and freakish. Out of this complexity a series of disputes and conflicts occurred, through which BP was 'made' or assembled.

These conflicts will be examined in three further sections: the first briefly concerned with the administrative issues posed by dual control of BP as shared between SIS and GC & CS; the second looking at greater length at issues of inter-service conflict and service–GC & CS conflict; and the third considering one of the central episodes in the history of BP's organization, the conflict in Hut 3.

The overall concern is with structures in the general sense of control of BP's activities and on occasion with the narrower sense of lines of command. Part of what makes organization is some such form of control, and at BP this was often indeterminate. The central argument is that, over time and through conflicts and negotiations, it became more determinate and that, to a degree, 'an organization' was constructed out of the flux of 'organization'. Thus by early 1942 BP was in some senses established in a form which was to endure thereafter.

That does not mean that the process of organization-making ceased after that date, but it became less visible and less acute as issues of structural control became crystallized.

THE COMPLEXITY OF BLETCHLEY PARK

In 1942 Joseph Eachus was posted to BP as the US Navy's liaison officer, and his first act was to ask one of his new colleagues for an organizational chart of BP. He was told 'I don't believe we have one'. Eachus went on to speculate: 'I didn't pursue this with him, but I was never quite sure whether he meant we don't have a chart or we don't have an organisation'[1]. In fact, a number of organization charts, at the time sometimes called 'organograms', were produced at different stages of the war[2]. They are neither consistent nor comprehensive, yet it is possible to piece together the broad outlines. These are reproduced in simplified form in Appendix D, where Figures 1 to 3 capture these outlines at various points, namely, early in the war, after the main structural reorganization of 1942 and after a second, more minor, reorganization in 1944. Figure 4 shows the outline structure in the immediate post-war period. But even had such charts been made available to Eachus, it is unlikely that they would have helped a great deal in making sense of the organization of BP, the complexity of which they largely concealed.

At the heart of this complexity was the process by which GC & CS was established in the first place. The amalgamation of Room 40[3] of the Admiralty and the War Office's MI1b in 1919 that created GC & CS was initially placed under the control of the Admiralty and headed by Commander Alastair Denniston. Its remit was to advise government departments on the security of their own ciphers and to study the cipher methods used by foreign powers (Smith, 2001: 17) as well as to provide cryptanalytic training (hence the 'school' of its title)[4]. But, because its peacetime role was mainly confined to diplomatic code-breaking, in 1922 it passed to the Foreign Office (FO) and then in 1923 was placed under the Secret Intelligence Service (SIS) or MI6, which was itself under FO control. This is the key to decoding one initially puzzling feature of BP's organization: the person in operational charge is referred to, prior to 1944, as the Deputy Director. Why? Because the Director of GC & CS was the Chief of SIS, known as 'C', a role held by Admiral Hugh Sinclair until November 1939 and subsequently by Colonel Stewart Menzies[5].

This in itself had implications for BP since on at least one authoritative account Menzies despised intellectuals, disliked and was incompetent at administration, yet was determined to take control of and credit for the Ultra intelligence produced at BP (Aldrich, 2010: 23–4). Other historians have taken a more positive view of Menzies' stewardship of GC & CS (Jeffery, 2010: 746–7), but either way the key point is that BP was not an isolated or stand-alone organization and cannot be understood independently of its location within SIS. One aspect of this was its financing, where, in Denniston's words, it was 'the adopted child of the Foreign Office, with no family rights'[6]. It is difficult, if not impossible, to reconstruct the ways that wartime intelligence operations were funded (O'Halpin, 1987: 187), but it would seem that as regards GC & CS it was in part through 'secret vote' funds (i.e. concealed from public accounts) channelled through SIS, which rose from £79,000 in 1940–1 to £1,302,000 for 1943–4 (Jeffery, 2010: 475). However, there were also 'open vote' funds channelled through the Foreign Office relating to the employment by the FO of permanent staff at GC & CS, amounting to £220,000 by the end of the war (O'Halpin, 1987: 202–3)[7]. Extraordinarily, given the extreme secrecy surrounding BP, the public accounts of this money refer to specific kinds of work, such as punch-card operators and tabulating staff, and the growth in their numbers could have provided a clue to the expansion (and hence, by inference, success) of British signals intelligence. But 'perhaps the security authorities believed that Germans did not consult British government publications; more likely, they did not read them themselves' (O'Halpin, 1987: 203). In addition to these sources of funding, some costs were borne by the military services (in particular salary costs of service personnel), whilst at least some machine costs were met by the Admiralty (Welchman, 1982: 140).

The placing of GC & CS within FO and SIS control had other, more far-reaching, implications. The services and their respective ministries – the army, navy and air force (RAF) and the War Office (WO), Admiralty and Air Ministry (AM)[8] – had acquiesced grudgingly to these new arrangements and all continued to have a stake and an interest in GC & CS. Their agreement was given in the expectation that in the event of war they would take over the operational use of decrypted material; on the understanding that the staff they in the meantime attached to GC & CS would work only on ciphers relating to their home service; and in the belief that they would retain respon-sibility for producing intelligence from signals (Hinsley, 1993c: 5). The ministries retained their own intelligence functions, with each having a Director of Intelligence because, of course, sigint was by no means the only source of intelligence material relevant to the ministries. Moreover, the first aspect of sigint operations – interception – was not under any single control. The army, navy and, in due course, the RAF each had a number of interception stations, as did the police and the General Post Office (GPO), whilst GC & CS itself had no intercept stations. Overall oversight of this entire complex of operations lay with a Whitehall[9] body which became called the Y Board, with which were associated a number of sub-committees bringing together the various parties involved.

From this very brief outline, it is possible to see how, by the time that GC & CS came to BP in 1939, there existed a complicated dynamic involving a multiplicity of different agencies with potentially compet-ing interests. These potentials became very apparent once Enigma keys began to be broken, with consequences both for the rapid expansion in the scale of BP and for the nature of its work, which will be discussed in the next chapter. The situation was described, by Frank Birch's internal post-war history of sigint, as 'a patchwork of extemporised expedi-ents'[10] which was 'freakish' and 'chaotic'[11], by the official history as 'creative anarchy' (Hinsley et al., 1979: 273) and by Nigel de Grey's internal post-war review as 'bad organization' without 'logic'[12]. Historians have described the situation as one of 'divided loyalties'

(Davies, 2001: 395) and having a 'chain of command so loose that it bordered on anarchy' (Budiansky, 2000: 229). In the remainder of this chapter I will try to unpick in greater detail what underlay this situation and what resulted from it, with reference to some illustrative examples.

DUAL CONTROL: BLETCHLEY PARK AS AN SIS WAR STATION

The complexity of BP from an administrative point of view was considerable. I have alluded, and will return, to the issue of the variety of employing institutions, but simply thinking about scale, the headcount increased from about 200 in September 1939 to 1,576 in March 1942[13] and then rose to a height of 8,743 at the end of 1944, before dropping back to 5,781 at the end of the war. These figures are drawn from personnel returns for BP[14], but it is the case that other estimates vary considerably, so that a figure of 10,000 is often given. What such discrepancies reflect is the organizational complexity of BP – what was counted as 'inside' or 'outside' its organization was not always clear, as will become apparent. But the main point for present purposes is the change in the *order of magnitude*. Nigel de Grey in his post-war review of BP made exactly these points in providing the rough figure of 10,000[15]. Of these, about one-third were civilians and about three-quarters were female.

As Dora, one of the interviewees, who worked in administration, remarked '[in January 1941] it was all the embryo of the organization and it just got too big, we couldn't be coping'. The growth of personnel entailed routine administration of the payroll, for example, but also all of the activity concerned with security vetting and security induction for new joiners. Beyond that, there was a massive logistical exercise involved in housing (or billeting, to use the term of the time), feeding and transporting this workforce, the bulk of whom worked a three-shift system running around the clock. Drawing again upon de Grey's post-war review[16], in July 1944, when BP was at its largest, there were about 4,000 billets (of various sorts) in force, with another 4,000 or so accommodated through the armed services. There were over 30,000 meals served at the BP canteen each week, on a near-24-hour basis. There were almost 34,000 miles of passenger journeys organized, using 115 drivers. Associated with the billeting was an organization of buses (with many personnel using their own transport, e.g. bicycles) so that, according to Ron, another one of the interviewees, in 1944 there were about 40 buses per shift, each with a seating capacity of about 40 (so, 1,600 in total), transporting the staff in and out. Dora, working in administration, recalls that 'it was a *huge* logistical exercise, and it had to take place every day round the clock ... that was a colossal administration in itself, the transport'.

This administrative effort caused many difficulties, not just because of its scale and secrecy, but because, quoting the annual report for 1942, 'the position was far from satisfactory because there was a complete cleavage between those responsible for the Station [i.e. BP] and those responsible for the work'[17]. This refers precisely to the fact that BP was initially a War Station, or temporary site, of SIS. In November 1939, Commander Bradshaw was charged with general administration of the GC & CS part of things, but from October 1940 the Station was placed under the Joint Management Committee (later the Joint Committee of Control), consisting of Bradshaw for GC & CS and Captain Ridley for SIS, and others. Bletchley Park was thus subject to 'dual control', a situation which grew directly out of the way that, back in 1923, GC & CS had been put under SIS control. The results, according to the internal history of sigint, 'brought GC & CS into disrepute'[18]. This was forcibly exposed in a 'Report on Military Intelligence at the GC & CS' prepared by Brigadier van Cutsem, Deputy Director of Military Intelligence at the WO, in January 1942[19]. Divided control, he concluded, meant that 'shortcomings in administration are already affecting the efficiency of the work of GC & CS'[20], with problems including poor planning of the site, poor heating, lighting and ventilation and overcrowding of buildings, a wasteful system of billeting and transport and poor staff welfare arrangements. These problems were not solely the result of growth. From the very first days of BP when the headcount was only 200 or so, Denniston complained that the site was inadequate, too crowded and had been allocated to GC & CS only because 'the Admiral' (i.e. Hugh Sinclair when Chief of SIS) had ordered it, and that SIS staff were receiving better treatment than those of GC & CS[21].

Van Cutsem's proposal was for a unified administration under a Chief Administrative Officer and, as part of the February 1942 reorganization discussed in the next chapter, this occurred, with the role being filled by Bradshaw, bringing results that were 'undoubtedly an improvement'[22]. Thus it is possible to see how encoded within the box in the organizational chart depicted in Figure 2 of Appendix D that says 'Assistant Director (Administration), Commander Alan Bradshaw' is a set of organizational developments which occurred over time, informed by *ad hoc* arrangements and political contingencies. What is true of this one segment of this organizational chart is, I suggest, true of all segments of all organizational charts and, for that matter, other representations of organization such as balance sheets and annual reports.

These administrative reforms did not, of course, sever the relationship between GC & CS and SIS, which continued until GCHQ became in effect, although not formally, independent after the war. What they did was to place the BP site itself under unified control, albeit dependent upon the Ministry of Works (MOW) for the development of its buildings and infrastructure (Evans, 2003), a matter of very considerable complexity given their rapid growth. Nevertheless, what was going on within the site continued to comprise an array of different organizations and agencies, and it is to these that I now turn.

INTER-SERVICE CONFLICTS: CONTROLLING
BLETCHLEY PARK

As I have already indicated, another consequence of the way that GC & CS had been set up was a complicated set of relationships with the armed services and their associated ministries. One result of this was that within GC & CS individual sections for navy (1924), army (1930) and air force (1936) were established, and continued throughout the war with the intention of ensuring that individual service interests were met[23]. Again, then, decoding the existence of these sections within the organizational charts requires a recognition of the play of interests at work. But, beyond this, it is important to recognize that these sections were in no clear sense the outposts of their respective services at BP. There were continual issues over control of staff and staff allegiance: 'GC & CS was very much an assortment of semi-independent sections with divided loyalties and subject to lines of dual control between GC & CS and their departments of origin' (Davies, 2001: 395–6). Service personnel were bound by their own hierarchies, leading to what Nigel de Grey called an 'intolerably complicated'[24] situation, growing out of the fact that service personnel had been loaned to GC & CS but initially were meant to work only on matters related to their own service. Moreover, as the war developed these regular service staff were joined, in much larger numbers, by others who had been mobilized 'for the duration' (i.e. of the war). In practice, as will be discussed elsewhere, BP sections brought together civilians and personnel of various services with little or no regard for rank or service. Whilst this seems to have worked well enough at 'grass roots' level, structurally it led to innumerable problems, as de Grey's post-war review explained:

> There was never ... any clear understanding about the staffing of the Service Sections or any uniformity of procedure between them [... and ...] the services were unwilling to mix civil and service men in the same station for administrative reasons[25].

Difficulties included the different commissioning, promotion and pay arrangements for the different services. As regards the discrepancy between civil and service personnel, the review referred to 'gross inequalities in pay ... monstrous cases where men were doing the same (not similar) work and some getting nearly double the others'[26]. Amongst high-profile examples of such inequalities was the fact that in December 1942 the Head of Hut 3, an RAF officer, was being paid almost twice as much as the civilian Head of Hut 6[27]. The same pattern was identified in Birch's internal history, in that 'from first to last, Service officers, nearly all of them civilians in uniform, were better paid than their plain clothes opposite numbers'[28]. However, it was not just pay which was at issue. De Grey also noted the 'very low standard of "military" behaviour in a civil institution'[29]; discrepancies in rank between service personnel in BP and those outside; and the sudden posting away of service personnel. More generally, the mixing together of civilians and different services gave rise to numerous problems of command and control. For example, de Grey identified that it led to 'divided loyalties' in Hut 3 (of which more below), and of the Teleprinter Room he says that 'WAAF resented civil controllers'[30]. An illustration of a similar issue is the occasion when the Director of the WRNS visited BP and asked '... in rather supercilious tones, "Why are my Wrens working with civilians?"' (Welchman, 1982: 147). Thus de Grey's general conclusion was that

> GC & CS created a most complicated structure internally violating the official ladder of command and at the same time causing an intricate and illogical series of channels of reporting ... [t]he history of relations of GC & CS to the Services consists almost entirely of the quarrels that resulted from this bad organization, having parallelism in no way as between the 3 Services or logic within GC & CS, and the efforts to straighten them out[31].

Whilst, as de Grey implies, they were never resolved, these kinds of issues were at least partially ameliorated with the agreement in 1942, again arising from the van Cutsem report, that service personnel would be brought under the control of the heads of the relevant sections at BP (i.e. Military, Naval and Air sections) rather than remaining under their formal service hierarchies. This had the effect of meaning that, regardless of whether a member of, say, Air Section was military or civilian, he or she would be within a single command structure. Even this agreement proved contentious in that in June 1942 the RAF repudiated it, causing considerable anger at BP until its reinstatement in August 1943[32]. Taken together, there seems to be considerable evidence to contradict the claim made by Ratcliff (2006: 82) that 'almost exclusively civilian at the war's start, GC & CS rather smoothly integrated an ever-increasing number of military personnel'.

Such issues were not confined to the services. The civilian workforce was composed of extremely diverse agencies, with individuals on loan from, amongst many other places, the Natural History Museum, Somerset House and the British Tabulating Machine Company (BTMC). It was not until spring of 1943 that all of these, with the exception of GPO staff, were brought into FO employment (at least in principle, for there appear to have been some minor anomalies).

The service-related issues, at least, can be seen to stem primarily from the way that GC & CS had been set up, but the issues of staff employment and lines of command were really only one aspect of a much wider set of problems, at the heart of which was the question of who was in control of its work. The story of BP organization during the first half of the war is littered with examples of ongoing arguments over just this issue (see Hinsley *et al.*, 1979: 267–74 for more extensive detail), which are referred to by Frank Birch in the internal history of sigint as the 'Y wars'[33]. In particular, during the period 1940–1 there was a sharp dispute between Major-General Davidson, then the Director of Military Intelligence (DMI) at the WO, and 'C'. In December 1940, the DMI proposed a considerable enhancement of military control of GC & CS, which he regarded as suffering from divided organization and as being overly dominated by Foreign Office interests. Moreover, he proposed a review of these organizational arrangements to be prepared for the Joint Intelligence Committee (JIC)[34]. In a series of memoranda and notes there was an ebb and flow of argument between the DMI and 'C', who rejected both the premise of the organizational criticisms and the need to involve the JIC. Despite a partial climb down in which the DMI admitted on 4 January 1941 that he had 'come in new to a show like this'[35], he continued to press for a review. In this he was successful, although 'C' avoided involving the JIC, and the Y Board initiated an investigation.

This review became the arena of some heated debate, with both 'C' and GC & CS resisting the proposal for enhanced military control. For example, in a strongly worded submission, Colonel John Tiltman (variously Chief Cryptographer and Head of Military Section at GC & CS) wrote of the DMI's proposal that it 'reveals a complete misunderstanding of the scope, functions and working of cryptography'[36]. The political negotiations were complex because it was not simply a matter of 'the services' versus GC & CS. Indeed, one reason for the failure of the services to gain control of GC & CS was that they were frequently divided amongst themselves (Davies, 2001: 399). For example, in this case the DMI's proposals were strongly criticised by the Director of Naval Intelligence (DNI), Rear-Admiral John Godfrey. But, at exactly the same time, the DNI himself proposed that all nomenclature used at GC & CS should be changed to match the system used by the Navy, a proposal unwelcome at GC & CS but in any case flatly rejected by the DMI[37]. At all events, the outcome of the Y Board review was to re-enforce the existing situation that, whilst interception remained under the control of the services, cryptanalysis must remain independently run at GC & CS. Nevertheless, new arrangements were made to co-ordinate service and GC & CS activities. These decisions, made in March 1941, 'brought to an end the period in which misunderstandings and emergencies resulted from inadequate high-level direction of sigint policy' (Hinsley *et al.*, 1979: 272).

Even so, there were continuing conflicts with, in particular, MI8 (the sigint service of the WO) over interception and traffic analysis, the areas where control of resources, such as intercept stations, was fragmented. For example, in a very strongly worded statement on 1 June 1941, Gordon Welchman accused its head, Colonel Butler, of 'continual obstruction' in relation to prioritization of interception resources, of pursuing initiatives which were 'not only unnecessary but a nuisance' and of 'interfering with the work of Hut 6'[38]. Significantly, perhaps, Butler was replaced on 16 June 1941[39]. On the other side of such disputes, although dating from some months before Welchman's devastating criticisms, one of the most curious documents in the archives – and one I have never seen referred to in studies of BP – is a kind of satirical sketch of the various agencies involved that was written in December 1940. The author was the very same Colonel Butler of MI8, and the document was formally circulated 'as an analogy to the present organization' intended as 'a serious attempt at giving a clear picture of the present position'[40]. Entitled 'The Kitchen Front', it satirizes GC & CS as the 'General Combined Cookery School' and treats all the main agencies in a similar way. For example, the Admiralty is 'Mr Sinbad', the Air Ministry is 'Mr Bird', the Y Committee is the 'Why? Committee', 'C' is Mr Smyth, Denniston is Mrs Smyth, the FO is Mr Effo etc. Butler (or MI8) himself is Mrs Atkins, whilst her husband is Mr Atkins, or the War Office. Using cooking as an analogy for cryptanalysis, the author amusingly, if perhaps heavy-handedly, re-creates a history of GC & CS up to the time of the document's writing.

It is a document which would repay more detailed analysis than is appropriate here. Its main significance is that under cover of the satire some really very sharp criticisms were made of GC & CS from an MI8 perspective. Thus, for example: '[i]t began to dawn on Mrs Atkins that whenever she found anything, the Smyth fraternity took control and got the credit while she footed the bill'. Chided by Mr Atkins that the results are good, Mrs Atkins opines that this may be 'in spite of Mrs Smyth', who is elsewhere described as being 'a superlative cook' (i.e. cryptanalyst) but an indifferent 'housekeeper' (i.e. administrator). Furthermore, as Mrs Atkins observes, 'there is more in housekeeping than just cooking'[41]. In short, the satire enabled Colonel Butler to opine that BP was poorly organized, bolstering the case for greater WO control over it.

Leaving aside the conflict with MI8, proposals for greater WO control of GC & CS were again made in December 1941, this time by MI14[42], and once more in the January 1942, in the van Cutsem report[43]. However, the combination of the arrangements made by the Y Board in March 1941 and the reorganization of 1942 which followed the van Cutsem report (discussed in the next chapter) meant that there was limited support for such proposals, and from that time onwards the issue of militiarization of BP (i.e. the demand by the WO for greater control over it) largely disappeared from the agenda. In other words, the status of GC & CS at BP as 'an independent organization' had been established, for all that it continued to have many inter-relationships with other agencies.

Relations between BP and the Air Ministry (AM) were in many ways smoother, for two reasons. Firstly, more than either the army or the navy, air intelligence benefited earlier and in greater volume from Enigma decryption, so the value of BP's work was clearly evident. Secondly, unlike the other services, the RAF retained some cryptanalytic functions in relation to some 'low-grade' codes and ciphers (Hinsley et al., 1979: 268–9). Conflicts over control of interception occurred from time to time, as they did over control of RAF and WAAF personnel, as mentioned earlier. Nevertheless, as the internal history of sigint records, whilst the AM tended to back up the WO in disputes with BP, it did so only 'from the touchline', being essentially satisfied with things as they were, 'as well it might be in view of the flood of GAF sigint'[44] it was receiving by virtue of the large volume of GAF Enigma being successfully decrypted.

Bletchley Park's relations with the Admiralty were rather more complicated. This may be partly because the Admiralty had had a greater cryptanalytic capacity than the other services prior to the formation of GC & CS and, as has been mentioned, initially controlled this new body. It is also relevant to note that the Admiralty actually conducted naval operations, whereas neither the WO nor the AM conducted army or RAF operations. In other respects, too, the navy 'was different'. I will talk in more detail about Enigma in the next chapter, but from what I said in the introductory chapter it will be clear that Naval Enigma was worked on in Huts 4 and 8 at BP, whereas Army and Air Enigma was the province of Huts 3 and 6[45]. Also, for much of the war, the WO and AM received Ultra in a form which was purported to have been gathered not from sigint but from other intelligence sources, whereas the Admiralty, from the beginning, was aware of the source of Ultra[46].

At all events, the creation of GC & CS had left the Naval Intelligence Division (NID) at the Admiralty 'reduced . . . to a shadow of its former self' (Beesly, 2000: 9) in that it no longer undertook cryptanalytic functions. Nevertheless, the Admiralty, and more particularly its Operational Intelligence Centre (OIC), which collected, analysed and distributed naval intelligence from all sources, including cryptanalysis, needed to work in concert with the Naval Section (NS) of GC & CS[47]. The issue was not just a matter of receiving decrypted material but also of linking cryptanalytic effort to naval priorities. This was made more geographically difficult with the move to BP in 1939, and the solution was initially to create a liaison section, ID8G or NID8G, located within the OIC and headed by Lieutenant-Commander Malcolm Saunders (Beesly, 2000: 22). However, this arrangement was not seen as satisfactory, apparently because of communication difficulties, although there is no information on the specifics of this, and in December 1940 Saunders re-located to BP (Hinsley *et al.*, 1979: 268; Beesly, 2000: 69).

Against this background, there were numerous disputes, leading the initial Head of Naval Section at BP until 1940, W. E. ('Nobby') Clarke (who had started out as a member of Admiralty Room 40), to describe his time at BP as the unhappiest of his life, due to the intrigues of 'high ups'[48] and the refusal of GC & CS to accept, in effect, the ways of working that had been established in the Admiralty[49]. Rear-Admiral John Godfrey, when DNI, was a forceful critic of BP's first head: 'Denniston has shown an amazing lack of imagination and pettiness of outlook' (cited in Budiansky, 2000: 202), and was certainly one of the many factors involved in his removal (discussed in the next chapter). But perhaps the most remarkable piece of evidence in this regard is the draft internal history of ID8G compiled in 1945. This lengthy document commences by noting that 'the story of ID8G [of the Admiralty] is one of constant tension and friction with German Naval Section [of BP]' and warns that 'this history has descended into personalities, often to a point on the boundary of good taste'[50]. It concludes by bemoaning 'the sordid existence of a unit whose functions were never clearly thought out and agreed upon by the heads of the two departments between which it stood'[51].

Whilst, indeed, often discussing personalities in rather forceful terms, the author of this history is cautioned by Commander (as he by that time was) Saunders that these were immaterial compared with the underlying structural issues, which he regarded as residing in the way that ID8G was serving various different agencies, including but not limited to the OIC and BP Naval Section[52]. As an aside, it is worth noting that this disagreement over how to analyse an organizational issue mirrors the structure–agency dualism mentioned earlier. That said, the main point to be made is this: BP was 'made' within a conflicted terrain and via a nexus of relationships. Thus, in this case, the box marked 'Naval Section' in the organization charts of GC & CS conceals or encodes a complex set of processes such as those I have very briefly indicated here. It may be, as the authoritative history of the OIC has it, that that body's relations with BP were ones of 'extremely close and fruitful co-operation' (Beesly, 2000: 255) and, as the internal history of sigint has it, that 'GC & CS dovetailed very neatly into the NID setup'[53]. But this had to be *achieved* in the face of the consequences flowing from, in particular, the rupture with the Admiralty caused by the creation of GC & CS in the first place[54].

Thus, in the various ways I have sketched, a series of conflicts, negotiations and agreements served to construct a boundary between BP and other agencies and in this way to make an 'inside' and an 'outside' in terms of the control of BP (cf. Strati, 2008: 1187). However, this did not simply entail conflicts with these other agencies, but also had an intimately interconnected internal dimension, the most dramatic and significant aspect being the case of Hut 3, which I will now discuss.

THE HUT 3 CONFLICTS: PUTTING THE HOUSE IN ORDER

The conflicts which occurred in Hut 3 at BP during 1941 and into early 1942 created a 'crisis'[55] which led, according to Birch's internal history, to the 1942 reorganization[56], although in the next chapter I will suggest that there were other factors in this. Hut 3, to recall, was the section of BP which, once provided by Hut 6 with decrypts of Army and GAF Enigma, emended them and translated them into English, indexed and cross-referenced the messages, identified and evaluated the intelligence they yielded and passed this on to the relevant ministry or command via the SLU network (see Chapter 5). It was in this sense one of the central and vital elements of BP (see Bennett, 1993; Millward, 1993; Calvocoressi, 2001), delivering a core part of the intelligence yield to end users.

According to the internal history of Hut 3, in the course of 1941 a series of 'interminable disagreements'[57] broke out amongst the Head of Hut, Commander Malcolm Saunders[58] (i.e. a naval officer, mentioned above in a different role), the Head of 3A – the air section of the hut – Wing Commander Robert Humphreys (i.e. an RAF officer) and the Head of 3M – the military or army section of the hut – Major C.R. Curtis (i.e. an Army officer). An indication of the tone of the dispute can be found in Frank Birch's[59] memo to Denniston accusing Saunders of 'interfering, intriguing, creating and magnifying difficulties and misunderstandings, causing friction, undermining confidence and, incidentally, making proper liaison impossible'[60]. Later, in the internal history of sigint, Birch recorded that

> The spate of arguments, cavilling, protest and recrimination that poured from the typewriters … bears bulky witness to the general discontent and, in some cases, to a breakdown of discipline[61].

Ralph Bennett, later to be Hut 3 Duty Officer, notes that 'something like chaos reigned' at this time (Bennett, 1993: 31), and there are many other accounts confirming this, with many of the disputes being referred outside BP, to 'C', causing significant embarrassment[62].

Smith (1998: 92) refers to this in terms of a 'clash of personalities' amongst the participants I have named, but, as I suggested earlier, whilst personalities may inflect institutional conflicts, the latter are rarely reducible to the former. So what was the dispute about? It concerned two inter-related things. One was yet another example of friction between services and between the services and BP, in terms of the authority which a naval officer might exert over an officer of another service, but also the relationship with ministries, because Humphreys had taken to bypassing both the Head of Hut 3 and GC & CS as a whole, instead making direct reports of intelligence yield to the AM: 'he tried to set up within Hut 3 a semi-independent and almost rival organization, responsible to himself and through him to the Air Ministry'[63]. In this he was supported by Major Curtis, who was himself passing intelligence directly to, in his case, the WO[64] and was also making unauthorized and critical reports to 'C' about the operation of Hut 3, for which he was reprimanded by Denniston[65].

The consequences of all this were not 'merely' political but also had significant potential for operational disaster. On 1 December 1941 MI8 of the WO issued an inaccurate document on the nature and extent of co-operation between the German army and air force on the basis of Enigma decrypts and traffic analysis. This they had received without the knowledge of GC & CS, constituting a breach of security as regards Enigma as well as a deficiency of intelligence analysis[66]. It is not clear from the archive material, but there must be a strong presumption that the source of this material was Major Curtis or at any rate that it derived from an unauthorized communication between Hut 3 and the WO.

The second, related, aspect of the conflict was something which sounds innocuous but was in fact central to the organizational story of BP: were the staff of Hut 3 intelligence officers or were they translators? Humphreys, himself a highly trained intelligence officer as well as an expert German speaker, was of the view that only such qualified intelligence officers should analyse, handle and distribute intelligence outputs[67]. The opposing view, expressed by F. L. Lucas, a senior member of Hut 3, when called upon to adjudicate in the dispute, was that Hut 3 watch members, whether trained as such or not, were 'intelligence officers NOT TRANSLATORS'[68] and that, in any event, the head of hut should have full authority over its sub-sections. I will explain more fully in the next chapter why this was such a key issue, but, briefly, what was at stake was whether BP was simply a crypt-analytic bureau or whether it was an intelligence organization: if Hut 3 staff were regarded simply as translators then this would imply that BP was not an intelligence organization.

The consequences of these conflicts were profound. Quoting Nigel de Grey, the internal history of sigint recorded that '[i]t was evident that the whole situation was getting out of control and that GC & CS was unable apparently to control it'[69]. This is an important observation in that significant change in organizations often requires the existence of a widespread sense of crisis (Munir, 2005). It was just such a sense which led to the DMI and 'C' jointly appointing Brigadier van Cutsem to prepare his report, which has been mentioned in a different context earlier. It had a very direct outcome. On 9 February 1942 a meeting was held at BP, the minutes of which record, baldly, that 'Commander Saunders will relinquish his post in Hut 3' and 'Wing Commander Humphreys will leave Hut 3'[70]. Both continued to have roles at BP, with Saunders being in charge of bombe building, although both, from 1943 were posted overseas[71]. Major Curtis simply disappears from the record, and certainly left Hut 3. What was then initiated was a 'triumvirate' arrangement consisting of the deputies[72] of the three orig-inal protagonists, with no one in overall charge and disputes to be referred to a 'referee' – with the need for a 'referee' perhaps suggesting the fragility of the supposed solution, as the internal history of sigint later pointed out[73]. Certainly this arrangement was very shortlived and in July 1942 a new Head of Hut 3, Eric Jones, was appointed.

Travis refers to this episode as one of 'taking a tick out of a dog' and of appointing 'a popular and respected Head [whose] even temper and calmness never fail to exert a deflationary influence upon a highly strung team'[74]. Jones is noteworthy for the fact that, unlike most at BP, his specialist expertise was not in languages, mathematics or intelli-gence but administration:

> He had left school at fourteen and had been in the cotton business in Manchester[75]. He was very intelligent, didn't know German but

understood organisation very well. He gave people a free hand. It all became crystal clear. Quite a lot of brainy people had the habit of resigning when they were miffed ... but Jones dealt with them.

(Jim Rose, quoted in Smith, 1998: 93)

Jones' key role at BP explains why, in the 1944 organization chart, he is the only one of the Heads of Hut to have the status of Assistant Director. Again, it is impossible to decode this particular piece of the chart without an understanding of the underlying process which made Jones' effective management of Hut 3 so vital: that is to say that, whilst Jones' personal managerial skills were important, their full significance resides within a broader structural narrative[76], for the resolution of the Hut 3 conflicts was a highly significant moment in BP's history. The high political profile they had came within the context of what was already a highly charged situation because of the way that GC & CS had been created and developed. It is easy to imagine, given in particular the various attempts by the WO to gain control over GC & CS and the lingering resentments of the Admiralty at the loss of such control (Lewin, 2008: 65), that the organization of BP might have proceeded quite differently had the conflict not been resolved in the way that it was.

It is therefore possible to see how, by early 1942, BP had been substantially 'made' in the form it was to remain in for the remainder of the war and, in many respects, thereafter. I do not mean by this that the processes of making and remaking organization ceased at that time – it was an ongoing process. However, from this time onwards attempts to militarize BP by putting it under, in particular, WO control all but disappeared, and many of the issues of lines of command were resolved by locating military staff clearly within BP rather than within service hierarchies. It is true that, as noted above, there were hiccups in the latter arrangement, and it is also the case, again as noted, that civilians did not come into unified FO employment until almost a year later. These are both examples of the process of organization-making being ongoing. Early 1942 also saw BP coming under its own administrative control, rather than being jointly administered with SIS, as outlined in the discussion of 'dual control' above. In these and other ways (to be discussed in the next chapter), early 1942 marked, as the internal history of sigint has it, 'the end of an era'. The problems and conflicts did not disappear, but the changes 'helped to clear the air', in a process which was 'not a reformation but a transformation'. Ministries became 'more sympathetic' towards and even 'respectful' of BP, and it was no longer seen as 'an FO institution meddling in service affairs'[77]. If the early years of BP were like a jigsaw, by early 1942 the pieces had been assembled so as to form a recognizable picture.

CONCLUSION

The 'making' of Bletchley Park's organization was an achievement rather than a given. It was stitched together over time in circumstances which, by the time of WW2, were quite different from those in which it had been created as a small amalgamated cryptanalytic bureau in the aftermath of the previous war. The multiplicity of agencies and interests that came to be involved meant that the making of BP was often marked by problems and conflicts, and gave the organization its widely remarked upon chaotic and anarchic character. These problems and conflicts left 'traces' that can be read both in the archive documents and in the organization charts, and the meaning of these traces can be understood only by considering the problems and conflicts they reference. I have given a few examples of how individual elements within the charts can be so understood. These have included understanding why, until 1944, the head of BP is designated as 'Deputy Director'; the significance of the role of Assistant Director (Administration); some of the issues embedded in the existence of the Service Sections; and why the Head of Hut 3 in 1944 had Assistant Director status. These – and other examples in the following chapter – may seem in themselves minor or arcane details, but collectively they are an important part of how an organization's structure is produced and reproduced.

I have stressed the role of conflicts in the process of structuring
BP. It is very important indeed in understanding BP, and I hope the brief
examples given have served to demonstrate the point, that any idea
that in the situation of war all bickering, disputes, rivalries and jeal-
ousies (both personal and organizational) were suspended is misguided.
Calvocoressi, for example, states that

> Intelligence-gathering has many sources and methods and breeds
> therefore a diversity of agencies which are frequently jealous of one
> another, but in wartime BP no such factiousness was apparent.
>
> *(Calvocoressi, 2001: 24)*

Whilst it may be reasonable to say that relations at BP itself – and, after
all, Calvocoressi worked there[78] – were free of faction at the level of
those working together 'at the coalface', and there is ample evidence of
this, it is emphatically not the case that, at a structural level, the
organizational complex of GC & CS and related agencies was one of
harmony. I do not mean to imply by this that there were not many
areas in which harmony obtained, or to deny that an easy co-operation
was sometimes achieved. Nevertheless, BP was 'made' through conflicts and negotiations amongst many different agencies[79]. These conflicts were inter-related and ranged from those between GC & CS and
SIS over control of the BP site to those within and between the services
and GC & CS over control of its activities. Although they never ceased,
the conflicts were especially acute and visible in the first half of the
war, during which time BP was substantially 'made'. But established as
what? Not the cryptanalytic bureau it had been set up to be in 1919, but
a signals intelligence organization. It is to the making of signals intelligence that I now turn.

NOTES

1. Obituary, *Daily Telegraph*, London, 19 December 2003.
2. For example TNA HW 3/152, TNA HW 43/1: 175–76; TNA HW 14/5; TNA
   HW 14/99.
3. Strictly speaking, NID 25.

4. See Denniston (2007: 54–5) for the full text of GC & CS's 1919 remit.
5. But note that Sinclair had been the Director of Naval Intelligence (DNI) at the time of GC & CS's formation and thus, in its days under the Admiralty, had also been its overall boss, so, in a sense, there was some continuity of oversight until Menzies succeeded Sinclair as 'C'. Colonel Menzies was, by the end of the war, Major-General Sir Stewart Menzies, but for ease of exposition I will refer to him throughout this book by the title he held for most of the war.
6. CCAC DENN 1/4: 2.
7. There is real difficulty in interpreting these figures, because Jeffery (2010: 475) refers to payment for 7,847 GC & CS civilians in 1944, whilst O'Halpin (1987: 203) refers to 3,789 such staff in 1945. If all of the former were being paid from the secret vote and all of the latter from the open vote then, even allowing for the fact that staff numbers were falling in 1945, that would give a combined total larger than the entire staff of BP, service personnel included. One possibility is that there is some double counting at play; another is that what is being picked up is payments to GC & CS civilians at locations other than BP, possibly in intercept stations or, which is more likely, at overseas locations. However, the key points to note are that GC & CS funds were not directly allocated, and, moreover, that they were channelled through more than one route.
8. In relation to the discussion at this point the RAF and the Air Ministry are less significant since, having been formed only in 1918, they had little in the way of intelligence functions (prior to their formation, air sigint had been the province of MI1b of the WO). This, however, rapidly changed in the inter-war period.
9. Whitehall is a generic term for the British government and, more specifically, for the permanent civil service administration of the state, as opposed to politicians.
10. TNA HW 43/1: 145.
11. TNA HW 43/1: 176.
12. TNA HW 14/145: 22.
13. This figure was actually lower than it had been in late 1941 because, as part of the reorganization to be discussed in Chapter 2, diplomatic and, a little later, commercial sections went with Denniston back to London. The headcount may have been 2,500 prior to this.
14. TNA HW 14/154.

15. TNA HW 14/145: 14. In some accounts it is suggested that the figure of 10,000 includes domestically based intercept staff, but it is not clear whether this is what de Grey had in mind. In any event, the previously quoted personnel returns suggest that the level of staffing at BP and the bombe outstations was not far short of 9,000.

16. TNA HW 14/145: 32–5.

17. TNA HW 14/ 67: 1.

18. TNA HW 43/2: 468.

19. TNA WO 208/5070. It is worth noting what a remarkable piece of work this report was. In the space of a few weeks van Cutsem not only got to grips with the complexity of BP's organization but did so in a way which, in the light of the heated conflicts which will be explored later in this chapter, was notably non-partisan. As Birch says in the internal history of sigint, the report was 'sane, disinterested and sympathetic' (TNA HW 43/1: 442).

20. TNA WO 208/5070: 11.

21. TNA HW 14/1. It is interesting, given the now iconic status of the BP site, to realize just how unpopular it was with many at the time. See also TNA HW 14/17 and TNA HW 43/2: 469 for the endemic problems created by the inadequacies of the site.

22. TNA HW 43/2: 469. Paymaster-Commander (later Acting Captain) Alan Bradshaw CBE RN, it is worth saying, is rarely mentioned in writings about BP yet, as the archives clearly show, was a pivotal figure as, seconded from NID, he worked throughout the war as (under various titles) GC & CS's chief administrator. This perhaps reflects the relative lack of profile and glamour of purely administrative functions. The interviewee Dora, who worked as his secretary, explained that Bradshaw had to fight the view that 'he's just an administrator' in order to get things done in the face of powerful lobbies who not only saw their work as more important but also acted as what Bradshaw called 'empire builders' – that is, pursuing their own sectional interests for resources. He was, according to Dora 'not a man to be trifled with' but he 'was a delightful man'. Gordon Welchman summarised Bradshaw's approach thus: 'it seemed . . . that Bradshaw worked on the principle of meeting any request with a stream of naval abuse. If the applicant crumbled, Bradshaw reckoned that the case was not a strong one' (Welchman, 1982: 128). A fuller, and slightly different, picture of Bradshaw is provided by his grandson, Tim Robinson (personal correspondence), who described him thus: 'he hated showiness and

bombast. He wasn't a swaggering deck officer with a red face and the argot of the lower deck. As a member of the Paymaster branch he was the epitome of the type that gave the Navy its "Silent Service" image. He fused ascetic Northern Irish Protestant pragmatism and probity with a naval officer's abhorrence of garrulousness. He never felt the need to speak if there was nothing to say. He was courteous. He never raised his voice to make a point. His words were polite and dry (to the point of sarcasm). He was a formidable presence – tenacious, relentless, almost menacing in his authority. Once in a while a flash of charm'. Robinson was told by Harry Hinsley that Alan Bradshaw was 'one of the most able men I have ever met', a significant accolade from someone of Hinsley's standing. It seems extraordinary that, alone of the leading figures at BP, Bradshaw has no entry in the Oxford Dictionary of National Biography.

23. In Chapter 5 I will discuss the Inter-service Distribution and Reference section (D&R) and its successor the Intelligence Exchange (IE), both of which are in some ways structural manifestations of inter-service issues, but are more relevant to my consideration of co-ordinative mechanisms at BP.

24. TNA HW 43/2: 474. The quote is from de Grey, but the document in which it is quoted is Birch's internal history of sigint rather than de Grey's post-war review.

25. TNA HW 14/145: 5 and 8.

26. Summary of TNA HW 14/145: 5–10, the quotation is from p.10.

27. TNA HW 14/61. The individuals in question were, respectively, (then) Wing Commander Eric Jones and Gordon Welchman.

28. TNA HW 43/2: 478.

29. TNA HW 14/145: 5. In a different part of his report, de Grey described Air Raid Precautions (ARP), firewatching and Home Guard duties of civilians at BP as 'little short of farcical . . . our record was thoroughly bad', TNA HW 14/145: 36.

30. TNA HW 14/145: 9.

31. TNA HW 14/145: 22.

32. TNA HW 43/2: 473–4. This event was itself an outgrowth of the conflicts over Hut 3, discussed below, arising from the Air Ministry 'feeling aggrieved at the time at not getting his own way in the appointment of a Head of Hut 3', TNA HW 3/120: 474.

33. TNA HW 43/1: 180–202.

34. Letter of 17 December 1940, TNA WO 208/5130.
35. 4 January 1941, TNA WO 208/5130.
36. 3 February 1941, TNA WO 208/5130.
37. TNA WO 208/5130: 10a.
38. TNA HW 14/16.
39. TNA WO 165/38.
40. 6 December 1940, TNA WO 208/5130. Note that this document is itself bound up with the wider discussions initiated by the DMI, discussed above.
41. All quotes in this paragraph are excerpts from 'The Kitchen Front', 6 December 1940, TNA WO 208/5130.
42. TNA HW 14/24.
43. TNA WO 208/5070.
44. TNA HW 43/1: 201–2.
45. There were technical reasons for this – Naval Enigma was differently configured, for one thing; Army and Air Enigma were more closely related. Hut 4 also undertook cryptanalysis of non-Enigma naval ciphers, whereas Hut 3 undertook no cryptanalysis.
46. TNA HW 25/2 and TNA HW 43/1: 195. Moreover, whereas distribution of intelligence to army and air military commands was controlled by BP via SLUs (see Chapter 5), that to naval commands was via the Admiralty, in large part because communication at sea required the Navy's W/T network.
47. In the early months of the war this was by no means smooth, with NS suggestions being met on occasion with 'something ranging from indifference to contempt' (Budiansky, 2000: 147).
48. Whom he blames (unfairly, one would think) for the death of Dilly Knox (TNA HW 3/16). Knox died from cancer in 1943. See Batey (2010) for an account of his life and work.
49. TNA HW 3/16.
50. TNA HW 3/134: 4.
51. TNA HW 3/134: 68.
52. TNA HW 3/134: 72.
53. TNA HW 43/1: 431.
54. I am skating over a good deal of complexity here, of course, in that OIC–BP relations and NID–BP relations were not the same thing, and NID8G–NID–OIC–BP relations were something else again. But I am concerned not with delving into these minute details so much as with giving illustrations

of Admiralty–BP relations. See Hinsley *et al.* (1979: 267–8) and Beesly
(2000) for more detail.
55. TNA HW 14/67: 5.
56. TNA HW 43/1: 492.
57. TNA HW 3/119 : 37.
58. This was not the first dispute involving Saunders at BP. He had been the
recipient of a sharp rebuke from Denniston himself on 27 October 1939
about interference in the work of others, principally relating to NID8G
functions *vis-à-vis* BP Naval Section, and was admonished 'not to butt in
on the jobs of others who are obviously better qualified to carry them out'
(TNA HW 14/1). A further sharp exchange occurred in August 1941 when,
following a direct appeal from Saunders to Captain Ridley of SIS for more
resources, Denniston threatened him with dismissal if he ever
communicated in such a way with someone outside GC & CS (TNA HW
14/18). This, of course, is a reflection of the underlying issue of conflict
between SIS and GC & CS over control of the BP site, discussed above.
Moreover, before the war, in October 1938, Saunders had been in dispute
with Denniston over Direction Finding and had appealed to 'C' (at that
time Hugh Sinclair) to have Denniston over-ruled (TNA HW 3/134: 74).
59. Head of Naval Section, in succession to W. E. Clarke, see above.
60. TNA HW 8/23. See also TNA HW 14/22 and TNA HW 3/119: 4–6.
61. TNA 43/1: 440.
62. TNA HW 43/1: 439.
63. TNA HW 3/119: 34.
64. TNA HW 14/24.
65. TNA HW 14/26. See also TNA HW 43/1: 441.
66. TNA HW 43/1: 440.
67. TNA HW 3/119: 37.
68. TNA HW 14/22, emphasis in original.
69. TNA HW 43/1: 441.
70. TNA WO 208/5070. This meeting was part and parcel of the broader
reorganization of BP at this time, which will be discussed in the next
chapter.
71. Saunders to Eastern Fleet Y posts, Humphreys to Mediterranean Air
Command. I am grateful to Jonathan Byrne, the Roll of Honour
Administrator at BPT, for this information.
72. Major Edgar, Squadron Leader Mapplebeck and Major Leatham.

73. TNA HW 43/2: 493.

74. TNA HW 14/67: 5.

75. According to the Oxford Dictionary of National Biography, Jones left school at 15 and the business was Samuel Jones & Son, textile manufacturers, of Macclesfield, Cheshire. He subsequently became Director of GCHQ 1952–60.

76. See also my comments about Ratcliff's (2006) account of this issue in the next chapter. In discussing the management of Hut 3, mention should also be made of Jones' deputy, Herbert ('Bill') Marchant, who was responsible for much of its day to day running. IWM 9390 has an interview recording. See also TNA HW 2/119: 43.

77. All quotations extracts from TNA 43/1: 452–7.

78. It is worth noting that Calvocoressi arrived at Hut 3 *after* the events I described earlier, and appears to have been largely unaware of them (Calvocoressi, 2001: 71).

79. It may be said that an archive-based study is methodologically biased towards finding disputes since documentary records will tend to register these more readily than harmony. I am grateful to Andrew Sturdy for making this very valid point. Even so, the combined weight of evidence and comment pointing to organizational problems at BP, not least in the histories written by those who worked there, does seem compelling. Moreover, even if there is an archival bias to recording conflict, it is still noteworthy that within the archive there is far more such recording in the period up to early 1942 than afterwards, which is again consistent with the claims made here.

2 The Making of Signals Intelligence at Bletchley Park

INTRODUCTION

Building on the analysis in the last chapter of how BP was made, with attendant problems, conflicts and structural complexities, I will now explore in more detail how these unfolded. In doing so, I will consider two issues, which I will later suggest are deeply interconnected. The first is the way in which the success in breaking increasing numbers of Enigma keys intensified an already embryonic issue, namely BP's construction as a signals intelligence organization rather than simply a cryptanalytic one. Indeed, I will suggest that signals intelligence as such was in large part a creation of BP's organization. Explaining this involves a more detailed consideration of the meaning of the Hut 3 conflicts discussed in the previous chapter and how this was related to an emerging redefinition of BP's purpose to encompass interception, cryptanalysis and intelligence analysis.

The second issue that will be considered moves back to the explicitly structural concerns of this section of the book. I will argue that the Hut 3 conflict was an aspect of a wider set of political issues. In particular, I will explore the politics associated with the appeal by a group of BP cryptanalysts to Churchill for more resources. I will suggest that this can be understood as a repudiation of the leadership of BP's head, Alastair Denniston, but that this itself relates to the way that that leadership was out of kilter with the emergence of a sigint organization. It is against this background that the major structural reorganization of BP in February 1942[1] is to be understood.

In the concluding section, I will draw together material from across the two chapters of this part of the book to make some preliminary observations about how the study of BP's organization might relate to the way in which organizations in general may be studied.

THE BREAKING OF ENIGMA AND THE MAKING OF SIGINT

The breaking of more and more Enigma ciphers and messages from January 1940 onwards was not just arguably the supreme, and now perhaps the most famous, technical accomplishment of BP. It was also organizationally pivotal because of the dilemmas and challenges it posed. Nigel de Grey, amongst others, noted how it created a very unexpected situation in terms of how the material should be handled and by whom[2]. This was for three reasons. Firstly, the sheer volume of messages being decrypted soon ran to many thousands per day – Red key alone generated over a thousand messages on some days in 1940[3] – reflecting the scale of German Enigma use, with some 100,000 machines being built in the course of the war (Lewin, 2008: 22). Yet these individual messages in themselves were of relatively little interest in an intelligence sense: their value came from the painstaking process of identifying their cumulative meaning (Calvocoressi, 2001: 19), which required data management, via indexing, and specialist linguistic and technical knowledge (matters I will return to in detail in Chapter 6). Secondly, this process often yielded immediately useable operational intelligence – for example about air raids or ongoing military operations – referred to by the interviewee Joyce, a Hut 3 analyst, as 'hot'. But if this 'hot' material was to be made use of, it needed to be dealt with very speedily, with minimum delay between message transmission by the German military and distribution to the British military, implying that it was best dealt with in-house. Thirdly, it was of paramount importance that the source of the intelligence be kept absolutely secret, since were it to be otherwise, the Enigma machine would be modified or abandoned and, hence, the continued breaking of the ciphers would become impossible. Taken together, these things meant that traditional ways of handling signals intelligence were increasingly inadequate: simply passing decrypted material to intelligence specialists in the ministries would swamp them with essentially worthless material[4] and, moreover, potentially compromise security. The intelligence work had to be done at BP, senior figures such as Nigel de Grey insisted[5], and the internal history of Hut 3 records that the key difference between Enigma and previous cryptanalytic work was that it was for Hut 3 (as regards Army/Air Enigma) to judge and assess intelligence, not ministries[6].

Moreover, the volume of Ultra and the secret of its source also implied that BP needed to exert control over the direction of intercept operations since decisions about the most important transmissions to be intercepted were inseparable from an understanding of cryptanalytic and intelligence requirements. The interception of transmissions required receiver sets and skilled people to staff them, both of which were in short supply. Thus decisions about which transmissions to intercept needed to be guided by which traffic was likely to be readable and, within that, which readable traffic was likely to yield useful intelligence. Beyond this general requirement a particular issue was which transmissions should be intercepted by more than one operator, and perhaps more than one station, so as to cover the possibility of failures or errors in their interception. This would again apply to the traffic which was most likely to yield useful intelligence and therefore the management of interception and the organization of cryptanalysis and intelligence became more and more closely related[7]. In the official history, it is suggested that this had been realized during WW1 (Hinsley, 1993c: 6), but, even if that were so, the organizational arrangements for integration were very far from having been established.

Such integration was problematic because, as explained in the previous chapter, Y (intercept) stations were controlled and staffed by a variety of different agencies, not by GC & CS itself. Thus, for example, Josh Cooper's internal history of Air Section records conflicts with the Air Ministry over control of interception going back as far as the Munich crisis of 1938[8]. Something of these conflicts is captured by this account of a later event:

When Josh Cooper, the head of the Air Section, suggested that an
RAF station should take [i.e. intercept] Enigma, the head of the RAF
Y service told him 'My Y service exists to produce intelligence, not
to provide stuff for people at Bletchley to fool about with'.

(Thirsk, 2001: 265)[9]

Even so, co-operation became more and more widely practiced and
accepted. For example, within Hut 6 there was from 1940 an Intercept
Control Room, under John Colman, which liaised continuously with
those stations relevant to German army and air force traffic in order to
prioritize their concentration on that most likely to yield valuable
results (Welchman, 1982: 76). Likewise 'close' and 'amicable' consul-
tation over interception between GC & CS and the Admiralty was
achieved from 1940 according to the official history (Hinsley et al.,
1979: 268), as part of the 'separate peace' (Davies, 2001: 399) between
the two. Admittedly, it would be wrong to say that these issues were
ever fully resolved, and disputes with MI8, in particular, persisted. For
example, in June 1942 MI8 criticised the duplication of interceptions
on the grounds that it was wasteful[10], whilst in his memorandum of 28
March 1943 Nigel de Grey was still having to raise concerns about the
control, staffing and training arrangements for Y stations, calling for
'control of interception by right – not by grace of the Ministries'[11].
Indeed, as late as July 1944 the general principles of control of Y
stations as between BP and MI8 was still being contested[12].
Nevertheless, the direction of travel was integrative and the more
established Ultra became as a valuable intelligence source the more
BP was able to dictate terms to the Y services, especially following the
1941 reforms which specified more clearly demarcations and means of
co-operation, discussed in the last chapter, and recommendations for
closer integration in the 1942 van Cutsem report[13].

Intimately related to interception was traffic analysis (TA), that
is, the analysis of, for example, the source, point of receipt, timing,
frequency, volume and technical characteristics of enemy transmissions but without their decryption. The relation was two-way in that,

on the one hand, TA required interception whilst, on the other, effective use of intercept resources was considerably enhanced by the findings of TA (for example by identifying promising frequencies to intercept). Traffic analysis could and did yield large quantities of useful military intelligence (for example with respect to concentrations of enemy activity) and in the period when no or relatively little Enigma was being broken became increasingly important, especially to the army. Army (and, for abstruse reasons, much GAF) TA was undertaken by MI8, and this became a central aspect of the disputes between that agency and GC & CS mentioned in the previous chapter. In December 1940, MI8's then head, Colonel Butler, proposed that its TA operations should move to BP so as to be in proximity to the cryptanalytic work there, given the many intersections and complementarities between the two.

At first sight, one might imagine that this would have been welcomed by BP, which in any case was undertaking TA in relation to naval and some GAF traffic. In fact, the proposal was rejected by Denniston, partly because Gordon Welchman and some other senior cryptanalysts at BP believed that TA was of little value, and even distracting from cryptanalytic work on Enigma, a view that Welchman later recognized as a mistake (Welchman, 1982: 156)[14]. Indeed, the internal history of military sigint states that the cryptanalysts regarded TA with 'contempt'[15]. But it was also rejected by Denniston because of 'fears of his own control of GC & CS' (Hinsley et al., 1979: 270), fears which might be seen as well-founded to the extent that the Butler proposal appeared at the same time as, and can be interpreted as an aspect of, the more general attempt by the WO to establish greater control over BP.

The resulting conflict led to the establishment of a Y subcommittee to look at the relation between wireless telegraphy intelligence (WTI), as TA was then often called, and cryptography (as cryptanalysis was then called). It reported on 2 July 1941 thus:

> There do not exist two mutually exclusive subjects that can be
> defined by these names. The two are so inter-related throughout the

process of extracting intelligence from the basic material obtained from the interception of enemy wireless transmissions that they form one indivisible mechanism[16].

This conclusion did not in itself resolve the issue since, as Frank Birch puts it in the internal history, in the absence of a unified organization it left the two as 'separate, then, yet inseparable'[17]. But it did establish the *principle* of inseparability and subsequently, when both Denniston and Butler had left their posts, MI8 TA did indeed come to BP in May 1942, to form what later became called SIXTA, the army and air TA section. In this way TA became bound into the emergent totality of 'sigint', and moreover bound into the Enigma operation, via the fusion room, as discussed in Chapter 6.

Nigel de Grey's comment referred to earlier notwithstanding, it is actually misleading to say that the situation arising from the large-scale breaking of Enigma was entirely unexpected. It had in fact to an extent been anticipated, most importantly by Gordon Welchman, the then Head of Hut 6, who was a key figure in establishing, before Enigma had been broken, much of the organizational infrastructure to deal with it if and when it happened. He anticipated the need for, and began to build, close co-operation between BP and intercept stations (Welchman, 1982: 56–7), but he also set in place the basic relationship between Hut 6 and Hut 3 which created a more or less unified complex linking the decryption and intelligence analysis of Army and Air Enigma, which was established in embryo before Enigma was broken. That is to say, rather than conceiving, as had been the case hitherto, of GC & CS as primarily a cryptanalytic operation, he 'developed an organization that would be ready to go into action as soon as code-breaking [i.e. of Enigma] became possible' (Welchman, 1982: 87), including the establishment of a three-shift, 24-hour system (Welchman, 1982: 89). Moreover, he recognized that these require-ments would grow as bombe capacity expanded, allowing the volume of decrypted material to increase (Welchman, 1982: 120–1). He also anticipated that the volume of traffic transmitted by the Germans on

Enigma would itself increase once plans to invade Britain were dropped and, instead, the war moved into more dispersed theatres in the Balkans and North Africa (Welchman, 1982: 120).

The combined impact of these insights was to create what was in effect a production-line operation geared to handling high volumes of Enigma traffic in an integrated process running from interception through decryption to intelligence analysis[18]. These initiatives were crucial not just for Hut 6 and Hut 3, but also for the analogous operations which developed in Huts 8 and 4, once some Naval Enigma keys[19] were being broken regularly from 1941, and which were largely modelled on the by then established organization of Army/Air Enigma handling, as Hugh Alexander's internal history of Hut 8 suggests[20]. The processes Welchman developed also had wider implications for the transformation of BP into a factory-like organization, which I will discuss in considerable detail elsewhere, especially in Chapters 5 and 6.

Whilst I am drawing here on Welchman's own account, which is admittedly slightly self-aggrandizing in tone, there is no serious reason to deny the essential accuracy of the claim that he was a key instigator of the emergent organizational architecture at BP as regards Enigma. This has been widely recognized in the literature on BP (e.g. Smith, 1998; Ratcliff, 2006; Lewin, 2008) and moreover is attested to by Welchman's successor as Head of Hut 6 at several points in his introduction to the internal history of the hut[21] and subsequently:

> [Without Welchman's] vision, which again and again proved his intuition correct, I do not believe that the task of converting the original breakthrough into an effective organization for the production of up-to-date intelligence could have been achieved.
>
> *(Milner-Barry, 1986: 141)*

Gordon Welchman's role matters to the extent that it cannot be assumed that without his actions the same things would have happened anyway, or would have happened as early, or in the same way; but the more important point is that it grew out of a situational logic arising from the breaking of Enigma. None of this explains BP's success in breaking Enigma – but it does help to explain the largely successful manner in which that technical achievement was exploited. But this is perhaps a little simplistic since, as Welchman himself stresses very strongly, it was only because of the persuasive case he made that Enigma would be broken that it was possible to make the case for resources to be devoted to the anticipatory organization to deal with its exploitation (Welchman, 1982: 164–5). So, just as there is an inter-play between individual and organization, so too is there an interplay between the technical and the organizational, a point to which I will return in the conclusion.

For now, I want to re-visit the conflicts in Hut 3 in 1941 outlined in the previous chapter and draw out their fuller implications, because what might there be understood as a conflict between the interests of different services, or between different individuals, can now be re-interpreted as a clash between old and new understandings of organiza-tional purpose and thus as a moment – a pivotal moment – in the process of constituting sigint. The attempt by Robert Humphries to insist that the Hut 3 Watch staff were translators, not trained intelli-gence officers, and his attempt to deal directly with the AM and circumvent the Head of Hut 3 ran directly contrary to what was emerging at BP, namely an entity which brought together crypt-analysis, intelligence analysis and, increasingly, both traffic analysis and a considerable degree of control of interception. In the last chapter I quoted the memo insisting, in opposition to Humphries' claim, that Hut 3 members were 'intelligence officers NOT TRANSLATORS'[22]. Now we can see the reason for this capitalized emphasis, and why this apparently rather mundane claim was of such significance: it pointed to the emerging unification of cryptanalysis and intelligence analysis.

What I suggest was occurring was not so much new ways of organizing signals intelligence, but, rather, the *making* of signals intel-ligence by virtue of what was occurring organizationally. Writing of Hut 3, but in words which apply to BP more generally[23], it had turned itself into a far more efficient intelligence organization than its Whitehall counterparts. The funny academics, in their tweeds and pullovers, had shown that they could understand certain military matters very well, and knew far more about the enemy fighting forces than Whitehall did. With their ever-growing indexes, research facilities, technical experts, specialised 'back room' groups – staffed by clever, hard-working people – Hut Three had become an intelligence organization the like of which had never been seen, or even imagined, in the antiquated, stuffy, military establishment. *(Freedman, 2000: 180)*

In the official history, it is observed in a footnote that from October 1943 there was a standardization of terminology (Hinsley *et al.*, 1979: 21n) so that sigint was adopted as the general term for all the processes and for any intelligence they provided. But this did not 'just happen': the emergent terminology was the outcome of, precisely, the organizational battles and innovations I have sketched. Similarly, in the internal post-war history it is stated that 'the comprehensive term "signals intelligence" was not evolved until 1943'[24] in the meaning of interception, cryptanalysis and intelligence. That is not to say that the term signals intelligence was unknown before, although it is the case that at the outbreak of war the term 'special intelligence' was more commonly used (Batey, 2010: 88) and, again according to the internal history, the term 'Y' was often loosely used to denote any or all of the processes of sigint[25]. But its emergent meaning as a unified set of operations was new, and it grew out of the organizational innovations at BP. It was the adoption of new ways of working, initially as a response to the breaking of Enigma, which 'made' signals intelligence.

My analysis here has many affinities to that of Ratcliff (2006) but differs in emphasis. She stresses the way in which BP centralized the organization of sigint but significantly downplays the contestations with the services by assuming that the creation of GC & CS in itself achieved a centralized inter-service structure (Ratcliff, 2006: 74–5). Perhaps more importantly, whilst identifying the ways in which sigint was centralized, Ratcliff does not consider the ways it was *constructed* by, rather than simply *brought together* at, BP; neither does she pay any great attention to the organizational processes through which 'centralization' occurred and the conflicts that attended it (cf. Ratcliff, 2006: 90). For example, whilst identifying that Hut 3 became 'highly efficient' under Jones (Ratcliff, 2006: 79), she does not discuss the pivotal significance of the Hut 3 crisis in the construction of sigint. Jones' 'efficiency' was not simply a matter of his management skills, it resided in the way that, unlike his predecessors, he was supportive of, rather than antagonistic to, the integration of intelligence analysis with cryptanalysis at BP. In general terms, then, I want to put far more emphasis than Ratcliff on how and why centralization occurred. Nevertheless, in the broad sense of identifying the bringing together of interception, cryptanalysis and intelligence, Ratcliff's analysis and that presented here are compatible[26].

That this integration was both novel and something accomplished over time at BP rather than simply resulting from its inter-service character is demonstrated by a note from Edward Travis dated 8 February 1943, outlining the 'perfect' organization:

> If I were asked to set up a new BP in the light of my experience since 1939 ... the organization would no doubt bear little outward resemblance to BP as it now stands ... experience has proved conclusively that Interception, Cryptography and Intelligence are indissoluble ... the whole process ... should be under one control[27].

In this regard, it is instructive to consider BP's annual report for 1942 dated just a few days later (18 February 1943), which is indicative of the crucial shift which had occurred. At the outset of the report it was noted that as little as a year before 'there was still the feeling that Intelligence was not the proper duty of GC & CS'[28]. The closing words, by contrast, read as follows:

> We have been particularly lucky in our friends at the Ministries[29] ... they have all accepted that GC & CS must be master in its own

house ... but if we were asked to cut the cackle and make a brief
statement of our aims and beliefs it would be this: we believe that we
should try to read every enemy signal, neglecting none however
apparently unimportant; we believe in the unholy trinity of
Interception, Cryptography and Intelligence ...[30]

This 'mission', be it noted, was very far removed from the much more
limited remit with which GC & CS had been established in 1919,
concerned as it was with cryptanalysis and training, and is explicit
and strong evidence of the case I have argued that sigint was constructed at BP during the period between the first breaks of wartime
Enigma in January 1940 and, say, December 1942 (one cannot say that
there is a precise date by which this process was completed). It would
not be an exaggeration to say that the conflicts over the control of
intelligence analysis all but disappear after this date by virtue of, on the
one hand, internal reforms of, in particular, Hut 3 management under
Eric Jones and, on the other, an acceptance by ministries and other
intelligence agencies of BP's legitimacy in this area. It is true that this
is less clearcut with respect to interception, as noted above, but, even
there, there was no repeat of the 'Y wars' of 1940–41. Sigint had not
simply emerged as a term in use; it had emerged as an organizational
reality initiated by and instantiated in BP.

A further point may be added to this. Early disseminations of Ultra
were given the cover name 'Source Boniface', a fictitious human agent
supposedly providing the intelligence. Now one reason for this was security in that this was a way of concealing the secret that Enigma (and other
high-grade ciphers) was being broken. However, another reason for this
particular form of concealment was the greater legitimacy in the eyes of
some in the military that human intelligence had as compared with
signals intelligence. Boniface formally ceased to be used as a cover name
from late 1941 (Andrew, 1985a: 449), after which Ultra was almost always
used[31]. Although that does not mean that its sigint derivation was known,
it does suggest that the need to gain legitimacy by the pretence of agent-
origin had disappeared. In this way, too, sigint had 'arrived' by 1942[32].

However, the author of the 1942 annual report and of the 'perfect sigint organization plan' just quoted was not Alastair Denniston, the operational head of GC & CS since its formation in 1919, but rather its new leader, Edward Travis. His appointment to this role was part and parcel of a major re-structuring, which I have already alluded to in passing and will now consider in detail.

THE REORGANIZATION OF BLETCHLEY PARK

Ralph Bennett, who left BP for North Africa in 1942 and returned in 1943 to become the Hut 3 Duty Officer, later remarked 'I had left as one of a group of enthusiastic amateurs; I returned to a professional organization' (Bennett, 1993: 38). This assessment has many echoes throughout the literature on BP (e.g. Davies, 2001) and what lies beneath it are the transformations in the scale, nature and purpose of BP's operations. These transformations were both a cause and a consequence of the major reorganization of BP in February 1942, which was, in narrow structural terms, the pivotal organizational event of the entire war[33], and, as I suggested in the last chapter, the point by which BP's organization was substantially made. That reorganization, in turn, led to and was symbolized by the replacement of Denniston by Travis as the head of BP. These linked events are typically expressed throughout the literature on BP (e.g. Budiansky, 2000: 202) in terms of the incompatibility between Denniston's personality and the changing nature of BP. Quoting Ralph Bennett again:

> He [Denniston] found himself in charge of a huge growing organization, a lot of us younger and in some ways thinking along different lines, and he got a bit outdated in some ways and was shunted out ... he was a very good chap but he was overtaken by events.
>
> *(cited in Smith, 1998: 93)*

This captures something of the situation – Denniston's own son records that 'he was not cut out for high-profile leadership' (Denniston, 2007: 74) and moreover was very seriously ill in 1941

(Denniston, 2007: 73) – but it denotes a more complicated set of issues, which I will now seek to explore.

The first thing to say is that Denniston did not disappear from GC & CS, although he did leave BP and was also removed from the Y Board[34]. Rather, he was moved sideways, and de facto demoted, by virtue of the Deputy Directorship (DD) of GC & CS being split between its 'service' (S) and 'civil' (C) operations, with Stewart Menzies – 'C' – remaining as its nominal overall Director. Travis was appointed as DD (S), much the larger part of GC & CS, and became the head of BP, which was now, as noted in the previous chapter, also separated from joint administrative control with SIS. Denniston, as DD (C), headed the smaller section concerned with commercial and diplomatic codes, which moved back to London shortly after the reorganization. Denniston himself never physically returned to BP, but is normally credited as having run the civil branch very effectively (e.g. Filby, 1988). It is obvious that this splitting of GC & CS was also bound up with its inter-war history in that the main reason it fell under FO control in the first place was because, in the early 1920s, the amount of military work was relatively small compared with diplomatic work. That situation had been reversed by virtue of the war, and in a sense the reorganization placed Denniston in a rather similar role to that which he had originally been charged with. This episode is not, then, one of the dismissal of someone in some general way incompetent, but carries a more complex meaning.

The crisis in Hut 3 was one element of this. Indeed, according to the internal history of sigint '[i]t was dissatisfaction with the running of the Hut [3] that had precipitated the reorganization of the command of GC &CS'[35]. The principal reason for this was the way that the Hut 3 disputes had spilled well beyond BP itself and had involved, as shown in the last chapter, 'C' at SIS as well as the ministries. It is certainly the case that in relation to a dispute between Denniston and Travis in 1940 about the conduct of a staff member, Travis threatened to raise it with 'C' and was chided by Denniston, who wrote '[C] is at this time con-cerned with the question of policy and administration of national importance, and I think it almost unfair to him to trouble him with what really are minor matters which we can settle ourselves'[36]. One interpretation of this is that Denniston was unwilling to have administrative disputes aired externally and that he believed that to do so would not commend itself to 'C'. If so, the much more extensive airing of BP disputes within the 'corridors of power' during the Hut 3 disputes must surely have damaged Denniston's credibility there. Certainly it is significant that, as mentioned in the previous chapter, the van Cutsem report was commissioned not by Denniston but jointly by the DMI and 'C'[37].

Perhaps even more damaging was one of the most famous events in the history of BP. This was the frustration about lack of resources which led Gordon Welchman, Stuart Milner-Barry, Alan Turing and Hugh Alexander to bypass Denniston (and 'C') to appeal directly to Winston Churchill (who had recently visited BP) in a letter hand-delivered to 10 Downing Street on 21 October 1941. The symbolism of that date – Trafalgar Day – would surely not have been lost on Churchill. At all events, his response, accompanied, famously, by the injunction to 'action this day' was '[m]ake sure they have all they want on extreme priority and report to me that this has been done'[38].

This letter is invariably invoked in accounts of BP to show Churchill's commitment to their work and is scored as a success story for 'the codebreakers'. But at the same time it was surely devastating to Denniston. It indicated a lack of confidence in his abilities to secure resources and the fact that this lack of confidence came from amongst the new breed of mathematical codebreakers[39] – known in some circles as 'the wicked uncles' (Smith, 1998: 80) – recruited by Denniston himself made it even more devastating. This interpretation of the letter as denoting a lack of confidence rests not least upon the fact that in it there is lavish praise for 'the energy and foresight of Commander Travis' and the statement that '[w]e do not know who or what is responsible for our difficulties, and most emphatically we do not want to be taken as criticizing Commander Travis who has all along done his utmost to help us in every possible way'[40]. These phrases, coupled with the fact that there is an eloquent silence about Denniston, indicate that, in effect and, it may plausibly be said, in intention (for these were highly intelligent men, who would presumably not have been casual in their chosen wording), the letter communicated a lack of confidence in Denniston quite as much as a plea for resources (Budiansky, 2000: 204). The person who actually delivered the letter to Downing Street, Stuart Milner-Barry, later recalled the following:

> I by chance met Commander Denniston in the corridors some days later, and he made a rather wry comment about our unorthodox behaviour, but he was much too nice a man to bear malice.
>
> *(Copeland, 2004: 337)*

That there might be 'malice' to bear is further support for the contention that the letter had a political meaning beyond its ostensible purpose.

Of course, it was not just Denniston who had been circumvented by the direct appeal to Churchill. So too was the Chief of SIS himself, which can only have added to the tensions of his relations with Denniston. Certainly Stewart Menzies – 'C' – was a key actor in the reorganization, both in formally ordering it[41] and also in terms of providing the political will. As the authorized history of SIS records,

> when he did act he did so both decisively and, on the whole, effectively. Menzies's demotion of Denniston and replacement [of Denniston] by Travis reflected an unsentimentality when it came to making tough decisions about the competence of longstanding colleagues ...
>
> *(Jeffery, 2010: 746)*

Politics and personalities (inevitably) mix together here. On the one hand, longstanding colleagues or not, there was a mutual dislike between Denniston and Menzies (Denniston, 2007: 79). On the other hand, displacing Denniston was perhaps the only, or at any rate the best, way that Menzies could respond to the repeated attempts by the WO to take control of BP from SIS and to the criticisms of the DNI (as discussed in the previous chapter). This was crucial to SIS since 'the fact that it survived the Second World War at all has been ascribed primarily to the supremely and perhaps incalculably valuable work of [GC & CS]' (Jeffery, 2010: 744), work which allowed Menzies to 'bask in its reflected glory' (Andrew, 1985a: 462). This is another instance of the point I made in the previous chapter to the effect that BP's organization cannot be understood in isolation from the wider dynamics of other agencies, in this case SIS.

However, beyond these political issues in relation to Denniston's leadership was something else, which I would suggest is the most important issue of all. It relates to the argument that what happened at BP in the period following the first breaking of wartime Enigma ciphers was the making of sigint as an entity. The credit for the success against Enigma belongs to many people, but one of them is surely Denniston himself, precisely because of the astuteness with which he recruited staff and the kind of creative and meritocratic culture he did much to foster, a matter discussed elsewhere. Yet, ironically, this success was in some senses Denniston's downfall. For what he was not willing or able to countenance was the consequence that flowed in large part from it. Instead, according to Birch's internal history of sigint, he wanted BP to remain as a pure cryptanalytic bureau and sought 'Canute-like to halt the inevitable tide that threatened to turn it into a Sigint centre'[42]. This preference was evident in Denniston's refusal to accede to WO requests to bring MI8 TA functions into BP 'on the ground that his establishment should continue to be a cryptanalytical centre' (Hinsley et al., 1979: 270). In this way, the issue is not so much about Denniston's personality, or about organizational expansion per se: it is about the consequences of the constitution of sigint qua sigint.

Of course, the 1942 reorganization was not just about the replacement of Denniston with Travis. Rather, it occasioned a wider re-structuring which is best understood in terms of a growing formalization and differentiation or, in other words, bureaucratization. This is evident in the growing complexity of the organizational chart and is also attested to by the many accounts which refer to the development of a more 'factory-like' work organization at BP (e.g. Welchman, 1982; Bennett, 1993; Ratcliff, 2006). In the internal history of Hut 6 this development is described in these terms:

> A natural consequence of the growth of work and numbers was an increasing degree of specialisation of most sections and a growing complexity in the general organization of the hut[43].

Within organization studies there are classic analyses which show and predict that changes in organizational size have an effect on organizational structure and function either as a direct, albeit diminishing, correlation between headcount and complexity or as an indirect consequence of the increase in the likelihood of repeated events (Blau, 1955; Pugh and Hickson, 1976). In general terms, increased size and the standardization of work routines correlate with increased bureaucratization and with shifts from 'organic' to 'mechanical' organization forms (Burns and Stalker, 1961). At one level the BP case is a textbook example of this 'structural contingency theory' and indeed the words of the Hut 6 history just quoted closely fit that theory. However, and I will return to this point in more detail later, it is important to recognize that this contingency was itself contingent rather than necessary – that is to say, it was not determined but, to a degree, chosen. Certainly it cannot simply be regarded as 'natural'.

Another aspect of this is the way that, over time, BP was arguably shaped by the demands of the 'customers' for its intelligence, that is, the ministries and the services. This argument is emphasised in Davies' (2001) discussion of GC & CS organization. He makes the interesting point that demand for intelligence operates in the opposite way to that of most goods in economic theory. The more that is produced, the greater the demand becomes: '[o]ne cannot really imagine [customers] turning round to Bletchley Park and saying "that's all the Ultra we need thank you, we've had quite enough now"' (Davies, 2001: 399). Davies suggests that this led (as I have traced) to various attempts by ministries to gain control and although these foundered, the voracious demand for intelligence forced BP to develop a more effective organization to cater for this. In this sense, too, a contingency-type explanation is in evidence – BP had to adapt in order to conform to external requirements – as well as a political one: the successful provision of Ultra made BP subject to the various political machinations that have been alluded to. However, it should be noted that there BP was also in a position to shape customer demands rather than simply responding to them precisely because of the strong degree of control it kept over both the provenance and the dissemination of Ultra.

This aside, whilst I have focussed on 1942 and the sidelining of Denniston, a further set of changes occurred in 1944 (see Appendix D, Figure 3). These can be read as a consolidation of the 1942 changes with a further elaboration of divisions and hierarchies. Now, Travis was installed as 'Director' and, whilst BP was still located within SIS, with Menzies retitled as 'Director-General', there is a sense of a growing independence[44] and this is directly related to the way that the sigint product of BP now far exceeded anything being produced by SIS's human intelligence (humint) operations (Boyle, 1979: 227–8; Jeffery, 2010: 744). With this being so, perhaps the enhanced status of Travis from 1944 – when he was also knighted – is best understood as a recognition of the centrality of BP, and sigint, within the intelligence hierarchy and, as discussed above, its importance to SIS. By 1944 BP had become the almost taken-for-granted provider of an extraordinary wealth of operational and strategic intelligence. Intelligence services are perhaps different from any other organization only because of the secrecy of their work and, as often occurs in organizations, success raises status, so it may be inferred that the success of BP led to an upgrade of its status, with Travis's elevation to Directorship as one result. There was also a corresponding 'upgrade' for the various Assistant Directors, who in 1944 became Deputy Directors[45].

This growing independence, which is to say the 'hardening' of the boundary which constituted 'the organization' as an entity, is further evident in the 1946 organizational chart (Appendix D, Figure 4). Although I am not concerned with post-war developments, this chart serves to emphasise one of the central points I have been making because it crystallizes the process that had been under way throughout the war. Firstly, 'C' has now disappeared: what was by 1946 officially called GCHQ had become effectively independent of SIS and formally constituted as a separate organization, albeit still, and for some years to come, under the loose control of 'C' (Aldrich, 2010: 67). In this way the issues of joint control discussed in the last chapter, which had proved so controversial and brought BP into 'disrepute', had now disappeared. Moreover, with Denniston's retirement in 1945[46], civil and service operations were re-united. Secondly, GCHQ was now quite explicitly a sigint organization with sections for interception, intelligence and traffic analysis, as well as cryptanalysis[47], whilst sections for each of the services had disappeared. Thus my contention is that this final chart can be decoded only by understanding the organizational processes of contestation and redefinition through which sigint was constructed at BP during WW2, whilst also serving to illustrate these processes by crystallizing them at a particular point in time.

The 1942 reorganization was pivotal in that, for it marked the way that, as the internal history of sigint puts it,

> GC & CS had developed from a parochially minded Cryptanalytic bureau into a Sigint Centre of global significance ... the old rivalry between 'cryptography' and 'Y' was giving way to a sense of partnership in Sigint ... Intelligence, it was coming to be realized, was as necessary to cryptanalysis as cryptanalysis to intelligence[48].

As with the making of BP, the making of sigint was not completed in 1942 – and in the above quote this is reflected in the expressions 'giving way to' and 'coming to be realized' – but after that date the understanding of sigint as an area of activity persisted, as indeed it has to the present day (Taylor, 2007).

CONCLUSION

In the two chapters forming the first part of this book, I have sought to capture some key aspects of the organizational transformations which occurred over time at BP. These transformations were the making of BP and of sigint, which were clearly intimately inter-woven: the construction of BP as 'an organization' and the construction of sigint as the 'business' it was engaged in proceeded in tandem. What linked them was the progressive establishment of a 'boundary' between BP and the 'external environment' and of the legitimacy of sigint as that which lay substantially within BP. Thus, what in 1939 had been a very small, primarily cryptanalytic, war station of SIS had been 'made' as a much larger signals intelligence agency which was not only to a considerable degree independent of SIS but also had defined a boundary (or series of boundaries) with the various armed services and ministries.

I now want to make some more general observations about these transformations. The first of these is to emphasise the importance of time and history. Organizations always carry with them, and in some significant way are made up of, the accumulated traces of the past. Thus, in the present case it is impossible to understand BP without understanding the way that GC & CS was set up after WW1. Of course, one could go much further and say that the way that GC & CS was set up can itself not be fully understood without digging back from that into WW1 and back again and so on. Similarly, one could go further forward and examine ongoing organizational processes at GCHQ after the war. That is absolutely the case and thus my point is not that in some way I have provided an exhaustive account but rather that I have provided an *illustrative* account of the temporal construction of organizational structures both in the narrow sense of part–whole relations and in the broader sense of the overall shape or form of organization. I hope that the analysis I have provided is persuasive on this point: that structures embody or crystallize temporally accreted meanings, and meanings which are typically bound up with conflicts, interests and politics.

This means that we cannot simply regard structures as ordained or determined by technical requirements, and on this point I should emphasise very strongly that there was no inevitability about the way that BP's structures developed. One might envisage an account which

explains these developments in terms of the increased scale of operations created by the breaking of ever more Enigma ciphers and messages – this, indeed, would be the contingency-theory account (Burns
and Stalker, 1961; Pugh and Hickson, 1976). But, whilst the increasing
size of BP is certainly relevant to the development of its organization, it
is emphatically not the case that it fully or even mainly explains that
development and, indeed, its increasing size was in part a consequence
of that development. What I have sought to offer is a subtly but
significantly different account in which the breaking of Enigma created the conditions under which it was possible for the new structures
to emerge. That they did so was itself contingent in the sense that it
could have been otherwise. To understand why the possibility of structural transformation was realized in the ways that it was entails a very
fine-grained consideration of, for example, individual actions (e.g.
those of Gordon Welchman) and of the outcomes of contingent political contestations (e.g. the Hut 3 disputes). We cannot infer from the
fact that such and such an organization in fact emerged that that
organization was bound to emerge. It is under-determined, and not
just in this particular case, but, I would suggest, in other cases. In this
way, as Child (1972) in a now classic article proposed, environmental
and other contingencies can never be understood in the absence of an
understanding of organizational choices and decisions.

However, matters are a little more complex than this. For it is
not just that individual agency and political contestations shape decisions about organizational forms. It is also the case that such decisions
are themselves structured by understandings of what forms organizations should take. Thus, in the BP case, the organizational innovations
initiated by Gordon Welchman were based upon his own understanding of what constituted efficiency and how a more factory-like operation should be run. This indeed is implicit in the suggestion in its
internal history that the changes in Hut 6 (of which Welchman was the
first head) were a 'natural consequence' of growth. What natural means
here is assumed or taken for granted, as it must be, since organizations
are social rather than natural phenomena[49]. Similarly, arguments over

dual control invoked (for example in the van Cutsem report) at least implicit models of administrative efficiency derived from military understandings of command and control. These then formed the basis of decisions made about re-structuring. Similar points could be made about other episodes described in these two chapters.

Thus there is more at stake than saying that there is an interplay between (social) structure and agency – not only is structure dependent in part upon agency but agency is itself socially structured. This has some affinity with various forms of institutional theory. For example, seeking to create (organizational) structures which conform to under-standings of what efficient organization looks like is a version of isomorphism (DiMaggio and Powell, 1991), whilst the politics of con-testation over organizational structure are bound up with legitimacy (Meyer and Rowan, 1977), both in the sense of what organizational forms are deemed legitimate and also in terms of who legitimately has control over those forms. This, indeed, was the basic insight of the 'old institutionalism' of Selznick (1949): the social construction of legitimacy.

In this way, it is possible to provide an account of organizational structure that draws together elements of contingency theory, institu-tional theory and, in a general way, structuration theory. To put it another way, from contingency theory we can draw an understanding of the kinds of organizational structures which are viable (but we can't conclude that they are therefore deterministically created) and this places limits upon the kinds of structure that can be institutionalized as legitimate. From institutional theory we can draw an understanding of the non-rational properties of organization structure and the politics through which legitimation is achieved. Furthermore, structuration theory allows us to insert what is palpably lacking in contingency theory and typically downplayed within institutional theory, namely the role of agency (cf. Willmott, 2011).

In some ways, as just suggested, this might be seen as a variant of strategic-choice theories of organizational structure (Child, 1972), or for that matter resource-dependence approaches (Pfeffer and Salancik,

1978) but the main difference would be that these rely upon a more rationalistic apprehension of decision making than I am suggesting here. In other words, alongside rational choice about organizational structures (or anything else), consideration needs to be given to chance and also to irrationalities of conduct of all sorts. For example, had Enigma not been broken – and it was clearly not pre-ordained – then Welchman's anticipatory organizational designs would seem not far-sighted strategic choices but pointless, even hubristic. Or had Menzies and Denniston not had a mutual antipathy then perhaps an organizational arrangement different from the 1942 reorganization might have been found. For that matter, had Denniston not happened to be seriously ill in the last half of 1941 then, again, a different organizational history might have emerged. These types of 'contingencies' mean that not only must contingency theory be modified by reference to strategic choice but also that strategic choice and resource dependence must themselves be modified to take account of them. Indeed, were this not so then it would be inexplicable that the Germans, unlike the British, largely failed to create a functional sigint organization (Ratcliff, 2006).

Moreover, one of the central arguments I have made in this chapter departs from both contingency and institutional theory. The former configures organization structure in terms of environmental fit, whilst the latter emphasises legitimacy of an organization within an organizational field. Yet the BP case illustrates the ways in which environment and field may be, at least to some considerable extent, shaped, as Barley (2010) suggests, as indeed do Pfeffer and Salancik (1978) and, in a different way, Weick (2001: 179–206). In other words, BP did not in isomorphic fashion emulate legitimate models of sigint organization; rather, to a large extent it rendered legitimate sigint as an organizational domain. In so doing it shaped or re-shaped what became the template for sigint organizations in other countries: those developments could be regarded as examples of isomorphism, BP cannot. They might better be understood in terms of a different outgrowth of institutional theory, namely institutional entrepreneurship (DiMaggio, 1988). Here, non-isomorphic innovations serve to create and legitimize new institutional and organizational forms. I will return to this point in the concluding chapter, but the more fundamental point is that what has been shown is the processual co-creation of both 'organization' and 'environment' by constructing the boundary between the two (Strati, 2008: 1187).

A different dimension of the making of BP and sigint is the matter of leadership. There was clearly a significant relationship between the 1942 changes and the replacement of Denniston with Travis. Here again a variety of theoretical perspectives, this time on leadership, can be deployed to make sense of what happened at BP. At one level the story of Denniston's leadership can be, and sometimes is, understood in trait terms (Stodgill, 1974). On this account his personal characteristics were unsuited to the role. The immediate rider to that would involve an invocation of situational theories (Hersey and Blanchard, 1993), in which framework one would say that there was a mismatch between Denniston's personality and the particular circumstances of organizational change and growth that occurred at BP[50]. To that could be added the ways that relational theories of leadership (Uhi-Bien, 2006) have some purchase: the breakdown of confidence in Denniston on the part of key actors fractured his capacity to continue as head of BP. Finally, institutional theories of leadership (Biggart and Hamilton, 1987) would suggest another explanation, that leadership links to constructed legitimate social and organizational norms: thus the emerging legitimacy of sigint contributed to the de-legitimization of Denniston's leadership.

It would seem absurd to imagine that leadership can adequately be explained by insisting that only one of these (or other) theories holds good. Indeed, it seems far more fruitful to recognize how, taken together, they can offer a more plausible account. Thus, in this case, there is evidence that Denniston was not personally suited to leading the new kind of organization which emerged, thus both losing the support of key actors and standing in contradiction to developing legitimated understandings of BP's purpose. We might say that, whereas the emergence of the more formalized sigint organization at

BP was under-determined, the demise of Denniston, given that more formalized organization, was over-determined. If breaking Enigma created the conditions of possibility for sigint organization, it also reduced the conditions of possibility for Denniston to act as its leader.

Does that, then, mean that the ongoing breaking of Enigma is the root cause of BP's organization? No, because the breaking of Enigma must in part be understood in terms of the organizational situation, including Denniston's leadership – for example in the way that he recognized the need to bring in mathematical expertise – and its exploitation in part attributable to Welchman's handling processes. Moreover, had the outcome of the conflicts over control of BP been resolved by, say, it being taken over by the War Office – as was perfectly possible – then a different organizational form would have been created within which Enigma would have been exploited. So, whilst the technical dimension is certainly important, it is but an aspect of the endless, recursive interplay between structure and agency which is why, as I suggested in the introductory section to this part of the book, an inevitable messiness emerges as soon as we cease to give priority to one or the other.

The particular details of how this interplay proceeds are, of course, ultimately unique to individual cases. I am not saying, for example, that all organizations so drastically shape and re-shape themselves and their environments as BP did. Indeed, on that specific issue, it must be quite rare for this to happen. Rather, my suggestion is that it is possible to adapt this general *style* of analysis to a wide range of organizational settings. That is to say, adopting a close, fine-grained reading of organizational processes over time enables us to approach organizational theory with fresh eyes, as a set of resources to make sense of organization, rather than as dogmatic categories to which we try to fit organizational processes which always elude such categorization. These are points which I will pick up in the concluding chapter of this book. For now, having set out at least some of the complexities of the structuring of BP's organization, I will turn to its – not, of course, unrelated – cultural aspects.

NOTES
1. Identified by Ratcliff (2006: 259 n103) as an issue requiring further research in order to understand BP's organization.
2. TNA HW 3/95.
3. TNA HW 43/70: 5.
4. Indeed, Enigma aside, this exact issue initially limited the effective use of low-grade GAF sigint (Bonsall, 2008: 832).
5. TNA HW 14/10.
6. TNA HW 3/119: 25–6. Nevertheless, 'to the end of the Hut's history it was often felt by the Watches that they and their work were looked down on by the Service intelligence sections', TNA HW 3/119: 38.
7. For a key example of the detailed way in which this happened, see TNA WO 208/5071.
8. TNA HW 3/83.
9. From Ralph Erskine's editorial introduction to the chapter.
10. TNA HW 14/40.
11. TNA HW 14/71: 2. The pluralization of 'ministries' shows that it was not just the WO which was being referred to.
12. TNA HW 14/107.
13. TNA WO 208/5070: 5.
14. This is an over-simplification in that Welchman and others were supportive of some forms of TA, notably those directly relevant to the Enigma effort. Relatedly, he was extremely hostile to Colonel Butler, as mentioned in the previous chapter.
15. TNA HW 3/92: 14. Not to be confused with the internal history of sigint.
16. Quoted in Birch's internal history of sigint, TNA HW 43/1: 186–7.
17. TNA HW 43/1: 187.
18. Beyond this, of course, was the issue of organizing the *distribution* of intelligence. Here the key organizational innovations were not Welchman's but the SLU system established by Frederick Winterbotham. See Chapter 5 for more detail, and Lewin (2008) for more still.
19. For accounts of Naval Enigma and its many variants see Erskine (2000) and Erskine and Weierud (1987).
20. TNA HW 25/1: 87.
21. TNA HW 43/70.
22. TNA HW 14/22, emphasis in original.

23. For example, Bonsall (2008: 827) suggests in relation to low-grade GAF ciphers that the AM's adherence to a division between producers and users of intelligence 'led it to obstruct the production of some of this intelligence for nearly half the war'. But, again, this situation shifted as sigint developed in the way outlined here.

24. TNA HW 43/1: 180.

25. TNA HW 43/1: 180. The term 'special intelligence' did continue to be used by the OIC, however (Beesly, 2000).

26. In indicating some points of contrast with Ratcliff, I should stress that her purposes are rather different from mine in that her analysis of BP forms only one aspect of her wider interest in Allied cipher security and German sigint operations. In terms of the latter, it is certainly true to say that they were less centralized than in the British case. I will discuss issues of centralization in more detail in Chapter 6.

27. TNA HW 14/66.

28. TNA HW 14/67: 1.

29. This is presumably intended ironically, since BP's capacity to be 'master in its own house' had been achieved in the face of opposition from the ministries.

30. TNA HW 14/67: 10.

31. Some people, including Churchill, continued informally to use the term Boniface for Ultra.

32. On the other hand, the 1942 van Cutsem report suggests that this fiction was in any case ineffective because the supposed source could not realistically have access to such varied material, TNA WO 208/5070: 4.

33. An assessment endorsed by the late Peter Freeman when in the role of GCHQ historian.

34. TNA HW 14/28.

35. TNA HW 43/2: 492.

36. TNA HW 14/8.

37. TNA HW 43/1: 441.

38. TNA HW 1/155.

39. And not just amongst these. Many of the older generation, including Travis, de Grey (Filby, 1988) and Birch (DNB entry), believed that Denniston must relinquish the helm. Indeed, Budiansky (2000: 203) states that Travis and de Grey were 'plotting to oust Denniston'. Of the leading players at BP, the only person who seems to have been strenuously opposed

to Denniston's removal was – ironically, since they had had many
disputes – Dilly Knox (Batey, 2010: 143–4). I will discuss inter-generational
issues in Chapter 4.

40. TNA HW 1/155.

41. TNA HW 14/28.

42. TNA HW 43/1: 183.

43. TNA HW 43/70: 82.

44. Denniston's situation after the 1944 reorganization was slightly
anomalous. Whilst retaining the title of Deputy Director in charge of the
civil section, he did not report to Travis, the Director of GC & CS, but still
to Menzies, Director-General of SIS. As noted shortly, on Denniston's
retirement in 1945 the separation of civil and service sections disappeared.

45. See TNA HW 14/99.

46. Many with an interest in BP's history believe that Alastair Denniston was
shabbily treated and I tend to agree. Unlike Travis and all other subsequent
Directors of GCHQ, he was never knighted (Andrew, 1985a: 488;
Denniston, 2007: 79); his pension arrangements were stingy (after
retirement he supplemented his pension with school teaching) and his
contribution to BP has perhaps been inadequately recognized.

47. Note how, by 1946, the term cryptography had officially given way to
cryptanalysis.

48. TNA HW 43/1: 455–7.

49. In this sense it is an example of what I referred to in the introductory
chapter as the self-understandings of social actors which social science
seeks to de-familiarize.

50. In other words, another kind of contingency-theory account, this time of
leadership rather than organizational structure.

Part II   Decoding Cultures

In this section of the book I seek to capture a sense of the complexities of organizational culture with reference to the BP case. Much of the analysis of organizational culture has been concerned with the nature (and, in more prescriptive literature, the desirability) of 'strong' organizational culture in which there is a homogeneous and deeply held commitment to shared values and beliefs across an organization, with consequent effects upon behaviour. On the other hand, it has repeatedly been noted that organizations are characterized not just by sub-cultural groupings but by schism and conflict – in other words, by what might be called 'weak culture'. My suggestion is that the distinction of strong and weak culture is a certain sort of encodement which is achieved only by a radical simplification of what culture in general, and organizational culture in particular, actually consists of. To put it another way, when organizational theory speaks of such things as 'power', 'role', 'task' or 'person' cultures (Handy, 1985) or any of the numerous other typologies, what is occurring is a form of 'code' that conceals meaning, and it conceals it by simplification, often gross simplification. Therefore, in order to decode culture it is necessary to set out its complexity.

If one aspect of this decoding of culture is to probe the simultaneity and inter-relationship of homogeneity and heterogeneity, another is to problematize the distinction of what lies inside and what lies outside organizational culture. There is a curious contrast between the ways that organizational theory typically treats organizational structure and organizational culture. In the case of the former, much emphasis is put upon issues of the organizational environment and the ways in which a structure is conditioned, perhaps even determined, by it. However, organizational culture is more usually treated as a primarily 'internal' phenomenon, something largely peculiar to, and generated by, itself. Even where they are made, references to 'external' factors are commonly tied back to generalized, and highly contentious, models of national characteristics, of which Hofstede's (2001) is the most frequently invoked. One explanation for this, which relates back to the prescriptive valorization of 'strong culture', may be that in recent decades organizational culture has been thought of primarily as something which is created and managed, at least aspirationally so. Thus the literature focuses either on how to achieve such management or on how these attempts are thwarted or resisted. In both cases, though, culture is discussed as something inside an organization. My suggestion will be that the distinction of internal and external again encodes through concealment and simplification a more complex set of relationships.

The BP case is an interesting one in this regard. Whenever I have presented or discussed it, the comment is invariably made that BP is surely mainly understandable in terms of the particular and peculiar culture of Britain at a time of total war, and in particular the notion of a shared sense of national purpose and solidarity. This seems to propose that BP organizational culture, at least, was externally generated. However, running alongside this is a received picture of BP as having, in fact, a very particular character. This is the image of the tweed-jacketed, academic, slightly eccentric, male, upper-class codebreaking genius, which, in a more extended version, is supplemented by a support cast of female, upper-class 'debs'[1]. There is some element of truth in both of these notions, as I will explore, but both need to be handled carefully.

As regards wartime culture, this is significant precisely because of the general point just made about 'external' aspects of organizational culture and specifically because of the extreme nature of wartime circumstances. Yet, as I will examine in the first section of Chapter 3, assumptions about a homogeneous and, as it were, 'strong' national wartime culture are themselves heavily contested by historians of the period. But, even if this were not so, it remains the case that not all organizations within Britain during WW2 had identical cultures. Thus, even if wartime culture was as homogeneous as the received image suggests, it would still be insufficient to account for every aspect of organizational culture in particular cases. This would be likely to be especially true at BP, which was in many respects isolated from the outside world because of its secret nature, but would be true in any case. In the second section of Chapter 3 I explore in depth how secrecy structured and gave a specific form to culture at BP. So far as the 'dons and debs' culture of BP is concerned, in the third section I will explore this with particular reference to the recruitment of staff at BP and suggest that, with a considerable degree of finessing, it captures a certain sense of the dominant cultural template at BP.

Taken together, my suggestion in Chapter 3 is that war, secrecy and recruitment may be considered to homogenize, to a degree, BP culture, and for this reason I refer to them as 'pillars' of culture, connoting elements which broadly bind together the construct of culture. However, these sit alongside a series of more heterogeneous elements, which I refer to as 'splinters' of culture. These are analysed in Chapter 4 and include distinctions between different services, between service and civilian personnel and between different types of civilian, as well as more sociological distinctions based upon gender, age, educational background and so on. It is a recognition of heterogeneity which leads me to use the plural term 'cultures' for this part of the book and also to refer to 'BP culture' rather than 'BP's culture' or 'the culture of BP', which I do as a reminder that we are talking of culture as something an organization 'is' rather than something it 'has' (cf. Smircich, 1983).

My analysis of BP culture here owes much to the approach outlined by Parker (2000) in which organizational culture is viewed as a kind of continual contestation between difference and similarity (Parker, 2000: 233). In a similar way, Martin (1992, 2002) argues that organizational culture is necessarily simultaneously integrating and fragmenting. In this way – in line with the overall approach of this

book – culture must be viewed as an ongoing process or accomplishment rather than a fixed or final 'thing':

> [a]s practice, culture is neither Bagehot's 'hard cake of custom' nor the
> realm of pure creativity idealized in notions of genius. It is made and
> remade in almost imperceptible small ways as well as occasional
> large bursts of innovation. As practice, culture is an achievement,
> not simply an environment.   *(Calhoun and Sennett, 2007: 7)*

In order to explore BP culture, then – but, I would suggest, the same
would be true in other cases – it is necessary to attend to the complexity and multiplicity of culture itself, to appreciate that 'it' is not a fixed
or homogeneous 'thing' but is rather multi-layered. Perhaps even that
is too clumsy a way of putting it – layers would seem to imply different
depths of culture, whereas a more appropriate metaphor might be of a
kaleidoscope of shifting and inter-relating elements (and each element
would itself be susceptible to a comparable analysis). This, it will be
shown, entails multiple cultural 'borrowings' from, for example, the
wider world of war and propaganda; from the cultural life of pre-war
Oxbridge colleges; from the cultures of military organizations and the
GPO; from different generations and so on. I have indicated that understanding this entails a decoding of culture[2] in the sense of exploring its
hidden complexities akin to the way that, at BP, splinters and fragments of information were brought together in order to reveal an
intelligible picture. In the following chapters I will seek to provide
such a picture of BP culture[3].

NOTES

1. Debs being a contraction of 'debutantes', literally, young women presented
   on their debut in 'society' at the Royal court; more figuratively, young,
   upper-class female socialites.
2. Having said that my approach is akin to that of Parker (2000), it should be
   noted that he is critical of writing which assumes that organizational
   culture 'can be "decoded" by the acute analyst' (Parker, 2000: 3), but in this
   he seems to mean the idea that a full and final reading of culture can be
   provided – which is not my meaning of 'decoding', as explained in the

introductory chapter. Rather, I mean by it something more like what Parker (2000: 4) describes as 'analysis'.

3. I should be clear that these chapters, whilst going into considerable empirical detail, in no way capture the full richness and diversity of culture at BP. Many highly readable accounts which fill out this picture are available (e.g. Smith, 1998; Page 2002, 2003; Hill, 2004; McKay, 2010).

3 Pillars of Culture at Bletchley Park

INTRODUCTION

In this chapter I will analyse those features of BP culture which tended to homogenize experience and values; specifically war, secrecy and recruitment. The relationship between BP and British society at war is clearly highly significant but also complex, not least because of its subsequent mythologization, in the sense of simplified images of society at the time. Thus I aim for an account which is sensitive to these complexities in part by reference to 'revisionist' histories of wartime society. This is not intended to deny that wartime culture is relevant to understanding BP culture, but to nuance that relevance. Yet, however nuanced, it remains the case that one of the shared cultural features of BP – although not unique to BP – was the experience of being part of a society engaged in a total war.

One popular slogan in Britain at the time was the injunction that 'careless talk costs lives'. This was intended to alert the population to the dangers of casual mentions of information that might be useful to enemy agents. This information might be in the form of off-duty military personnel mentioning operational matters, or civilians identifying areas where bombs had fallen short of target and so on. But at BP it resonated with a much more profound and all-embracing emphasis on absolute secrecy about the work of its staff, secrecy both from the outside world and between different sections within BP. My suggestion is that this, more than any other single factor, was defining of a unitary organizational culture, since it was an experience, and a highly significant one, that was shared in some way by everyone.

The third homogenizing element also related to shared experiences, but in a more diffuse sense. Early recruitment methods meant that there was a degree of similarity in social and educational background. This was not all-encompassing and, as the war progressed and BP grew, became less evident, although it did not disappear. Nevertheless, my contention is that this early history significantly shaped BP culture by providing a kind of cultural template derived, primarily, from middle- and upper-class pre-war Oxbridge.

WARTIME CULTURE

It would be impossible to understand culture at BP without giving attention to the culture of Britain at war. To call this the cultural 'context' of BP would seem to be far too anaemic a term, given the profundity and power of the ways that war permeated every facet of British society. In accounts of BP, invocations of wartime culture are ubiquitous. For example,

> everyone was willing to put in all he or she had and to put up with a lot of inconveniences and even, in some cases, real hardships. This advantage was typical of the national feeling of 'all being in it together', which – paradoxically perhaps – made Britain a wonderful place to live in during the war years.   *(Welchman, 1982: 125–6)*

Such sentiments are to be found at some point in almost all recollections of BP and figured in many of the interviews in one form or another. For example, Daphne recalls that 'the only thing that went through your head was "we're helping, we're doing war work, we're helping the war"'. The same notion is present in academic analyses of BP's work, for example

> The obvious need to defeat their common enemy convinced everyone at Bletchley that 'there was no room for any rivalry at all'[1].
> *(Ratcliff, 2006: 89–90)*

The notion of a 'common enemy' is clearly an enormously powerful one in terms of culture formation, since there is hardly a more effective way of cementing group identity than by reference to a significant external threat. That this was so at BP is perhaps most clearly revealed not so much by direct examples as indirectly by this interesting story:

> When the war with Germany ended on 7 May 1945, there were no more logs to read. But before many days passed more logs appeared, this time from French and Russian traffic. Many of the log-readers[2], astounded to learn that we were intercepting Allied signals, refused to take part. We formed a group and protested. A captain ... attempted to justify the work, but we could not agree, 'In that case,' he said, 'you are redundant'. *(Thirsk, 2001: 276–7)*

This culture of common purpose in the face of a common enemy and national emergency is linked, in many accounts, to a sense amongst those at BP that they had a relatively safe and 'pleasant' life when compared with those in the fighting services and, moreover, that the work that they were doing had the capacity to impact directly upon the fate of those in these services, even though that work itself might be of a humble sort. To take, again, just one example from the interviews, but one which links together some of these themes in a clear way, the Wren Vera commented as follows about her work as an indexing clerk:

> Mundane, yes, a bit boring. Well it could have been but ... I had a brother in the Merchant Navy and it meant a lot to us. You know, there were several girls ... who had people in the Navy, family and this sort of thing. So we really did take it very, very seriously and it meant we knew that we were in a difficult situation, that we had, that the country was in a difficult situation, that we all had to work very hard to get us out of this problem. And we took it all very seriously indeed.

Of course for many others the relationship between their work and the prosecution of the war was very obvious both in terms of the cumulative impact of the intelligence being gathered or, sometimes, in terms of the consequences of a single decrypt. For example, the sinking of the German battleship *Bismarck* followed just such a decrypt in Hut 8 – an event which rendered Hitler 'melancholy beyond words'

(McKay, 2010: 135). Sometimes the realities of war were brought into sharp focus even for the most humble office junior, such as when Daphne was instructed to have copies made of 'captured documents [that were] all curled and wet'.

It is undeniable, I would suggest, that this sense of shared purpose, sacrifice and duty to the war effort structured many aspects of BP and of wartime life in general. Yet there are some complexities. It is enormously difficult to apprehend the wartime culture of Britain and this is not so much because it lies in the past but because of the many ways in which it continues to be present. Memories and mythologies – and by this word I do not mean 'untruths' but simplified, yet meaningful, stories – of the 'Dunkirk spirit', the 'Blitz spirit' and the more general sense of Britain as an island that 'stood alone' continue to inform, in very powerful ways, contemporary senses of British identity. Equally, images of social solidarity and shared purpose continue to structure a sense both of the nature of the British people and, in more complex ways, of what has been lost. That is to say, these images are held both to disclose something of the essential nature of British culture and also to represent a contrast with subsequent cultural developments which are taken to be more individualistic, selfish and less purposeful:

> When reading books on the Second World War years, it is very often difficult to resist being enticed into the atmosphere of nostalgic patriotism which they evoke. Today the nation may be divided, but then things were different: everyone knew the job that had to be done. All agreed that Nazism was a terrible nightmare and that the Axis simply had to be defeated. Almost nobody, therefore, had any reservations about pulling together to win the war. *(Croucher, 1982: iii)*

In a similar way, Summerfield and Peniston-Bird's (2007) history of the Home Guard notes that it proved impossible to write that history without extensive reference to the popular television comedy *Dad's Army*[3] because this had so heavily inflected cultural memory and understanding of the topic. This is a very particular and perhaps extreme example (i.e. for a single TV series to be so influential), but it is illustrative of the more general significance of the interpretation and re-interpretation of the war in subsequent decades. It is well beyond the scope of this book to do more than gesture to such issues in order to flag up how difficult this terrain is. At the same time, it should be noted that such difficulties would attend any attempt to grasp organization within its wider cultural setting and perhaps would be even greater when dealing with contemporary situations. After all, the complexities and mythologies of culture are most heavily encoded in that which we take for granted and do not notice: at least a more historical case helps to make them visible.

Indeed, one of the reasons why it is possible to do this is precisely the now considerable body of work by historians which seeks to provide a more nuanced and sophisticated account of British wartime culture than the received one. Seminal within this body of work is Calder's (1969) study which calls into question the notion of an overweening national unity. Instead, he suggests, there were considerable levels of social discontent, criticism of the government in general and of Churchill in particular, and significant industrial unrest, including strikes. On the final point, specifically, Croucher (1982) extensively chronicles poor industrial relations in manufacturing industry which at the time, of course, meant primarily the armaments industry, which was clearly central to the war effort. Calder's later work (Calder, 1990) explores 'the myth of the Blitz' and here, again, the suggestion is that the received sense of 'all pulling together' was at least in large part a matter of propaganda, concealing deep social divisions as well as looting and rape undertaken under the cover of blackouts and bombing.

It is important not to misunderstand the meaning of such studies. They are not depicting wartime Britain as an entirely, or even primarily, divided or unpatriotic country, uninvested in war aims. Rather, these and similar studies act as a corrective to the view of wartime Britain as an entirely united society. This is in part a matter of recognizing the very considerable variety of individual experience and also the ways in which culture varied between different periods of the war (Hayes and Hill, 1999), for example between the period in 1940 in particular when invasion was feared to be imminent and the later years when victory seemed in prospect but was not yet assured. The veracity of this stress upon variety becomes very evident in what is now a large, and growing, volume of material published from Mass Observation Society (MOS) diaries of the period (e.g. Sheridan, 1990; Garfield, 2005; Hinton, 2010). In a similar vein are the now published reports of the home intelligence division of the Ministry of Information (MOI), comprising the daily observation of informants on the state of popular morale (Addison and Crang, 2010). In such material scepticism and complaint are as much in evidence as patriotic fervour and stoicism.

Again, none of this means that there is not a genuine sense in which one can speak of British wartime culture. It is just that – unsurprisingly, were it not for the extent to which it continues to be unrecognized – it was a culture every bit as complex as any other human culture. A key aspect of this complexity is explained by Calder (1969) in his analysis that repeated invocations of the collective – the 'we' or 'us' – were highly influential but interpreted differentially so as to mean whatever social group one was a member of – professional classes, miners, fighting services and so on. In other words, Calder's analysis suggests that there was a widely shared sense that 'we are all in it together' at the same time as there being a fragmented sense of who 'we' were. In this sense, it can perhaps be concluded that wartime culture did not supplant so much as supplement existing features of culture and, in this way, did not so much *simplify* culture by creating a sense of collective purpose as make it more *complex* by adding another layer to it.

Certainly an absolutely central aspect of wartime culture was the very intense effort which went into attempts – at national level – to manage it. This effort was massive and multi-layered, encompassing everything from, say, the provision by the BBC of inspirational radio talks from J. B. Priestley – which, just in themselves, did much to forge enduring cultural images of the war, such as those of Dunkirk (Hanson,

2008) – through to comprehensive programmes for post-war reform which laid the basis of the welfare state via the Beveridge Report, and so promoted a sense of 'what we are fighting for'. Within this, the propaganda activities of the MOI (McLaine, 1979) are worthy of particular mention. One especially potent part of these activities was the numerous and widely watched[4] public information films[5].

Viewed as a collection, these show a remarkable homogeneity of message: the need to play one's part and to make sacrifices for the greater good and a stress upon common responsibilities. At the heart of almost all of them is the idea that every individual action, no matter how tiny, from throwing away a used bus ticket to talking needlessly on the telephone is linked by a causal chain to the effectiveness of the fighting forces. This chimes directly with the sense at BP that the most mundane of work tasks mattered to the war effort. Indeed, the very notion of the 'home front' which featured prominently was designed to emphasise that domestic life was as much a part of war as the front line. Other common themes were, as noted earlier, injunctions against 'careless talk' (i.e. gossiping about things which might be of value to enemy agents), and amongst these a particularly interesting example from the point of view of BP is the film *You Can't Be Too Careful*. This recounts the shame felt by someone in civilian clothes doing secret work and the importance of him not being tempted to tell his family and friends of this work in order to gain their approval. Taken together, these often very well-made films are enormously powerful and, just in themselves, help to explain the dominant image of wartime culture which we still have. Even today, in Britain some of the common catchphrases are widely understood, recognized and, occasionally, still invoked – 'dig for victory', 'keep mum', 'careless talk costs lives', 'coughs and sneezes spread diseases', 'make do and mend' and 'is your journey really necessary?' all being examples[6].

Yet these films also tell us something else. They do not so much reflect the reality of the times as the concern amongst the authorities that such sentiments were insufficiently widely shared. That is, had everyone already realized that each tiny action on their part impacted upon the war effort, it would hardly have been necessary continually to remind them of it. So, in themselves, they point to precisely the cultural variations which more recent historical analysis of the war insists upon. A central point to re-emphasise here is that such analyses do not deny the formidable power and indeed the reality of wartime solidarity as something both depicted by and to a large degree produced by propaganda; rather they suggest that this was grafted on to something equally powerful but much more complicated in terms of contested realities and experiences of different social groups and identities (Rose, 2003).

Perhaps I should also re-emphasise the point that, whilst I have repeatedly used the terms 'myth' and 'mythology' in referring to received images of wartime culture, it would be quite wrong to regard myth as synonymous with untruth. In the realm of culture one might almost say that there is only 'myth' in the sense of stories which are meaningful to members of a culture and allow them to make sense of both past and present (and perhaps future). The very fact that it is possible to speak in a meaningful way about shared purpose, social solidarity and so on in the context of the war is culturally important, so long as its complexities and limitations as an explanation are recognized. And, beyond even this, there is a need for some care in not replacing one mythologized image with another. Historical studies of wartime culture have, since Calder, acted as an important corrective to unproblematized received accounts, yet some recent additions to this stream of work seem almost to go to the other extreme. Can it really be true, for example, that 'nothing could hide the fact that the informing purpose of the national effort was mass murder' (Hinton, 2010: 13)? No doubt some such concerns were held by some people, but as a general statement about apprehensions of the national effort this seems considerably more overblown than the received account of a nation united in pursuit of a 'good war'.

The other point that should be made as a qualifier to any implication that a more complex account of wartime culture denies that there was any such thing is this. What is undoubtedly the case, and the propaganda effort was a part of it, is that the war saw a massive extension of state activity and state direction of activities (Middlemas, 1979; Cronin, 1991; Edgerton, 2011). This in itself significantly transformed cultural life in terms of everything from the state direction of labour to rationing, and created as a result new types of identity and, to some considerable extent, homogenized experience. Whilst there are continuing debates about the nature and extent of the social change which is attributable to the war (see Marwick (1988) and Smith (1986) for the two poles of this debate), it would be idle to deny that it stands as one of the most significant periods within the cultural landscape of Britain and to that extent it would be equally idle to downplay the ways in which it both shaped and 'contextualized' organizational life at BP.

This very brief account of wartime culture in Britain has done no more than raise some general issues, yet I hope that the contours of these are clear. If Bletchley Park is to be understood primarily as an instantiation of that wartime culture then it will not serve to conclude that an overwhelming shared purpose leading to individual sacrifice, conformity and duty tells us all we need to know. Whilst there is no doubt that such elements were present within BP culture, they were not by any means all there was to BP, any more than they were all there was to wartime culture in general.

SECRECY

Whilst I have already indicated (and will explore in the following chapter) that there was great cultural variety at BP, there is one element which was universally shared and perhaps more than any other gives a sense of a distinctive BP culture, different from those of almost all other wartime organizations. Many kinds of wartime service entailed discretion and, as mentioned earlier, there was a general imprecation to the population to avoid 'careless talk'[7], but BP entailed a degree of secrecy which was almost unparalleled. Even amongst intelligence-related organizations the degree of secrecy at BP was, perhaps, extreme[8], and certainly there is no example (or none that is known!) of a *greater* degree of secrecy. This means that everyone[9] who worked at BP had the experience of being required to sign the Official Secrets Acts (OSA) and, more vividly, of receiving very stern instructions on the matter of secrecy. There are some stories, possibly apocryphal, of new recruits being told, with a pistol on display, that security breaches would result in being shot. Slightly less dramatically, 'we were told in no uncertain terms that this [signing the OSA] was a very important thing and we would go to the Tower if we breathed a word' (Hill, 2004: 27). What is certainly not in doubt is that every person working at BP was told on joining, and repeatedly thereafter, that they must say nothing whatsoever about their work to anyone in the outside world, including families, friends and spouses; nor must they talk about their work to people at BP beyond those they actually worked with, and not to them when outside their working area at BP. Frequent written notices and lectures continually re-enforced the fact that staff must not talk about their work at meals, in BP transports, when travelling on public transport, in lodgings or at home, and even had to take care within their own hut, lest cleaners or maintenance staff overhear[10]. Staff were instructed to respond to queries from outsiders about their work with vague answers[11] about working in an office, or for the foreign office, or, possibly, that they worked 'in communications'[12], and they should not make reference to working at a place called Bletchley Park (even though, of course, at the time this name would have meant nothing to most people). Special arrangements were made for postal deliveries, telegrams, telephone calls and rail warrants so that it would not become obvious that there was (as the years went by) a huge concentration of personnel working at this one site.

Although they were not necessarily aware of it, everyone who worked at BP had security checks made upon them, in many cases leading to short delays between being appointed and actually taking up duties. These checks would relate to general issues of trustworthiness as well as to vulnerabilities to blackmail and political sympathies. It has proved impossible to gather any significant level of detail on these practices[13]. Hayward (1993: 182) recounts being 'subjected to the full positive-vetting[14] procedure' on joining BP, although also reports being informally inducted to save time, given the two-week delay in getting formal clearance, so there was some flexibility in play. A further glimpse is provided by the comment of Dora, an interviewee who worked in administration and saw some of the paperwork relating to this: 'I can remember there was somebody who had a record that he went out to Spain and he'd been fighting the Spanish Civil War ... he was under suspicion'[15]. More generally, she recalls that in the administration office there were files on each employee 'and they were fairly penetrating as to who you were and where you'd come from and what you'd done. They knew about you, plus your clearance'. The extent of the knowledge gained was considerable, as one staff member discovered when accidentally seeing a file on a colleague: 'I simply couldn't credit the extraneous detail of this girl's life that was contained in the dossier – concerning her parents, her extended family and even her friends. It sticks in my mind that her grandmother had once had an affair with a Turk!' (unnamed ATS officer, quoted in Hill, 2004: 61). This extensive checking process also lead to what for some was the disconcerting experience of finding, on arrival at BP, that one was already 'known'. For example, the interviewee Joyce found that '[my boss] knew the names of some of my teachers and what subjects I was good at' (cf. Hill, 2004: 19). By contrast, no one arriving at BP knew any details whatsoever of the work for which they had been recruited.

All of the many published accounts of life at BP provide numerous illustrations of the strength of the culture of secrecy, but a few cases from the interviews for this study will serve to illustrate the point. For example, Daphne recalled that 'my sister worked in Hut 10 ... I've no idea what she did, she never told' (and neither did Daphne tell her sister what she herself did); Vera remarked 'it was so impressed upon us that we'd got to keep this secret and we must never, never, never tell it'. Neither Daphne nor Vera was 'enwised' – which is to say they had not been indoctrinated[16] into the fact of Enigma (or other ciphers) having been broken – whereas Joyce, because of her assessing work in Hut 3, was. She recalled not just the instruction that this secret must never be told but also it being burdensome 'knowing this terrible secret'. Others who worked at BP have described the strain that working in secret imposed, for example 'I used to be terrified that I would say something in my sleep. There were women who refused operations in case they said something under anaesthetic' (Hill, 2004: 130). One revealing story concerns a BP worker who became ill when on leave, prompting her doctor, suspecting a work-related cause, to write to chief administrator Commander Bradshaw stating '[she] has hypertrophy of the conscience to such an extent that she will not divulge the smallest detail of what she does, even though it is against her own interests. As I find it difficult to believe that this young girl is on work which is so important … I thought I would write to ask …' (McKay, 2010: 103–4)[17].

Alongside a culture of 'not telling', the other element of secrecy was 'not asking'. All of the interviewees just quoted, and many other published accounts of life at BP, emphasise this element. No doubt it again relates in part to wider wartime strictures about careless talk. In Vera's words:

> This is what I find astonishing, is my lack of curiosity. It's something to do with wartime, being brought up in a very Naval family, my father was away at sea, my brothers were away at sea, that was part of our lives. You didn't talk about where ships were … You'd go out with your friends in London, you just simply didn't ask them where they were going …

This account is interesting because it invokes the war in general but then immediately positions this in terms of a particular kind of personal and social background, a matter I will return to. The general point is the way that secrecy was linked not just to discretion but to lack of curiosity. But at BP there was a very significant additional element to this, namely the extremely rigid compartmentalization of work and restriction of information on a 'need to know' basis. I will discuss this in greater detail in Part III, including some of the problems it gave rise to, but it is vital to grasp here how central it was to BP. To give one of many examples:

> It was a very curious organisation. We were very, very departmentalised [sic][18]. You never discussed your work with anyone except your little group you worked with. I hadn't a clue what was going on in the rest of the Park and nobody else had a clue what we were doing. *(Susan Wenham, Hut 6, quoted in Smith, 1998: 37)*

A nice illustration of compartmentalization is provided by Ron, who was interviewed for this study. He came to BP to work as an engineer on the teleprinters used to handle Fish decrypts. Throughout the war and until the 1970s he thought that BP was simply a communications station, and that the only secret, sigint aspect of the site was his section: 'I thought it was a brilliant idea, to bury this little unit amongst thousands of others working on communications'. In a similar way, Naval Section recruit James Hogarth 'never really understood the BP organization – I imagine very few people did – and I never met the head of the whole organization' (Hogarth, 2008: 25). This again was commonplace: those joining BP were given no induction into its overall scope and purposes, only, at most, information on those of the particular section or sub-section where they worked or perhaps just their individual task within that.

To re-emphasise, it is absolutely crucial to understanding the secrecy culture at BP to recognize the nature and extent of this compartmentalization. It meant that the majority, probably the overwhelming majority, of those who worked there did not know the reality of what they were working on. Ron, just quoted, at least was enwised to Fish being read. Amongst the much larger number of people[19] working in some way on Enigma and other ciphers only a minority was enwised[20] and, although others certainly guessed that Enigma was being broken, many did not even realize that they were engaged in a codebreaking operation at all[21], or understood only in the haziest way. For example, for many all they were aware of was their own tiny, perhaps clerical, task: what they were actually filing and indexing they did not necessarily know or, even if they knew, they had no idea where the material came from or what it meant – although they did know that what little they were aware of must never be spoken of. Again the implications of this for BP operations will be discussed further elsewhere, but, for now, what is central is that the secrecy at BP was not just a secrecy from the outside world but also an internal secrecy. Many who worked at BP died not knowing what work they had been involved in. Some who lived long enough had the, no doubt extraordinary, experience in 1974 of learning the truth (or some of it, since the full details emerged over a period of years[22]).

The extreme secrecy at BP extended beyond vetting, constant reminders of security and rigid compartmentalization. Security officers also frequented public places in the area around Bletchley Park – staff were billeted in towns and villages for many miles around – checking for any signs of security breaches. An extract from one of these reports, from security officer James Bellinger on 23 March 1941, can serve to illustrate their nature, as well as making interesting reading in itself:

> During the course of my investigation I have visited nearly every hotel, public house and club in Bletchley and the surrounding districts ... I do not believe that any information as to the nature of the duties undertaken [at BP] has been imparted to [local residents]. The greater majority are very patriotic and [are] satisfied that whatever is done is all for the good of the country. There are some however who have a different idea and refer to the civil employees as persons who have dodged out of London, either to avoid the air raids or being called upon for military service. On the other hand there are a few people who have a shrewd idea as to what may be going on, by referring to some of the employees as Doctors of Science, Mathematicians and Professors from various Universities who are undertaking work of great national importance ... [Others, specifically women] have a lot to say as to the way that some of our young ladies dress for business; I suppose it is a natural topic with

women. Nevertheless at 9.15 am on the mornings [sic] of 19th, 20th and 21st March 1941 I have seen a young married woman leaving the Park, coming off night duty, dressed as if she had just left a Turkish Harem[23].

There are several points of interest here, including issues relating to gender, which will be discussed later, and the fact that some 'shrewd' guesses were made by the public (and, in fact, very often by family members) as to the nature of the work being done by BP staff. However, the point I want to highlight is how the very strong secrecy culture at BP had three elements. One was about ignorance – not knowing what was going on beyond one's immediate work; one was about silence – not speaking to anyone at all about any aspect of one's work; one, as the quoted extract illustrates, was about surveillance – vetting checks and ongoing monitoring of behaviour.

Despite the quite remarkable strength of the secrecy culture at BP, there were throughout the war minor security breaches. It would be a daunting task to document these, but throughout the TNA HW 14 sequence of directorate-related papers there are numerous references to lapses and injunctions to staff to recall the strict rules in place: 'month after month instances have occurred where workers at BP have been found casually saying things outside BP which are danger- ous'[24]. Most of these cases were relatively trivial, and many seem to have been to do with individuals explaining, or perhaps boasting, that they were doing work of importance. It is easy to understand why this might have been a temptation, especially for civilians who might be viewed with the kind of disdain implied in the security officer's report just quoted (cf. McKay, 2010: 220). Indeed, in this way the more general culture of war cut in two directions: on the one hand discouraging 'careless talk', on the other putting considerable pressure on individu- als to be seen to be 'doing their bit' – an example of the way that such culture was neither homogeneous nor uncontradictory. Even a very senior person at BP, Gordon Welchman, broke the security rules by telling his father something of his work (Hill, 2004: 80). Nevertheless, there is no evidence of any significant security breach at BP – although there is one account of a 'spy' being taken off the premises by 'two burly MI5 men' (Hill, 2004: 52) – and no suggestion whatsoever that the Axis powers ever breached BP security[25]. A different question is how much of BP's work was known to the Soviet Union, since John Cairncross, a Soviet agent, worked there for a period[26] (Aldrich 2010: 36–7; Smith, 1998: 155–6). However, this was not a matter of 'careless talk' but of purposeful espionage, and does not in itself undermine the wider point about a culture of secrecy.

What is perhaps the most striking feature of the secrecy culture at BP is the way that it persisted for so long after the war, which is remarkable considering the number of people who worked there. It is straining credulity to think that no one subsequently told any family member of their work, but there are many cases which have emerged since BP became public knowledge of how silence was kept within families. Particularly delicious are those cases where spouses both worked at BP but never told each other, for example,

> My husband John and I had been married for 30 years or more when one spring we visited a stately home ... The magnolia trees were in full bloom. John said, 'there were two such lovely magnolias where I was stationed for a time during the war'. 'Oh' said I, 'I knew two such trees too – beside a lake'. 'Really,' said John – same lake, same magnolias at Bletchley Park. In all those years we had kept the secret from one another!! *(Joan Unwin, Wren, quoted in Page 2002: 70–1)*

Such stories and the very fact of the silence that was maintained are a testament to the centrality and solidity of secrecy in BP culture and, in fact, many who worked there will still not speak of it. Indeed, even amongst those agreeing to be interviewed for this study there was sometimes evident a residual sense of reluctance, even guilt, about speaking, so strong was the injunction to silence (cf. Hill, 2004: 48).

The process through which the BP story came into the public domain is itself an interesting and complex one, which can only very briefly be outlined here (see Moran, 2012 for a detailed account). The original reasons for keeping it secret were, firstly, that it was still operationally relevant to post-war sigint techniques (Kahn, 2010) and, secondly, to avoid any suggestion in post-war Germany that the Nazis had not been beaten by 'legitimate' military means. The fear was of a belief developing, analogous to the 'stab in the back' belief that followed Germany's defeat in WW1, that defeat had been based on trickery (Herman, 2007: 2)[27]. By the 1960s the latter concern had become irrelevant, although the former was held still to have some, albeit diminishing, purchase[28]. But bit by bit the secret was leaking out through various more or less oblique references in published books in English, French and Polish (Herman, 2007: 3–5; Thirsk, 2008: 61–8). At the same time, it had been decided in 1969 that there would be some form of official history of British intelligence in WW2, and it was difficult to see how such a history could realistically exclude the Ultra secret. It was against this background that Winterbotham published his 1974 book with the tacit, albeit ambiguous, agreement of the authorities (Herman, 2007: 7). This book's publication, and its serialization in the *Sunday Telegraph*, provoked massive public interest. Although it did not by any means tell the whole story of BP, and in some respects was inaccurate in what it did say, it led to further revelations and, eventually, near complete declassification of official documents. Meanwhile, despite some ongoing political machinations, the magisterial official history was being prepared under the leadership of former BP luminary and Cambridge historian Professor Sir Harry Hinsley, with the first volume being published in 1979 (Hinsley *et al.*, 1979). Four subsequent volumes appeared over the next decade, despite some considerable delays caused by opposition from the then Prime Minister Margaret Thatcher, culminating in an abridged edition summarising the series (Hinsley, 1993c).

Whilst this process of disclosure is not directly relevant to my analysis, it is indicative of how entrenched the culture of secrecy surrounding BP was. Winterbotham 'was violently criticized by former colleagues as the man who had let the side down' (Herman, 2007: 7), although it will be clear even from the brief account I have given that disclosure was happening anyway, and would almost certainly have continued to do so. Many BP veterans interviewed or otherwise supplying information to me for this book spoke very negatively about Winterbotham's book having been published, more than thirty years after the event, again showing how far-reaching the culture of secrecy was.

What does this culture of secrecy mean organizationally? Firstly, it marks the main, shared feature of BP culture: the thing above anything else which would allow us even to entertain speaking of 'a' BP culture. Secondly, of course, it indicates that this was a highly unusual culture. For reasons which are presumably obvious, studies of organizational secrecy are rare (Anand and Rosen, 2008; Jones, 2008). Although secrecy can take a number of forms within organizations (Costas and Grey, 2011), the BP case conforms to a classic definition of secrecy as that which 'intentionally conceals knowledge, information and/or behaviour from the view of others' (Bok, 1984: 5–6) in order 'to protect an informational asset perceived to be of high value – whether tactical or strategic' (Dufresne and Offstein, 2008: 103). This precisely describes the situation at BP, where secrecy had a clear and very high value of this sort. But culturally the protection of secrets has some interesting effects. In Georg Simmel's seminal sociological treatment of secrecy he remarks as follows:

> Not quite so evident are the attractions and values of the secret
> beyond its significance as a mere means – the peculiar attraction of
> formally secretive behaviour irrespective of its momentary content.
> In the first place, the strongly emphasized exclusion of all outsiders
> makes for a correspondingly strong feeling of possession . . .
> [m]oreover, since the others are excluded from the possession . . . the
> converse suggests itself psychologically, namely that what is denied
> to many must have special value.   *(Simmel, 1906: 442)*

Michael Herman, mentioned above, subsequently became a leading scholar in the field of intelligence studies. Drawing explicitly upon Simmel, he points out that the very existence of strict secrecy bestows upon intelligence practitioners a feeling of 'specialness' into which newcomers are inducted through special rituals, secret language and elaborate precautions. In this way, he suggests that a deeply ingrained and lifelong sense of being a member of a privileged inner circle develops (Herman, 1996: 328–30).

This would seem to capture the potency of secrecy as an element or – as I have suggested – a *key* element of BP culture. This is not to say that BP staff felt particularly special in the sense of 'important'. As noted, many were doing mundane jobs whose true nature they did not know, and at a time when their peers were sometimes engaged in far more 'glamorous' activities. Nevertheless, all seem to have been permanently 'marked' by secrecy and a sense of standing in contrast to 'outsiders'. Moreover, as I will explore further in the next chapter, because there were different circles of secrecy, for example and in particular between those enwised to the breaking of Enigma and those not, there was a sense in which it gave rise to sub-cultural groupings within BP.

There is another consequence of a secrecy culture, though, which is worth mentioning: it can become an end in itself. Thus 'in practice, peacetime secrecy is often overdone; special codewords and limited distributions become departments' badges and means of protecting and extending their territory' (Herman, 1996: 93). Bletchley Park was not, of course, a peacetime situation, but even so there are some indications of this. In a general way, mirroring Herman's point, Commander Malcolm Saunders, head of Hut 3 until 1942, remarked 'I have often noticed with men in secret positions that they tend to project their secrecy into realms where it should not exist'[29]. To take some more specific consequences, Hill (2004: 57) gives the example of a technician leaving Hut 3 for a few minutes to get a spare part and being refused re-admittance since he had left his pass in the hut: 'The hapless engineer pointed to the badge on his coat hanging on the chair, but [the officer] still refused'. This is perhaps a fairly trivial example, but of more significance is this, from the internal history of Hut 3:

It was laid down (fortunately the rule was never strictly obeyed) that Hut 3 workers were not allowed to discuss their work with Hut 6 workers, nor to have direct access to the Hut 6 Decoding Room. In practice it was always of great importance that members of Hut 3 Watch should be able to take corrupt decodes personally to the decoders, a procedure which naturally gave better results than the contacts at third-hand via official channels[30].

I will discuss some of the issues posed by these kinds of restrictions arising from a culture of secrecy in more detail in Part III. For now, I will resume the exploration of those elements of BP culture which tended towards homogeneity, turning now to recruitment.

RECRUITMENT

It is a truism that organizational cultures are significantly shaped by recruitment (Legge, 1995: 75). It applies particularly strongly in the case of BP for two reasons. Firstly, indeed, it applies to the way that recruitment was done in secret, and considerations of trustworthiness were central. Secondly, the phenomenal growth of GC & CS from a couple of hundred to many thousands meant that culture was actively and rapidly formed in ways which are different from the more gradual entry and exit of staff that is perhaps more common in organizations.

The core staff of GC & CS consisted of its inter-war personnel, many of whom had been members of Room 40 during WW1 and had either stayed on during peacetime or had been recalled for service in WW2 or, in a few cases, had been recruited during the inter-war period. This group included many of the senior people at BP, such as Alastair Denniston, Edward Travis, Nigel de Grey, Frank Birch, Dilly Knox, John Tiltman, Nobby Clarke and Josh Cooper. To these was added a further complement of staff gathered during the pre-war planning process or very early after the outbreak of war. In this, 'men of the Professor type' – a telling phrase – were identified and in many cases given some training in anticipation of hostilities. This planning process is described by Alastair Denniston[31] and details of early recruits are

provided by Erskine (1986). I will discuss in detail some of the methods
and consequences of this process in Chapter 5 but, for now, the point to
make is that those being recruited were academics, mainly Oxbridge
academics, and almost entirely male; and they were being recruited
primarily as cryptanalysts. Within this group were many of those who
became central figures at BP including Gordon Welchman, Alan
Turing, Hugh Alexander, Harry Hinsley, John Jeffreys, Peter Twinn
and Stuart Milner-Barry[32]. Many of these were mathematicians, some
were also expert chess players. Roy, interviewed for this study, was one
of precisely this group of recruits, a Cambridge linguist recruited following an interview with, as he later discovered, Alastair Denniston
and John Tiltman in 1939. Both in the pre-war group and in the newly
recruited group some were widely considered to be eccentric in manner – Turing, Knox and Cooper being widely mentioned in this regard –
but it is highly misleading to claim that this was generally the case.
Throughout the war, with a few exceptions in terms of gender – such as
Joan Clarke (later Murray) (Burke, 2010), Ruth Briggs (Morris, 1993:
243), Margaret Rock (Erskine, 2010: xv) and Mavis Lever (later Batey)
(Batey, 2010) – recruits of this type formed the core of the cryptanalytic
staff at BP. The pool of universities increased somewhat, although less
for cryptanalysts than for other staff[33].

Alongside this early recruitment of mainly male cryptanalysts, a
cadre of female support staff was brought to BP. This continued the
pattern established both in WW1 and in the inter-war period, when
about half of GC & CS staff had been women (Aldrich, 2010: 16). In
other words, the subsequent employment of large numbers of female
employees at BP should not be read just as an example of the widespread
mobilization of women during WW2 but also as relating to the pre-
existing practice at GC & CS. Within this group of women in the early
days of BP were Barbara Abernethy[34], Diana Russell Clarke, Joyce Fox-
Mail, Elizabeth Granger, Claire Harding and Phoebe Senyard. Many of
these women came from very privileged social backgrounds and gave rise
to the 'debs' stereotype which is still associated with BP. A flavour of this
can be seen in Diana Russell Clarke's account of her recruitment to BP:

> My mother simply rang up Commander Denniston whom we'd known all our lives. She said 'Liza [Denniston's nickname] have you got a job for Diana?' He replied 'Yes, send her along'.
>
> *(quoted in Smith, 1998: 14)*

A similar sense is conveyed by Clarke's account of her arrival at BP: 'I simply went in my car. I had a Bentley. It belonged to a friend. He said it was better for it to be driven than stuck up on blocks. So I had this beautiful car all through the war[35]' (quoted in Smith, 1998: 2). Colourful examples of 'the debs' abound, such as the Honourable Sarah Baring, god daughter of Lord Mountbatten, who spent her days off at Claridges Hotel in London; or the unmissable parties given by the future Comtesse de la Falaise (McKay, 2010: 121–2).

However, it is important not to over-state the significance of these stories. Firstly, the social composition of the workforce in general and of its female members perhaps in particular, changed markedly in the ensuing years. Secondly, it is a misnomer to think that these privileged women were selected out of sheer snobbery. On the contrary, consider one of the most famous of the early groupings of women at BP, the so-called 'Dilly's girls' who worked in Dilly Knox's section (later known as ISK): 'Dilly had made it clear that he did not want any debutantes whose daddies had got them into Bletchley through knowing someone at the Foreign Office ... he wanted to know our qualifications' (Batey, 2010: 107). Indeed, many of the women who worked at BP had exemplary academic records, quite apart from any social credentials they may have had (and, clearly, given the restricted nature of female university education at the time, there was inevitably some correlation between social class and such education). More generally, in the post-war review it was noted that 'for lower grade labour, especially girls, large numbers were raised through the FO ... the standard of labour produced in this way was on the whole exceptionally good'[36]. Thus whatever else may be said, any suggestion that these female civilians were mere social adornments must be rejected.

I will return to issues of gender in the next chapter, but my point for now is that the received image of BP as being populated by 'dons and debs' derives from the nature of these early phases of its history. I am not, however, implying that this was of no importance. On the contrary, to a degree this set a cultural template which in various ways endured and which shaped and gave homogeneity to BP, even when the actual background of the workforce became more heterogeneous.

This began to occur almost immediately because of the growing demand for staff. It is notable that it is possible so easily to give the names of early members of BP. The reason is simple: at the outbreak of war there were just 200 members. Thereafter, as mentioned elsewhere, numbers grew very rapidly. The majority of this growth took the form of military personnel – typically volunteers or conscripts, rather than regular or career personnel – and most of these were female. By far the largest single contingent, then, were female service personnel, predominantly Wrens. Although members of different services could be found in a wide array of different functions, there was some specialization, with Wrens in particular providing the staff for the bombes and other devices at BP and its outstations, ATS personnel often assigned to Traffic Analysis (TA), WAAFs assigned to teleprinter work and so on[37]. Although, as I have stated, GC & CS had a history pre-war of employing women, this tendency grew as more and more men were deployed to frontline duties and in particular women were recruited to staff Y stations (i.e. listening posts).

Regardless of whether they were civilians or service personnel, considerable efforts were made to identify people with appropriate work experience. Sometimes this was quite perfunctory, such as the Wren who was asked whether she was sufficiently mechanically minded to put the chain back on her bike if it came off and, on giving a positive answer, ended up working on the bombes (Page, 2002: 23). In other cases it was more rigorous, such as the interviewee Joyce who was tested on her proficiency in German before being allocated to a responsible role in assessing weather decrypts in Hut 3[38]. Banks, insurance companies and department stores (especially John Lewis[39]) were scoured for clerical and managerial staff. One now famous recruiting strategy was to approach winners of the Daily Telegraph crossword competition, although, for all that this is a nice story, very few staff came via this route. By contrast, very low-grade labour (cooks, cleaners etc.) was simply directed by the Ministry of Labour or provided by the services from amongst the ranks of those unfit or incompetent for military duties (Hill, 2004: 74). A particularly important source of skilled labour was the GPO, where people with pre-existing technical expertise in electrical engineering as well as wireless telegraphy, Morse typing and similar specialist skills could be found. Ron, interviewed for this study, was one of those gathered during a sweep of the GPO, whose managers were asked 'to identify their brightest individuals'. Indeed, it is important to note that, despite what might be imagined, whereas there was no significant difficulty in recruiting sufficient cryptanalytic staff, the perennial problem was finding skilled technical labour such as mechanics and intercept staff. The latter, in particular, posed challenges because of the length of time needed to train them – up to two years to become highly skilled, whereas a Typex operator, by contrast, could be trained in ten days[40].

With this growth of staff, recruitment methods inevitably went beyond the informal methods of the very early days of BP and involved a multiplicity of agencies. The results were not always happy. For example, speaking of the Civil Service Commission (CSC), Nigel de Grey wryly noted that 'it was difficult to persuade them that people were not necessarily suitable just because they were queer and difficult to place elsewhere'[41]. This does suggest, perhaps, the enduring imprint (here in the minds of the CSC) of BP's early cultural template as a place of eccentricity. This image is captured in Churchill's oft-quoted although possibly apocryphal remark on visiting BP in September 1941: 'I know I told you to leave no stone unturned to get staff, but I didn't expect you to take me literally' (Smith, 1998: 78). Eccentricity aside, whatever the increasing formalization of recruitment, social considerations continued to play a part in it. It is impossible to gain a comprehensive picture of the class composition of BP staff and it was surely very varied, including many from working-class backgrounds (Hill, 2004: 71). Yet, again and again in published recollections and interviews there are unmistakeable traces not of aristocracy but of a kind of educated, middle-class respectability even amongst those doing quite mundane jobs. As the post-war review records, an 'unusually high percentage of supporting staff were i) university trained ii) Higher School certificate standard. This in the services applied especially to the WRNS and ATS ...'[42].

This generality is illustrated by the interviewee Vera, who, describing her recruitment interview, commented in passing on 'the fact that I'd been to grammar school, that was of interest', which seems, given the fact that the actual work she did was fairly routine filing of index cards, perhaps to suggest that it was social as much as educational standing which was being probed. In a not dissimilar way, Dora learned, after the war, that she had been identified for BP when the head of the secretarial college she had attended had been approached to identify 'girls of integrity' for confidential war work[43]. Integrity is not, of course, a specifically middle-class attribute, but there is a sense again here of a search for a certain 'type' of person both educationally and socially: 'girls from good families and good schools' (Hogarth, 2008: 26). This is very impressionistic, and even more so is the following observation. When I started the research upon which this book is based I was working at the University of Cambridge and, almost invariably, when I mentioned the project to colleagues I would be told that a relative of the person in question had worked at BP, usually in a fairly routine role. Given the small number of people who worked at BP relative to the population as a whole, my sense is that the social networks which still somewhat structure a place like Cambridge were disproportionately represented at BP.

What can be said with rather more certainty is that the cultural life of BP – in the sense not of organizational culture, although it is relevant to this, but in the sense of artistic and intellectual pursuits – in some ways retained as its template that of Oxbridge Colleges. This was compounded by the fact that, even when recruiting became more broadly based, graduates were recruited on an annual cycle, matching that of the academic year. In the early days, staff were catered for by a chef brought in from the Savoy Hotel, and the entire staff met for lunch (Welchman, 1982: 34), rather like in a College dining hall. This, of course, could not persist – as staff size grew a canteen was built – but what did were other inheritances from Oxbridge culture: a very rich array of clubs and societies dedicated to music, amateur dramatics, chess, languages, highland dancing, ballet and so on (see, for example, Simpson, 2011: 131). As McKay (2010: 245) notes, these activities were of a more 'highbrow' nature than that of wartime Britain more generally, which he ascribes, indeed, to the university background of many members of staff. Nevertheless, these activities were not purely spontaneous in character. Whilst it would be an anachronism to speak of 'culture management' at BP, what was very much in evidence was a managerial concern with staff morale. I will discuss aspects of this managerial approach in Chapter 5 but, for now, note that it was part of an understanding that operational efficiency was affected by the provision of recreational facilities[44], and indeed there was a Bletchley Park Recreational Club to co-ordinate these (McKay, 2010: 251). Again, though, there is a complexity. Some, perhaps many, at BP had no involvement with these kinds of recreational activities. For example, the GPO engineer Ron stated 'I didn't take part in any social activities at the Park. I didn't have the time … I was studying for my City and Guilds exams by correspondence course', and his was not an isolated case (see, for example, McKay, 2010: 250)[45].

Leaving aside leisure activities, what else might the relatively restricted nature of recruitment have meant for organizational culture at BP? Again many aspects of this will be examined in Chapter 5, but for now my suggestion would be that it tended to promote – I choose this word deliberately, rather than 'create', to imply influence rather than determination – a culture of intellectuality and a meritocracy based upon intellect (which is clearly not to be confused with egalitarianism) rather in the manner of an Oxbridge college, a culture fairly informal in style (which is clearly not to be confused with non-hierarchical) and suffused with a 'tradition of amateurism' (Ratcliff, 2006: 77). In a way, and this may account for its enduring power, it was an imaginary ideal of a certain apprehension of British – or perhaps English – middle-class cultural identity. But, to be absolutely clear, this was not 'the culture' of BP: it was an element of culture which shaped and inflected BP rather than, except perhaps in its present-day image, totally defining it.

CONCLUSION
In this chapter I have examined some of the main elements tending towards cultural homogeneity at BP, the 'pillars' supporting and running through a form of organization which was in other ways fragmented. My suggestion has been that wartime culture impinged very considerably on BP but was itself more complicated than is normally recognized. It would clearly be idle to deny that the circumstances of total war, including, at least in the early years, the genuine possibility of invasion and subjugation, impacted on BP, as they did in various ways upon every person in the country. The very fact of being mobilized into (in most cases) new occupations and re-locating to new accommodation and away from family and friends, as well as daily experiences of rationing, transport, cinema, public information films and so on were all a part of the 'context' of BP. However, I do want to resist the notion that these general factors can be taken at face value, either as a description of British society or as a sufficient account of BP culture.

Secrecy, on the other hand, was a very context-specific and highly significant part of BP culture, and is absolutely central to understanding that culture. Although general imprecations against 'careless talk' were widespread, at BP secrecy was a cardinal principle, impressed so forcibly on those who worked there that it endured for thirty years thereafter and there are still many traces of it left today. It was a secrecy that was enshrined and enforced in law, by virtue of the Official Secrets Acts, and backed up by vetting and security checks. But it was also ingrained into everyday practice and understanding so as to be embedded and taken for granted not to talk about work and not to ask about it.

Recruitment is perhaps a more ambiguous 'pillar' of culture than these other two. My argument has been that to some considerable extent the practices of the early years in particular but also, in a more diffuse way, during the later expansion served to provide a kind of template for organizational culture. This template owed much to a particular class-based educational system inherited from Oxbridge Colleges, which continued to have purchase even when the social background of staff became more heterogeneous and in the face of the many cultural cleavages which I will discuss in the next chapter.

NOTES

1. The quotation inside this extract is attributed to a research interview with Alan Stripp, who worked at BP and has contributed to the literature upon it, e.g. Stripp (1993).

2. See the Glossary for a definition of log-reading and Chapter 6 for discussion of this work (part of SIXTA).

3. *Dad's Army* was a British TV situation comedy based upon the wartime Home Guard, a defence force comprised mainly of former servicemen who were too old for regular military duties. Its 80 episodes were originally broadcast between 1968 and 1977 and attracted very large audiences. The programme is still regularly repeated today, both in the UK and around the world.

4. Cinema was perhaps the most popular form of entertainment at the time, and feature films and newsreels were almost invariably accompanied by public information films.

5. 'Public Information Films of the British Home Front 1939–1945', available via www.strikeforcetv.com/.

6. The rough meanings of these phrases are, respectively, as follows: grow your own vegetables to reduce the need to import food; don't talk about matters related to the war effort; again, don't talk about matters related to the war effort; don't spread illnesses by coughing and sneezing without a handkerchief; repair damaged goods such as clothes rather than waste resources by throwing them away; don't make use of transport resources unless it is vital to do so.

7. For example, the interviewee Daphne: 'You see the thing is this, that the war had broken out and everywhere, all over the country, "careless talk costs" and all that kind of thing'.

8. For example, a person who had worked in military intelligence during the war might be required to keep the details secret thereafter, but would not necessarily be precluded even from saying that he had worked in the area of intelligence.

9. Almost everyone – some domestic workers, e.g. canteen staff, did not.

10. TNA HW 14/36.

11. There may be more to say here. In Nigel de Grey's post-war review of BP in the section on security he includes the single, gnomic remark 'Cover stories. Oh be careful. We were very silly sometimes' (TNA HW 14/145: 31). I have been unable to find further material which might shed light on what this refers to (indeed, it may refer to cover stories for the provenance of Ultra rather than to staff cover stories).

12. For example, one of the interviewees, Joyce, told her parents that she 'worked on captured documents'.

13. I am not aware of any published material on this process. There are some examples in the archives of references from school teachers attesting to general reliability of potential employees, but that would seem to be quite a low level of checking. In other cases there were certainly police and MI5 checks made (TNA HW 14/145). My assumption is that the extent of security vetting would be related to the degree of access to secret material. Of course, at least some of the recruiting practices (discussed later in this chapter and again in Chapter 5) were very highly personalized so that those recruited were well known, and it may be that this acted as an informal vetting process.

14. That is, not just background checks but detailed examination of a person's past conduct, associates, affiliations etc.

15. The story here is very 'thin'. It is not clear from it whether the person in question was or was not accepted for employment at BP; neither is it clear on which side he fought in the Spanish Civil War.

16. The term 'indoctrinated' did not come into wide use at BP until after the USA had entered the war; the term 'enwised' was normally preferred, especially with respect to Enigma. See Chapter 4 for more detailed discussion of the cultural meaning of enwisement.

17. Unfortunately, the referencing in McKay's book is unsatisfactory and the documentary basis of this event is given simply as 'National Archives' with no further detail. I have been unable to find the original document.

18. Almost all other accounts use the word 'compartmentalised' not 'departmentalised'. This is a significant distinction because the compartments were typically smaller than departments or sections so that, for example, those working within the same Hut might be in different compartments. Moreover, the word 'compartments' captures the sense of these being 'sealed' units, rather than conventional organizational sub-divisions.

19. Probably only about 400 people at BP were working on Fish in some form. Most of the others were probably working on Enigma in some form but the lines between working on this and on other codes and ciphers were not always clearcut because of the ways in which, as discussed in Chapter 6, attacks upon other ciphers (e.g. weather) provided ways into Enigma ciphers.

20. There is no definitive figure for the number of people enwised to the breaking of Enigma at BP. My guesstimate, based only on having read an enormous number of accounts and studies of BP, would be that perhaps a total of 1,000 people knew (I am referring to BP staff – others in ministries and in the services were also enwised, but I have even less idea as to what that figure might be).

21. For example, again, Daphne: 'I certainly didn't know then that we were breaking codes'.

22. This in itself created some strange situations. The interviewee Ron, realizing from press reports in 1974 that the BP story had now been disclosed and that veterans were now freed from their obligations of secrecy, told a workmate of his experiences during the war, only to receive a letter a few days later telling him that despite the general revelations about BP his own work was still classified (it no longer is).

23. TNA HW 14/13.

24. TNA HW 14/36.

25. The fascinating question of why Germany did not realize that its ciphers, especially Enigma ciphers, had been compromised is beyond the scope of this study, but is extensively examined by Ratcliff (2006). See also Erskine (2001b).

26. Calvocoressi (2001: 119) is surely wrong to state that Cairncross never worked at BP, although correct to say that Kim Philby did not (Philby was, however, involved in recruiting BP staff).

27. This unpublished text of a talk is quoted with the permission of Michael Herman. Herman, a former senior manager at GCHQ, also served as Secretary to the British Government's Joint Intelligence Committee (JIC) during the years 1972–1975, thus encompassing the period in which the secret of BP was first substantially revealed. See Herman (2001: 164–79) for an account of his time in this role. It is worth noting in passing that, as a GCHQ staff member, Herman attended training courses at BP (which, indeed, occurred there until 1987).

28. Indeed, some documents remain classified on (presumably) this basis, e.g. Frank Birch's internal history of 'GC & CS and Naval Sigint', TNA HW 43/10–15 (anticipatory catalogue references).

29. TNA HW 3/134: 73. The context of this comment was Saunders' response to the draft internal history of NID8G and its relationship with BP, discussed in Chapter 1.

30. TNA HW 3/119: 23.

31. CCAC DENN 1/4.

32. All those listed were graduates (or, in Hinsley's case, an undergraduate) and in some cases staff of Cambridge University, except Peter Twinn, who was from Oxford.

33. One important exception is that the School of Oriental and African Studies (SOAS) was a particular source of cryptanalysts and translators for Japanese ciphers, since this was at the time the only British university where Japanese was taught. Other universities were certainly targeted – for example both Edward Simpson and Rebecca Simpson (then Gladys Gibson) who worked on Italian and Japanese ciphers, were amongst several graduates of Queen's University Belfast recruited to BP in what would appear to have been an orchestrated process (personal conversation with Edward and Rebecca Simpson).

34. Barbara Abernethy (later Eachus) was in the first group to enter BP in the pre-war 'shooting party' (the cover name for the initial SIS entry to the site) and was the last person to leave after the war.

35. It was very rare to have a car at all at BP, because of petrol rationing, let alone a Bentley.

36. TNA HW 14/145: 4.

37. TNA HW 14/145: 5–7. To prefigure the theme of the next chapter, this indicates one way that sub-cultural groupings were established, in turn alerting us to the relationships between organizational structure and culture.

38. Pure linguistic ability was not enough for such roles. Knowledge, or the capacity to gain knowledge, of technical and military German was vital.

39. This was because John Lewis used a card-punching system similar to the Hollerith machines used extensively for data management and analysis at BP.

40. Except where indicated otherwise, the account in this paragraph is drawn from Nigel de Grey's post-war review (TNA HW 14/145). For accounts of the arduous work of Y station intercept staff see Page (2003) and Clayton (1980). Typex, to remind the reader, was the British high-grade cipher machine.

41. TNA HW 14/145: 6.

42. TNA HW 14/145: 7.

43. Dora was subsequently interviewed by Miss Moore of the FO. It is impossible to read accounts of the recruitment of female civilians at BP without coming across mentions of this civil servant, invariably described as 'formidable' (e.g. Batey, 2010: 107; Blacker, 1993: 300), who played a pivotal role in its staffing, as the post-war review acknowledged (TNA HW 14/145: 4). This is not just a point of detail but indicates how very micro-level issues may impact upon the way that organizational cultures are shaped.

44. For example TNA HW 14/20.

45. There may be some class basis to this variety – Simpson (2011: 139) makes passing mention of his perception that 'low grade' staff did not join in much in leisure activities.

4 Splinters of Culture at Bletchley Park

INTRODUCTION

In the previous chapter, I outlined some of the more homogenizing elements of BP culture. This second chapter of Part II will continue the attempt to 'decode' culture at BP by identifying the various complex ways in which that culture was fragmented and fissured (cf. Parker, 2000). I put it in those terms because it is not simply my intention to identify 'sub-cultures' – although that is sometimes at stake – but, rather, I seek to capture the 'splinters' of culture. That is to say, I am concerned to draw out the range of ways that aspects of culture operated, sometimes overlapping and re-inforcing each other, at other times remote from or contradictory to each other. I will not seek to elaborate in detail each and every feature of these splinters, which would be a huge task. Instead, in line with the tenor of the book as a whole, I seek to convey a broad sense of the range and diversity of culture, albeit giving some highly detailed illustrations to make particular points.

Whilst attempting to depict the cultures of BP, this inevitably intersects with the structural issues set out in Part I and I should say a brief word about that. Within organization theory, the literatures on structure and on culture are to a large extent separate and indeed this book, in devoting separate sections to these two topics, reproduces that division. Yet it is clear that structure and culture may be intimately linked. Most obviously, it is commonplace within organizations to find sub-cultural or group distinctions based upon different divisions, departments or job functions, for example. Thus one might say that as well as there being cultural accounts of structure, most influentially in institutional-theory explanations of normative and mimetic isomorphism (DiMaggio and Powell, 1991)[1], there are also structural accounts of culture and in particular the way that structural fragmentation links to cultural heterogeneity (e.g. Trice, 1993).

At BP this interlinkage of structure and sub-culture was of particular significance for two reasons. Firstly, as the discussion in Chapter 1 makes clear, BP was assembled from a range of organizations, each with its own culture or, no doubt, if one were to look at them in detail, its own mix of cultural elements – and this caveat is not a minor point since it is suggestive of the complex layering and re-layering of culture. It is also relevant to recall that this 'assembly' occurred over quite a short time period during which BP rapidly grew and so there was relatively little in the way of accreted, established organizational cultural norms. Secondly, because of the compartmentalization and secrecy discussed in the previous chapter, the potential for separate sub-cultures to develop in relative or even complete isolation from each other was considerable. Thus one might, perhaps, speak of the sub-culture of this or that Hut, of the different rooms within them (and I will give some examples of these) or even, given the shift system in force, of sub-sub-cultures deriving primarily from the structuring of the work process. As a matter of fact, different shifts did have different characters, primarily because the volume of work was generally less during the night shift, although it would be too strong to speak of these differences as sub-cultural, not least because of the rotation of staff between shifts (the shift system is discussed further in Chapter 5)[2].

At all events, it is possible to see how, as well as or even instead of a cultural identity of, and identification with, BP, identities of and with service or employing organization, hut or work section, or some combination of these were viable and indeed likely. These kinds of distinctions are somewhat softened by historical distance, and the dwindling number of those who worked there, so that it is now commonplace to speak of 'BP veterans' as if this were an obvious or unproblematic identity or category. This is an example of one of the potential methodological traps of conducting an historical study of organizations. So it is important to recall that at the time this was by no means necessarily so and that, for example, 'for Hut 3 most of BP was the outside world' (Calvocoressi, 2001: 82).

In what follows, I will seek to capture BP's cultural heterogeneity first by looking at what are primarily structurally related elements, namely the issues relating to the way that civilian and military groups were deployed together and the consequences of this. The second main section of this chapter is concerned with issues that cut across the first, primarily the broad distinction of 'Chiefs' and 'Indians' and, nested within this, distinctions relating to gender, secrecy and age as well as some more fine-grained distinctions such as academic background. As I have already implied, such distinctions relate in principle to cultural identities, since they are all various forms of delineating 'us' from 'them'; markers of, indeed, 'distinction' (Bourdieu, 1986). It does not follow, however, that this in fact occurred or that it gave rise to unitary identities based on each of these delineations. On the contrary, many of these distinctions cut across each other and so offered the potential for multiple identifications. It might be best, then, to see them as a set of cultural resources and possibilities rather than as discrete and solid entities mechanically giving rise to discrete and solid identities.

CIVILIAN AND MILITARY

The most obvious structural source of cultural variety at BP was the distinction of civilian and military staff, something remarked upon in various ways in almost all accounts of life at BP. Indeed, it is singled out in some analyses as central to the 'chaotic' nature of BP's organization: 'Relations between the military and civilian sides was strangest of all at Bletchley Park, where the chain of command was so loose that it bordered on anarchy' (Budiansky, 2000: 229). Yet what it meant in practice was far more complex than might be implied by the apparent binary of the two categories of 'military' and 'civilian'. For a start, its meaning in terms of workplace organization was very varied. Some sections and work groups at BP were run as unitary military sections[3] – for example, the bombes were staffed by Wrens[4] working within the

standard hierarchy of their service (albeit that their work and its prioritization was ultimately determined mainly by civilians). Some sections, for example administration, were almost entirely civilian and
might be run, again hierarchically, but on civil service rather than
military lines. But many sections, notably some of the 'central' segments of BP in Huts 3, 4, 6 and 8, consisted of amalgamations of
civilians and various branches of the military. I will explore in detail
how these modes of work organization operated in the next two chapters:
my point here is that the issue of civilian and military cultures did not
necessarily map directly onto work groups, but intersected with these.

Nevertheless, these cultures were a significant part of the landscape at BP, very visibly flagged by the fact that the civilians did not
wear uniforms (and, of course, appearance and ways of dressing are in
all sorts of contexts important cultural markers). However, there are
considerable complexities arising even from this apparently simple
statement. First of all, not all military personnel did, in fact, wear
uniforms: 'those of us who were commissioned officers wore uniforms
only when we felt like it – or when some top brass were expected on a
visit' (Calvocoressi, 2001: 83). This in itself suggests a distinction
within the military between officers and others, but in fact there was
more to it than that because this laissez-faire attitude to uniforms
seems to have applied only amongst BP's more elite staff and in this
sense connects with the issue, discussed below, of the distinction
between 'Chiefs' and 'Indians': no such licence was granted to the
Wrens, for example, regardless of their seniority. So already a quite
subtle set of distinctions opens up, in which the sub-cultural marker of
a uniform, denoting both service allegiance and rank within that service, is conflated with a further marker in which the discarding of uniform could be used to denote status[5].

A second complexity, of course, is that the distinction, symbolized by uniform, was not simply between civilian and military but
amongst the large variety of different branches of the military – the
male and female branches of the three services – present at BP. One
consequence of this was to make conventional military behaviours

such as saluting superiors (again a very visible cultural marker) diffi-cult to implement on the BP site itself. This is sometimes taken to be a sign of egalitarianism, but it was more a matter of necessity than principle and did not negate the many ways in which military hier-archy manifested itself. In particular, many service personnel were required to undertake physical and military training over and above their duties at BP, which did not apply to civilians (who, nevertheless, did have to contribute to home guard and fire-watching activities). An additional aspect here is that, whilst it is possible to speak of military staff, there is a distinction to be drawn between those who were 'regular' service personnel and those, the majority, who were mobi-lized for the duration of the war either by virtue of having volunteered or by conscription. The regulars often sought to impose 'proper' mili-tary discipline and, to the extent that they succeeded, created signifi-cantly different conditions for those under their command as compared with civilians (see Copeland, 2006: 166). It should be explained that the regular officers running, in particular, service accommodation sites were completely unaware of the nature of the work being done at BP and therefore the demands being placed upon the personnel of whom they had charge, leading to a somewhat unsym-pathetic attitude in many cases (see Hill, 2004: 72–4; Watkins, 2006: 148–59; Thirsk, 2008: 77–82). Thus Joyce, interviewed for this study, who was in the ATS, described how her life became much more regimented when, mid-way through the war, she was moved from a private house (shared with other ATS women) to a military camp run by a regular army officer who insisted on running the camp as if it were a conventional barracks.

For someone such as Joyce, this gave rise to a fragmented cultural experience at BP. She worked in Hut 3^6, where civilians and military staff were mixed together and the overall ethos was described in the post-war internal history thus:

> Ours ... was an exceptional freedom. Those who did their work well were left, within the inevitable limits, to do it their own way ... [i]t

was the exact reverse of the HITLER principle of the greatest possible meddling with the greatest possible number. That trust was repaid. And if mistakes were made (as of course they were) by ignorance or negligence, the remedy was found not nearly so much in reprimands, or witch-hunts for the delinquent, as in the mortification decent persons felt at having let things down[7].

I will consider in the following chapter this and other examples of 'management style' and their significance, but for now the issue is to appreciate the contrast between a relatively free and trust-based work culture at Hut 3 (and also some other huts) and that of a military camp where some, at least, spent their off-duty hours and how experience was thus 'splintered'.

One very important part of the civilian–military distinction indeed lay in accommodation arrangements. These were crucial because for most people at BP, except when on leave, their lives consisted largely of work and billets, the various organized recreational activities referred to in the previous chapter notwithstanding. Thus accommodation defined a major part of their experience in general as well as being intimately enmeshed with civilian–military relations in particular. It is not my intention to recount the many detailed stories of billeting experiences (see Hill, 2004: 104–21; McKay 2010: 59–69), but rather to indicate how they relate to cultural heterogeneity. Civilians were typically billeted in private homes in a wide area around BP[8]. Conditions here were very varied indeed in terms of the quality of accommodation, ease of travel to work and so on, but they did in principle allow a certain degree of freedom (Watkins, 2006: 149). Some military personnel were billeted in this way, but many were accommodated by their services in various hostels and dormitories and in this sense lived much more constrained lives both in terms of military duties, as just mentioned, and also in terms of having set bedtimes and being directly subject to military discipline in various ways. Thus it is easy to envisage that staff such as the Wrens, who worked on the bombes and were almost invariably also housed and managed by their service, can be regarded as inhabiting a particular sub-culture within BP, understandable primarily in terms of WRNS culture[9]. This was indeed the experience of many Wrens (Page, 2002) and, given that some 3,000 of them worked at BP and its outstations, it is a particularly important example to give.

So, even from the few cases I have mentioned, it is possible to see the varieties of cultural experience according to whether one, both or neither of work and off-duty periods were subject to military discipline. And even within these broad varieties of experience there was further variation. For example, I have referred to the generality of the Wrens' experience as being one of military discipline in and out of work, but the interviewee Vera, herself a Wren, was not required to drill because she happened to be allocated to the Wavendon outstation where it was not required, whereas her colleagues at the Gayhurst and Eastcote outstations were[10]. So this would be an example of a cultural 'splinter' – it would be too strong, I think, to speak of a 'Wavendon sub-culture' – which, in conjunction with the senses of a BP culture, WRNS culture and so on would combine to create a particular configuration of experience.

Just as there were distinctions between military personnel in terms of service branch and other factors, there were also fragmentations amongst civilians, who should not be regarded as a homogeneous group. Amongst civilian cryptanalysts, translators, intelligence assessors and so on it is to an extent plausible to see the dominant culture as being, as discussed in the previous chapter, one linked to the universities from which most had been recruited. Yet, even here, it is possible to identify more fine-grained distinctions. First, there was a distinction between mathematicians and linguists, which itself relates to two other distinctions, that between pre-war and wartime GC & CS practice and that between cryptanalytic and intelligence staff. Before the war, GC & CS had traditionally been dominated by linguists and more especially classicists and, indeed, one of Denniston's most important contributions to BP had been to recognize that machine ciphers such as Enigma would increasingly require mathematical expertise. This also points to a cultural fault line of 'generations', which I will return to shortly, and it is worth noting how radical a change it was. One of the first mathematicians to be recruited was Peter Twinn:

> The classics professors who dominated GC & CS were highly sceptical that recruiting a mathematician would help, Twinn recalled: 'they regarded mathematicians as very strange beasts indeed. They required a little persuasion before they believed they could do anything practical or helpful at all'. *(Smith, 1998: 16)*

On the latter issue – the linkage of the mathematical/linguistic distinction to the cryptanalytic/intelligence distinction – Calvocoressi (2001: 19–20) goes so far as to posit that amongst the 'Chiefs' (of which, again, more later) there were 'two distinct groups', the mathematical codebreakers and the linguistic intelligence staff[11]. In a similar way there were

> chronic tensions between cryptography [sic] and intelligence which were notable at least in Bletchley's Naval Section. It may exemplify the friction between production and sales management that is liable to emerge in any industry[12]. Each party looked somewhat askance at the other. To the intelligence officer, cryptographers were apt to appear as unworldly, absent-minded, eccentric, ill-dressed academics. To the cryptographer, the intelligence officer could appear to be too political by half and often as a shameless empire builder. *(Morris, 1993: 242)*

To this notion of 'distinct groups' can be added a further, if subtle, sense not just of distinction but of hierarchy. Nigel de Grey's post-war review suggests that the growing need for intelligence analysts at BP was satisfied partially from amongst the ranks of 'failed cryptana-lysts'[13] and, although it would be wrong, I think, to take that to mean quite the derogatory distinction that might be inferred, it does point to a certain pecking order. A similar notion was articulated by Roy, interviewed for this study, who suggested that Hut 6 had a higher proportion of staff with first-class degrees, whether in mathematics or other subjects, whereas an upper second was more common elsewhere. He went on to recall hearing Nigel de Grey say that 'there was a distinct grading of intellectual level between Huts 6 and 8 [i.e. the two main Enigma cryptanalytic sections] and everywhere else'. This is of course highly impressionistic[14], yet it does provide a glimpse of some of the more subtle inflections of cultural distinctions.

It should not be thought that the gradations and distinctions I have identified here were trivial or of little practical importance. In Stuart Milner-Barry's introduction to the internal history of Hut 6 there is an account of the decision to merge two sub-units of the hut – the Machine Room (MR) and the Crib Room (CR)[15]. Reflecting that it was a mistake that this had not happened before, leading to 'a serious crisis of personnel management'[16], the reason given was that

> It had been argued by the supporters of the status quo, on the one hand that the CR were not mathematically minded and would therefore be ill-fitted to cope with the more technical aspects of the machine; and on the other that the MR were mathematically minded and were therefore not likely to be proficient at cribs and re-encodements, which were thought to require a linguistic or humanitarian [sic] background. There was an element of truth in this reasoning but also a good deal of prejudice[17].

Thus a cultural distinction and beliefs associated with it impacted upon work operations and indeed, at the micro-level, upon organizational structure[18]. That these beliefs were based upon 'prejudice' (which really, or at least presumably, denotes a cultural assumption) is confirmed by the fact that, as the account goes on to explain,

> It was soon found that the mathematical education was as good as any other for cribbery and re-encodement work; and that those unversed in the mysteries of mathematics could nevertheless make a surprisingly good showing at the more technical aspects of machine cipher ...[19]

Whilst these distinctions are highly nuanced, other sub-cultures amongst civilians were more pronounced, the best example being the GPO. These staff stand out firstly because, as mentioned in Chapter 1, when the diverse civilian employees were brought under FO control in 1943, GPO staff remained outside that. Secondly, GPO staff were, uniquely amongst BP staff[20], unionized and, as the de Grey report notes, attempts to mix non-GPO civilians in with them 'led to trouble'[21]. Thus GPO employees formed a fairly clearcut sub-culture and one particular manifestation of that was, as the interviewee Ron explained, that the working methods of his group of technicians in the Testery and Newmanry were taken over lock, stock and barrel from the GPO, which also undertook the training of his group (but not just them) at their central experimental and research station at Dollis Hill. These working methods also applied when, as was the case, the group included former GPO employees enrolled into the RAF. But, again, there is a need for more subtlety than simply identifying a sub-culturally distinct grouping. For, whilst in many ways the GPO is the best example of such a grouping, it is also one of the best examples of a group attuned to the wider, homogenizing cultural factors discussed in the previous chapter. There, I suggested that secrecy was one such factor, and in this respect GPO staff, unlike almost everyone else who came to BP, were already strongly encultured since their pre-war work had also often been confidential and had even in some cases required signing the Official Secrets Acts.

In these various ways, then, there was a patterning of cultural experience at BP which mirrored its somewhat fragmentary structure. I have taken pains to suggest that the civilian–military distinction, whilst relevant to understanding the heterogeneous culture of BP, itself conceals some further distinctions. Nevertheless, that basic distinction can be seen to have given rise to some significant tensions[22]. There was some resentment on the part of some service personnel of the apparently more relaxed life enjoyed by civilians, in some cases very strongly felt:

One [unnamed] ATS officer commented bitterly: 'Their [the civilians'] brains were overdeveloped to the detriment of their personalities. This led to an atmosphere of egotism, not to mention spitefulness and backbiting. The precept of public service was unknown to them and though they would do what they were paid to do, the thought of doing a bit more did not occur to them. There was no generosity of spirit, no feeling of loyalty to the unit as is the case in, for instance, an infantry regiment'. *(Hill, 2004: 85)*

This is an extreme example of such views, and needs to be carefully contextualized. There is no indication of where this person worked and, whilst purporting to be a general comment about civilians, compartmentalization makes it extremely unlikely that she was in a position to make such a generalization. Certainly it should be counterposed with the large amount of evidence of civilians and military staff working harmoniously together, as discussed elsewhere, but something similar, if less forcefully expressed, can be found in, for example, resentments about civilians supposedly having more luxurious or geographically closer accommodation. Yet these tensions cut both ways, with civilians sometimes feeling that military people looked down on them for not being in uniform and that the military were better catered for in terms of communal facilities and comradeship. Indeed, the latter point was recognized by military personnel such as Vera, who felt

very sorry for the civilians who were billeted out in small houses and this sort of thing around, and not able to talk, not able to talk to their people to say what they were doing, not able to answer questions. It must have been very difficult for them. At least we had companionship.

Certainly, whilst some civilians did indeed have good experiences of billeting, this was often not the case and was a cause of constant unhappiness and complaint. As Nigel de Grey pungently remarked in the post-war review, 'the whole process is unpleasant and unpopular even to the patriot'[23]. I will pick up on issues of discontent – not just those related to billeting – in the next chapter, but for now I will turn to other sources of cultural heterogeneity at BP.

CHIEFS AND INDIANS

Largely cutting across civilian and military lines, BP was characterized by a fairly sharp distinction between what Calvocoressi called 'Chiefs' and 'Indians':

> The Chiefs . . . were distinguished from the Indians because they were fewer and preponderantly male and had the better jobs – better because they were more responsible and closer to the brush of real events.
>
> *(Calvocoressi, 2001: 19)*

This distinction is identified in different language in other accounts: 'Most [at BP] saw themselves as "minnows" alongside the "Boffins"' (Hill, 2004: 62). It also features by implication in the way that many who worked at BP, examples including both Dora and Ron amongst the interviewees, made references to 'the academics' and 'the university people'. This is, admittedly, not quite the same distinction in that Calvocoressi notes that many of the 'Indians' were university-educated. However, all of these usages share the sense of there being a smaller, central group of great importance and a larger, more marginal, group of lower status[24].

This distinction is one of considerable importance, and I would suggest that it is very much in play in terms of what is now the dominant received image of BP[25]. That is to say, it is all of a piece with the foregrounding of the 'boffins' – the mainly male, academic codebreakers – in this received image; an image which this book, with its wider organizational focus, seeks to problematize. One reason why it is problematic is because it renders if not invisible then certainly marginal the majority of those who worked at BP. And this has one very particular effect, which is to downplay the role of women at BP. For, as Calvocoressi's comment suggests, gender was highly significant at BP.

I have noted elsewhere that about three-quarters of those at BP were women, and, although it is impossible to give precise figures – not least because the categories involved are not precise – it seems clear that women were found overwhelmingly amongst the 'Indians'[26] or 'minnows'. The simple fact that almost all of the 3,000 Wrens were working in 'minnow' roles is confirmation of this. It is certainly the case that a small number of women were to be found amongst the cryptanalysts, as mentioned in the previous chapter, and rather more amongst the translators and intelligence evaluators, but the general picture is clear. Nevertheless, amongst the women working in more humble roles many were highly educated, and there is some evidence of resentment on the part of some of these women[27], as, for example in Hut 6, where

> among the girls especially, we had a staff which was doing a job that ... was desperately dull routine work, and much more monotonous than girls with an academic background ... felt they could expect[28].

Or, less sympathetically, in the post-war review: 'Girls in main T/P [Teleprinter] room who were skilled got bloody-minded'[29]. Or, finally, in relation to Wrens working in the Newmanry on 'by-hand' solutions to short messages, they

> all had to have a qualification in mathematics – quite a number with Honours Degrees – and here we were asking them to do mathematical jobs without explaining it ... [Newman] had the attitude that 'women wouldn't like to do any intellectual work'.
> *(Hill, 2004: 79)*

There were examples of women being promoted from humdrum roles:

> Miss White ... who originally served as a secretary to the Naval Section head ... was 'found to have the makings of a quite passable' cryptanalyst, high praise in these circles[30], and so she moved into that capacity. *(Ratcliff, 2006: 81)*

However, it is very hard to find such examples; more common were experiences such as the way that

> Despite their acknowledged worth, Wrens still encountered a 'glass ceiling' obstructing their promotion and imposing on them, almost without exception, male bosses ... [a] woman's role was typically seen as servicing the needs of other, more senior staff ... [one] Wren wryly comments: 'we could make tea or coffee and handed it out to the elite, the linguists'.
>
> *(Hill, 2004: 78)*

Within this context, the often-mentioned meritocracy of working methods (e.g. Calvocoressi, 2001: 83) in accounts of life at BP, which will be discussed in the next chapter, has to be qualified by a recognition of its gendered limits, a recognition found, indeed, in one such account:

> [The] whole structure [of Hut 6] was one where you might readily find a Major working under a Lieutenant or under a civilian, somewhat younger. Whoever was in charge was the person who had been judged to be more effective at doing it. It was meritocracy in spades and without regard to where you came from or whether you were a man or a woman, although I think we had a very large majority of men in the senior positions.
>
> *(Bill Bundy cited in Smith, 1998: 136)*

Of course, very little of this is specific to BP. Rather, it reflects wider cultural apprehensions at the time about gender and the kinds of work that women were suited for[31], something which the war changed somewhat with the mobilization of women, albeit more variably than is sometimes supposed (Summerfield, 1998). Such apprehensions are woven, in a very low-key way, into the fabric of archive documents from the time and, of the literally hundreds of examples, a couple may give a flavour. First, from the internal history of Hut 3:

> [Two] of the specialist watches were entirely composed of women who, though never found to reach the standard of No.1's or No.2's on

the Main watch, always showed a special talent and readiness for dealing with matters at first sight trivial or dull, which by the frailty of human nature were habitually pushed on to them[32].

The second example, more pithily, from the post-war review in comments on 'medium and low grade labour', is the observation that '[i]t was astonishing what young women could be trained to do'[33]. However, not all aspects of gender distinctions at BP can be subsumed into wider societal views. For example, Hugh Alexander's internal history of Hut 8 records that in Hut 8 'girls with University degrees' were not used for clerical work, whereas 'Hut 6 held the opposite view'[34].

There is much that could be said about the role and work of women at BP, and in recent years far more has been written about this than in the early accounts of its history (e.g. Page, 2002, 2003; Hill, 2004), but for present purposes my intention has been to show, again, the fragmentations within BP culture. That includes the ways that distinctions such as those of 'Chief' and 'Indian' (or the earlier issues of civilian and military) ran alongside distinctions of gender. But, by the same token, distinctions of gender were cut across by those other distinctions. In other words, it would be wrong to think that women's experiences of BP were themselves homogeneous since they, too, were fragmented by virtue of the other cleavages that I am describing – this, indeed, is one good illustration of what I mean by the notion of cultural 'splinters'.

Just as the 'Chiefs' and 'Indians' distinction intersects with others, such as gender, so too did it mesh with another highly important distinction at BP. In the previous chapter I discussed issues of secrecy as a broadly homogenizing cultural experience. Yet I also drew attention to one quite sharp division within that experience – that of different levels of 'indoctrination' or 'enwisement' into particular secrets. There were many different versions of this. One interesting and little-discussed example is that those who needed to be privy to knowledge about when and where the D-Day Normandy landings were planned to occur were indoctrinated into this under the codename 'bigoted'. But by far the most important was between those enwised to the breaking of Enigma and those who were not. As with gender, this maps fuzzily onto the 'Chiefs' and 'Indians' distinction in that almost certainly all of the 'Chiefs' who worked on Enigma were enwised, but so too were a good number of the 'Indians', depending on precisely what kinds of work they were doing.

Calvocoressi (2001: 23) uses the term the 'Ultra community' to refer to the Enigma-enwised[35] and makes a very revealing comment: 'The Ultra community at BP saw itself as – perhaps was – an elite within an elite'. This is significant for two reasons. Firstly, it points to a specific way in which, as discussed in the previous chapter in relation to Simmel's (1906) theorization, secrecy has the effect of creating feelings of 'specialness' amongst those in the know. That seems to be very much the sense conveyed by Calvocoressi and, in relation to being indoctrinated into the D-Day secret, a BP veteran informally interviewed at a reunion[36] recounted how, precisely, 'special' she felt coming off duty the day before D-Day and knowing as she returned to her billet that she, unlike her hosts, knew what was to happen. Secondly, and of course related, there is the notion of a conscious knowledge of and identification with a group (it *saw itself* as an elite). This is a commonplace of any kind of cultural analysis since it is a large part of what culture means. But it is variable in extent and perhaps not always strongly present. For example, in the case of gender, just discussed, there is not a great deal of evidence of a sense of there being a 'male' or 'female' community at BP although there was a Women's Welfare Committee[37], implying some sense of a distinctive, gendered set of concerns.

To a large extent because of the stringencies of secrecy, the existence of an Ultra community within BP had the effect of creating what Calvocoressi (2001: 81–4) describes as a series of 'concentric circles', the innermost being Hut 3 together with Hut 6 and the Naval Section, the next being BP itself and the third being life outside in billets[38]. This, of course, is all of a piece with the more general point about how secrecy creates in and out groups, but there are some important points to note about it. Firstly, these concentric circles do not apply in this form across BP. For example, Calvocoressi's equivalent in Hut 4 would presumably position that and Hut 8 as being the central circle; someone in Hut 6 would include SIXTA (for reasons which will be explained in Chapter 6) and so on. Thus we should envisage a multiple series of concentric circles across BP. Secondly, it should be noted that these circles are not identical with, although they relate to, work sections (thus, in this case, the central circle is not simply Hut 3). So, again, it is necessary to consider culture as a complex series of overlapping and intersecting elements (cf. Parker, 2000).

A further such element is that of age. One of the most remarkable features of BP was that, although GC & CS had been established for many years, its expansion and the new era of machine ciphers opened up some quite sharp generational divisions. In Chapter 2, I noted how this played its part in the 1942 reorganization, with Denniston becoming associated with an 'old guard' to the extent of being described in one account as having 'spent his life in the time of the Battle of Hastings dealing with hand codes' (Ralph Bennett, cited in Smith, 1998: 93). That is a particularly pointed, perhaps even slightly dismissive, form of words, although, as I explained, there was more to Denniston's removal than this, and certainly many of his contemporaries continued to occupy pivotal roles at BP, including Travis, de Grey and Tiltman. Nevertheless, each year brought in more and more young recruits, many of whom rapidly became very senior figures at BP, such as Harry Hinsley – later to become the official historian of British intelligence in WW2 – who was recruited in 1939 having not even completed his undergraduate degree and yet, amongst other things, by the end of the war played a key role in negotiating sigint agreements with the USA.

Recruited in the same year – although just after having graduated – Roy, a cryptanalyst interviewed for this study, commented as follows:

> We regarded anyone over 40 as very unlikely to be of any use and quite a lot of the Room 40 people were moved into undemanding

jobs, for example Clarke[39], Head of German Naval Section before Birch, [was] moved but was very unhappy about it.

Roy went on to refer to other Room 40 staff who in various ways became 'fixed in their ways' and reflected that 'this was a totally new problem and older people found it harder to adjust', and it is difficult to resist the sense here and in the many other accounts of cryptanalysts, in particular, of the emergence of a new generation. Indeed, Dilly Knox 'was probably the only codebreaker in any country to make a successful transition from breaking manual ciphers and book codes in the First World War to solving complex cipher machines such as Enigma and their traffic, in the Second World War' (Erskine, 2010: ix). Also, as pointed out in Chapter 2, the 'Wicked Uncles' letter to Churchill was in part to do with a generational shift. Issues of youth were not confined to cryptanalysts or to the 'Chiefs' in general. It seems to have been a feature of BP staffing as a whole that it was fairly youthful[40], one reason being the way that so much recruiting took the form of approaches to university students. There is perhaps a methodological bias in this, since published reminiscences of BP are, by virtue of the long period of secrecy before any could appear, inevitably tilted towards those who, at the time of the war, were amongst the younger members of staff. Nevertheless, and accepting that it is impossible to be precise (there are no available data on the age profile of BP staff), the contemporary archive material confirms my overwhelming sense[41] that it was so.

In partial support of this contention, and of more general relevance, Nigel de Grey's post-war review contains a section on the issue of age (in relation to staff of all sorts) and it is worth quoting in full:

Recorded opinion[42] lays emphasis upon youth because it is more trainable, more prepared to accept directions, better able to stand the strain, more flexible in mind – all obvious considerations. There are factors to set against this: i) experience has a value and was none too prevalent, ii) cases of mental breakdown occurred equally among young and old, iii) both men and women are often tougher in middle age than in youth, iv) flexibility is not always as valuable as judgment. In 6 years people grow older. Impossible to be dogmatic but the right side of 50 at the beginning of the war would appear to be the upper limit, then only picked men with some definitely needed qualification for a particular post, not for instance general watch-keeping. For the latter an upper limit at the outbreak of 35 appears to be the consensus of opinion. Boys were taken straight from Public School – i.e. at age 18. Girls from the age of call-up[43].

As with other cultural issues discussed in this chapter, there are complexities which tend to splinter the apparent clarity of categories such as, in this case, youth. For alongside the general sense of a new generation it is possible to find evidence that the 'new guard' itself fragmented into a kind of 'old new guard' and a 'new new guard'. The cryptanalyst Roy commented that 'The ones who arrived later in the war sometimes complained that all the real work had been done already and they weren't given a fair chance'. And, indeed, there is a sense of a division between the early, almost heroic, days before and just after wartime Enigma ciphers began to be broken and the later period when operations became more large-scale and factory-like. This is captured by the memories of one of the most eminent of Hut 6 staff, Derek Taunt: 'I found myself, in the middle of August 1941, transferred to GC & CS at Bletchley Park ... [had I been recruited via a different route] ... I might just have arrived at BP in its great pioneering days, rather than at "the end of the beginning"' (Taunt, 1993: 101)[44]. The latter phrase is, of course, the key one to note.

Thus culture divides and re-divides if not endlessly then at least extensively and even in its smallest elements may be meaningful for those involved in it (e.g. coming to BP in 1941 rather than 1940) in a way perhaps not immediately obvious to those outside it. Precisely because of their multiplicity, my account here of cultural splinters is not exhaustive. There are others that can be identified, but, partly for reasons of space, though mainly because I have not been able to uncover much information on them, they are omitted from detailed discussion. Examples include ethnicity, because, although most at BP were white British people, there were members of other nations, races, religions or cultures present, including North Americans, Poles and people from the various countries of the British Commonwealth, Empire and Dominions. Perhaps particular mention should be made of the considerable number of Jewish staff at BP (Lewin, 2008: 123), of whom there were at least 205 according to Sugarman's (2008) account, although the true total, he believes, rightly I think, was higher. Some of these were refugees from Nazi Germany or occupied Europe, and they were to be found across the various functions and groups[45]. Whilst Sugarman (2008: 3) describes these as a 'Jewish community' at BP, it is not clear that this was manifested in any particular way, and the term is probably being used in a generic sense, although Eytan (1993: 60) suggests that he and other Jewish staff at BP 'had an extra interest in fighting Hitler'.

Another example of a possible 'splinter' is that based on sexuality. Alan Turing, as is now well known, was gay – although not openly so at BP. Others were more open about their sexuality (albeit within the constraints of the fact that homosexuality was then illegal), and there are a few references to this in some accounts, including some by modern standards startlingly homophobic remarks, for example: 'Angus Wilson was my first conscious encounter with a "queer" and I found him simply repulsive. He used to mince into the room, swaggering, and wore ... outrageous clothes ...' (Hill, 2004: 67). Again, one would be hard-pressed to find evidence for there being any sense of a discernible sub-culture or even 'splinter' based on sexuality, but the possibility that this may have been so cannot be discounted, especially given the legal position at the time.

I mention these examples (to which could be added others, for example a few references to a north/south divide amongst some British staff) both to indicate the extensiveness of the notion of heterogeneity and also – or rather, relatedly – to pick up on a point made in the previous chapter about the way that subsequent accounts of WW2 in general have tended to downplay the multiplicity of groups, identities and experiences in favour of a received, more monolithic, image of culture at the time (Rose, 2003).

CONCLUSION

In this chapter and that which preceded it, which together represent my account of BP culture, I have sought to capture its complexity in terms of, firstly, more or less homogenizing elements of culture, namely war, secrecy and aspects of social background, primarily education and class; and, secondly, the various ruptures, splits, distinctions or, as I have tended to call them, splinters which contributed to heterogeneity.

I have suggested that the capturing of this complexity is a way of 'decoding' culture. Why? Because it serves to probe what underlies, firstly, the received image of BP which tends to stress as universal the experience of a particular segment of BP, namely the cryptanalysts, and, more generally, to link this image to a particular, received version of British wartime culture. This image is not entirely false, but it is certainly not complete or accurate, and I hope that I have demonstrated this.

But, secondly, it calls into question the way that – leaving BP to one side – organization theory, at least in its more popular and prescriptive manifestations, apprehends organizational culture, the most gross example being Peters and Waterman's (1982) highly influential work; hardly less gross are some related works of the same era (e.g. Pascale and Athos, 1982; Deal and Kennedy, 1988). There, culture is envisaged in terms of 'blocks' of strong culture across organizations or sub-groups, potentially amenable to management and describable in terms of general typologies. Of course, such an understanding is not found in the many sophisticated, ethnographic studies of organizational culture (e.g. Kunda, 1992, Watson, 1994, Parker, 2000; Weeks, 2003) which followed, reacted to and undermined the normative literature, and which are altogether more attuned to the complexity of culture. Indeed, such studies have considerably more purchase than mine in terms of accessing the daily practices of culture and the richness of its symbols, meanings, rituals and so on. Although I will provide more detail at least on daily work in the following chapters, I cannot capture culture in that way because to do so would require an ethnographic study which, in the case of BP, is impossible.

What I have done instead is to focus on potential sources of sameness and difference, and these are indeed central to any account of culture since this, fundamentally, is what culture is about: who 'we' are and who 'they' are (see Dupuis, 2008). That is why uniforms, for example and amongst many other things, are important, since they provide markers of cultural membership. Yet it is a truism of anthropology that cultures vary as much within themselves as between each other, and the same is true of sub-cultures (Fetterman, 1998; Jenks, 2005). Thus, as soon as one identifies some basis of cultural membership, it begins to fracture. To give some obvious examples, we can speak of the 'military' at BP, but this fractured amongst different services, between those who chose to wear uniform and those who chose not to wear uniform, those who were regulars and those who were not and so on. Or, again, we can speak of secrecy, but this fractured between different levels of clearance. Or we can speak about a work group, but this fractured between different genders, so then we might speak of gendered groups, but this fractured between different educational backgrounds. So the issue of who is 'us' and who is 'them' is necessarily a process which is endlessly constructed and reconstructed and with it, of course, not just culture but individual identity, since the possibilities of this are predicated in very large part upon group identifications.

In the BP case it is possible to see how there is a kind of 'matrix' of different elements: war, secrecy, prior social background and educational experience, Chief, Indian, boffin, minnow, army, RN, RAF, ATS, WAAF, WRNS, regular, volunteer, conscript, civilian, enwised (and to what), male, female, age, graduate, mathematician, linguist, non-graduate, hut member, room member, privately billeted and so on which can be – and were – thrown together. The various possible combinations of these, and other, cultural splinters are enormous rather in the way – although perhaps not to the extent – that huge numbers of combinations of Enigma settings were possible. And, as with Enigma, it is possible to make sense of this complexity: to decode it.

It is difficult to render this into words, and I have used the metaphor of a kaleidoscope and the associated image of cultural splinters to try to capture the way that different cultural distinctions are set into interaction with each other. This entails both a holding together – without the kaleidoscope the splinters of glass would scatter everywhere – and a pulling apart – as the splinters shift around and make new patterns with each other. And so with culture, which is both pulled together by homogeneity – if this were not so then any notion of culture as something shared would collapse – and fragmented by its heterogeneity – without which culture would be dead and automatic. Of course, the particular nature and balance of that is highly context-specific, with BP being one such context. However, in the best of the writings on the subject, it is proposed that organizational cultures are always somewhat integrated, somewhat differentiated and somewhat fragmented all at the same time (Martin, 1992, 2002; Parker, 2000), which suggests that a similar analysis to that provided here could be made, in principle, of any organization.

NOTES

1. Normative isomorphism being the ways that shared (e.g. professional, educational) backgrounds amongst organizational actors lead them to favour common organizational structures and mimetic isomorphism being the ways that a desire for social legitimacy leads organizations to emulate the structures of others within their field. These can both be seen as cultural bases of structure. The third type of isomorphism in institutional theory, coercive isomorphism, has a more legal character – being based upon the demands of governmental and regulatory agencies for certain kinds of structures, although this, too, can ultimately be seen as rooted in culture. See also Meyer and Rowan (1977) on the 'non-rational' and 'ceremonial' (i.e. cultural rather than economic) basis of legitimate organizational structures.

2. Such splinters of culture might also be thought of in terms of the dynamics of groups and of inter-group relations (Knowles and Knowles, 1972). However, the nature of the data and the methods of this study do not allow one to carry out much in the way of a rich analysis of such dynamics and so I have not pursued this frame of analysis. The conceptual boundary between groups and sub-cultures is of course a rather plastic one, so that many studies treat them as almost interchangeable (e.g. Schein, 1997).

3. It may be recalled from Chapter 1 that there was considerable resistance from some branches of the military to mixing their personnel with those of other services, or with civilians.

4. The bombes were operated entirely by Wrens and the majority, although by no means all, of the Wrens worked on bombes. The bombes were maintained by RAF mechanics.

5. And perhaps more complex than this: Watkins (2006: 97–8) suggests that *all* air force personnel could choose whether or not to wear uniforms, rather than this just being a choice for officers, but that this licence did not apply to other services.

6. Although in the interview Joyce did not spell this out, it is almost certain from what she said that she worked in Section 3L, assessing and prioritizing traffic (cf. Lewin, 2008: 122).

7. TNA HW 3/119: 5, emphasis in original.

8. For an account of the impact of the war on the surrounding area see Taylor (2009).

9. That is not to say that there was no intermingling. For example, the interviewee Dora, a civilian, 'had a number of friends amongst the Wrens and if I had a day off or something I might go and spend the night at Woburn Abbey with a Wren friend'.

10. To remind the reader, some of BP's work, especially, as in this case, the running of the bombes, took place at a number of nearby outstations, mainly other large mansion houses in the area and not just those mentioned here.

11. It is, in passing, of note that for Calvocoressi, joining BP in 1942, the doubts that Peter Twinn had encountered just three years before had evaporated and the essentially mathematical nature of cryptanalysis was now assumed and unproblematic. Of course, it was not the case that cryptanalysts were uniformly mathematicians, but these progressively

dominated this area of work. Nevertheless, in some sections, e.g. the Testery, linguistic cryptanalysts were commonplace.

12. Note how this implies a 'structural' basis of cultural difference.

13. TNA HW 14/145: 6.

14. It also seems to relate to the German Enigma huts rather than to those working on other ciphers.

15. Broadly speaking, the MR was concerned with finding possible mathematical solutions to the daily Enigma settings to be sent for testing on the bombes, whilst the CR sought to identify possible textual clues to solve a daily setting (e.g. repetition of stereotypical phrases). Note that the meaning of the MR in Hut 6 changed as a result of the developments described here. What had been MR1 merged with CR1 to form 'The Watch', which was itself divided into the Army Watch and the Air Watch, whilst what had been MR2 and CR2 merged to become the Hut 6 Research section. What had formerly been the Netz room was henceforth known as the Machine Room. See TNA HW 43/70: 107.

16. This is from the main, multi-authored, text of the Hut 6 history, rather than Milner-Barry's introduction. TNA HW 43/70: 106.

17. TNA HW 43/70: 10.

18. More precisely, what we see here is the two-way relation of culture and structure. On the one hand, an organizational division (in this case MR and CR) gives rise to a cultural distinction (academic background), whilst on the other hand, cultural beliefs about the functionality of that distinction serve to reproduce an organizational division.

19. TNA HW 43/70: 10.

20. Many GPO staff worked in Y stations or at the Dollis Hill research section rather than at BP itself. However, Ron, quoted in this paragraph, worked on the BP site.

21. TNA HW 14/145: 8.

22. In addition, as noted in Chapter 1, there were widespread discrepancies in pay rates and promotion prospects both amongst the different services and between service and civilian staff.

23. TNA HW 14/145: 33. Dora, the administrative assistant interviewed for this study, worked closely with the billeting officers and recalls high levels of dissatisfaction from staff with the billets they had been allocated.

24. There is some implication of social class distinctions in this but, if so, it is a subtle one. Because of the class structure of education at the time,

university graduates might well typically (although, of course, by no means ubiquitously) be from more privileged social classes. However, because of the small numbers of people attending university at the time, the converse does not apply, i.e. plenty of people from socially privileged groups did not go to university. Moreover, although many or most of the 'Chiefs' are likely to have been graduates, so too were many 'Indians'. Indeed, in some sections, there were graduates employed in quite low-skill work.

25. Most obviously in the now almost ubiquitous linkage in the public mind between BP and Alan Turing, but this is also evident in the widely read collection of memoirs of BP in Hinsley and Stripp (1993). Since 'chief' and 'indian' are ill-defined categories, it is impossible to be exact, but in my judgment the vast majority of those featured in that collection would fall into the 'chief' category and certainly only four (out of thirty) are female, of whom at least one, Joan Murray, was very much a 'chief'.

26. Perhaps, then, one might envisage a distinction amongst the 'Indians' between 'Braves' and 'Squaws'?

27. Interestingly, in Robert Harris's novel *Enigma* (1995), the character Hester Wallace is depicted in just this way, as having been recruited by virtue of having won a crossword competition, following which 'the two male finalists became cryptanalysts whilst she, the woman who had beaten them was despatched to a bedlam called Control . . . [where] . . . she was a glorified clerk' (Harris, 1995: 214–15). The Control in question refers to Hut 6 and is presumably the Intercept Control Room. The idea of recruitment via crossword competitions has a basis in fact, although very few were recruited to BP in this way, as noted in the previous chapter.

28. TNA HW 43/70: 22. It is worth reflecting on the use of the term 'girls' in this passage, which carries, especially for the modern reader, a slightly patronizing connotation. It is used almost ubiquitously in BP documents in preference to 'women'. The term 'boys' is also found, referring to young men specifically, but 'men' is far more frequently used to refer to male staff and, although, as is explored elsewhere, there was a preponderance of young people at BP, this was true of the men quite as much as of the women. There is, then, a gendering of language in this respect, although one which was widespread at the time rather than being specifically an attribute of BP.

29. TNA HW 14/145: 9.
30. I am not convinced that this is so: elsewhere one finds quite extravagant praise for individuals. On the specific milieu of Naval Section it is worth noting that 'some of [its] best cryptographers [sic] were women' (Morris, 1993: 243).
31. Which should lead us to recall the point made in the previous chapter about the inter-relations between BP and the wider cultural and historical context(s). Assumptions about gender in this context are, in terms of organizational culture analysis, an example of what Schein (1997) calls the basic, shared assumptions which are largely sub-conscious.
32. TNA HW 3/119: 41–2.
33. TNA HW 14/145: 7. Aside from specifically work-related issues, the bringing together of large numbers of young men and women was, in line with the standards of the time, sometimes seen as 'a problem'. For example, there were worries over the morality of mixed-sex night shifts (see TNA HW 43/70: 4; Welchman, 1982: 89; Millward, 1993: 20), and more generally relations between the sexes were to an extent 'policed'. In particular, there are a great many accounts of permission to marry having to be obtained or in other ways being discouraged (e.g. Wilkinson, 1993: 66; Smith, 1998: 152; Watkins, 2006: 174; Thirsk, 2008: 49). The post-war review also refers to 'much difficulty over girls and American pilots: drink mostly', TNA HW 14/145: 31.
34. TNA HW 25/1: 91.
35. Strictly speaking, since Ultra referred to the product not just of Enigma decryption but also of other high-grade ciphers such as Fish, the 'Ultra community' and the Enigma-enwised are not identical expressions. It was the case that some were enwised to Enigma, some to Fish and some to both. Nor were Enigma and Fish the only sources of Ultra, there were others, e.g. JN-25, a Japanese naval code, and those enwised to this were by no means necessarily also enwised to Enigma. One might say, then, that the Enigma-enwised were a subset of the Ultra community, but my sense is that Calvocoressi is using the term to refer to the Enigma-enwised in particular, given that he worked in Hut 3. Of course, it also bears saying that knowledge, certainly detailed knowledge, of the full range of Ultra sources (e.g. the range of different keys within Enigma etc.) would have been confined to a very small number of people indeed. Also note that those with 'bigoted' indoctrination were by no means

confined to the ranks of the Enigma-enwised – again, the 'communities' cut across each other.

36. See the introductory chapter for details.

37. TNA HW 14/145: 36.

38. Note that this corresponds to my earlier point that for those at BP life, work apart, consisted mainly of billets.

39. This is a reference to W. E. F. 'Nobby' Clarke, who was indeed sidelined, and discontented as a result, as Roy stated. See Chapter 1 for more detail and TNA HW 3/16 for even more.

40. It is perhaps worth pointing out that, as a generality, the wartime mobilization of the population at large led to young people taking on many responsible roles which perhaps in other circumstances would have been denied them.

41. Nor am I alone in this sense, e.g. BP was a 'community of young people' (McKay, 2010: 195).

42. One case of such an opinion is to be found in Hugh Alexander's internal history of Hut 8. TNA HW 25/1: 91.

43. TNA HW 14/145: 7–8, formatting of original simplified. Note in passing the sidelight thrown on class and gender here. Male recruitment, only, is referred to in terms of education, and that education in terms of Public (i.e. private) School.

44. However, Briggs (2011: 36–7) takes issue with Taunt's account and says that he himself had no such feeling, even though he did not arrive at BP until 1943. Clearly experiences were not uniform, so it would be wrong to over-state this point.

45. And included some of the 'Chiefs', such as Walter Ettinghausen (later, as Walter Eytan, to be Israel's Ambassador to the United Nations), who worked in Hut 4, Harry Golombek, a chess champion who worked on *Abwehr* (Intelligence) Enigma ciphers, and Rolf Noskwith, who worked on Naval Enigma in Hut 8. See Sugarman (2008) for more details.

Part III   Decoding Work

The first two parts of this book have provided a broad background to the way that BP worked. In this part, I build on this background to offer a more detailed explanation of that working, and by 'working' I mean two different, albeit related, things. Firstly, although I have already provided some glimpses of this, I want to examine at least aspects of the work itself and in particular the various ways – themselves entailing some work – in which the fragmentations of structure and culture I have outlined nevertheless co-existed with a co-ordinated set of activities which collectively constituted signals intelligence. Secondly, in Chapter 6 I will try to make sense of how BP worked by reference to various 'standard' ways of thinking about work organizations. In both cases, and in line with the points I made in the introductory chapter, it should be understood that 'working' is a process – that is, an ongoing effort to produce and reproduce organization. In other words, it is not just a question of the organization of work but of the work entailed in organization.

There are obvious reasons for addressing these issues. One can speak of the organization of all kinds of activities, but much of organization and almost all of organization studies is concerned with the organization of work. Arguably, as organization studies has become increasingly distinct from one of its main progenitors – industrial sociology – it has also become decreasingly attentive to work (Barley and Kunda, 2001). This is one reason why organization studies has become overly abstracted from organizational experience, of which work is so central a part. Illuminating work requires digging beneath established understandings and, in the case of BP, these relate, as I have explained before, to received images of 'the codebreakers' as a small group of male academics engaged in work of genius. I hope I have already gone some way to 'decoding' this image. But there is more at stake than this in asking how BP worked.

As I enumerated in Chapter 1, both contemporary and subsequent accounts have invariably emphasised the chaotic, anarchic, freakish and incoherent characteristics of BP. It should already be clear that the work of BP was extremely varied in character and generalizations about it are therefore difficult. This might be true of many large organizations, but the compartmentalization of BP because of secrecy makes it perhaps especially so in this case. Lewin (2008: 137) characterizes the situation thus:

> A honeycomb – this must be the final and dominating image of Bletchley Park: a honeycomb of cells some of which may appear to have functioned independently of the main structure. But distance and perspective allow the significant patterns to emerge. It is now clear that huts and sections, individuals and teams, the Wren at her bombe, the cryptanalysts at their ciphers, the calculations of the mathematicians and the creative ingenuity of the technologists were all parts of a whole – of an organism which, like the honeycomb, had evolved to secrete a single product: in Bletchley's case, intelligence about the enemy.

However, whilst useful, the honeycomb image is misleading in that it perhaps summons up a sense of a series of identically sized and shaped compartments, whereas those at BP were of widely differing sorts and sizes. In March 1944 there were some thirty-one formally constituted operational sections at BP (i.e. not including the sub-divisions within some of these), plus a further sixteen administrative sections. These ranged in size from the 1,704 staff in 'Hut 11a and the WRNS outstations'[1] to the 3 employed in 'Dr. Wynn Williams' section'[2]. Insofar as the administrative sections were concerned, these encompassed the Transport section, employing 147 staff, mainly drivers and maintenance crew, down to the five-strong Barber's Shop[3].

Nor does the honeycomb notion really help us to understand the processes and mechanisms through which this 'organism' was

co-ordinated. At the heart of this is a very longstanding issue in organization theory, namely the various ways that autonomy and control co-
exist. Thus:

> Bletchley Park ... managed to combine organizational fluidity and
> an apparently anarchic disregard for hierarchy with success in
> getting its key areas under firm control.   *(Herman, 1996: 332)*

The questions to be explored in this part of the book are the following:
how did this occur and how can it be understood? I will approach these
questions in terms of the ways of working that were in evidence at BP.
These ways of working were a complex entanglement of different
kinds of practices. Thus, in relation to co-ordination, an array of different 'mechanisms' can be discerned, some based upon personal, trust-
based relations, some on explicit approaches to management seeking
to elicit commitment, efficiency and so on, some on formalized practices ranging from routine meetings embedded in daily conduct to
specific structural arrangements. In a similar way, Chapter 6 tries to
address the question of what 'kind' of working this was, and here the
argument is that categories of organizational theory do not speak very
adequately to the messy intermingling of organizational practices. In
particular, I seek to show how broadly bureaucratic and non-
bureaucratic ways of working, exemplified by standardization on the
one hand and knowledge work on the other, were twisted together and
cannot be untwisted. Similarly, I address the key issue of centralization to show that this, too, is indeterminate because BP's work was
both centralized and decentralized.

   So the core argument which I want to illustrate through the BP
case is that, if we want to understand work organization, we need to do
so not through 'top-down' typologies of organization which abstract
and impose sense upon the practices of work, but through 'bottom-up'
consideration of work practices which concretize and make sense of
organization.

NOTES

1. This refers to the bombe room and outstations.
2. This section was involved in the development of various machine devices, most famously the 'Heath Robinson machine', forerunner of Colossus. It worked in conjunction with the GPO experimental facility at Dollis Hill, so the true numbers involved would have been larger than the three listed at the BP end of the operation, but the point holds that some sections were very small.
3. TNA HW 14/154: table of contents, section II.

5 Making Bletchley Park Work

INTRODUCTION

In this chapter, the first part of the answer to the question 'how did BP work?' takes the form of an account of three key areas, all of which are concerned in some way with the co-ordination of work. First, the role of highly personalized networks in enabling informal co-ordination will be explored. The suggestion here is that digging deeply into the recruitment process for some parts of BP reveals not just common background in the generic sense identified in Chapter 3, but a dense web of pre-existing personal connections and friendships which facilitated trust and communication across the structural fragmentations of BP.

The second area I will consider is that of management and, in particular, 'management style'. The key point here is to explain the diversity of such styles in different parts of the BP operation, ranging from collegiate to factory-type control. Allied to this are considerations of morale in the face of work which was often physically and intellectually demanding, frequently dull and sometimes incomprehensible.

Finally, consideration will be given to some of the more formal mechanisms and methods of co-ordination, including meetings, committees, cross-departmental communication channels and intelligence distribution systems.

TRUST AND NETWORKS

I have already shown how the structural and cultural fragmentations of BP meant that in many of its sections – especially Huts 3, 4, 6 and 8 – the workforce comprised a large diversity of service and civilian personnel working without a clear hierarchy, which, indeed, is one of the main reasons why the organization has been described as anarchic. I have also indicated how recruitment, especially to the huts just mentioned, was achieved through informal networks centred on universities, especially Oxbridge and even more especially Cambridge. I now want to put these points together to suggest that the consequence was to foster a degree of trust and an ease of communication that was able to 'patch' the schisms and consequent ambiguities and uncertainties about, for example, hierarchy. Within organization studies, there is an almost limitless way in which social networks in organizations can be understood and analysed (see, for example, Kilduff and Tsai, 2003; Kilduff and Brass, 2010), but here I am concerned with the interrelationship between pre-existing social and educational networks and informal organizational networks at BP. With respect to trust, specifically, a survey of the literature explains that

> All [models of trust development] highlight that trust is based on a body of evidence about the other party's motives and character, from which a belief, prediction or faith judgment about that party's likely *future* conduct is derived.
>
> *(Dietz, Gillespie and Chao, 2010: 11, emphasis in original)*

It is clearly the case that shared background is relevant here, since it is one source of evidence about another's motives and character from which beliefs about future conduct may be derived. However, there is more to this than what I said in Chapter 3 about recruitment patterns. For these patterns were not simply about shared background, but in many cases arose from highly personalized 'micro-networks' in which the individuals concerned did not just come from similar backgrounds but also were already well known to each other. There are so many examples of this that it would be tedious to recount them, but the contours can be indicated by, first, considering a kind of 'standard' case of shared background:

> In April 1940, about the end of the phoney war, Hugh Last, Professor of Ancient History, asked me to come to his rooms in Brasenose

College, Oxford. He explained in a roundabout way that there was important but highly secret war work to be done, and that my studies in ancient languages and Egyptology might make me suitable for it. He advised me to go to a house called Bletchley Park and offer myself. And so on 6 May 1940 I took a train to Bletchley and entered BP . . .   *(Dakin, 1993: 50).*

But now consider another case which shows the even more personalized networks of recruiting:

One day at Oxford in the summer of 1940 I was asked by someone – I believe it was Alec Dakin – if I would be interested in intelligence work for the war effort, and I said I would.   *(Eytan, 1993: 57)*

Here we can see personalized chains of recommendation and approach – from Last, to Dakin, to Eytan – and these were commonplace, as in this case:

I was recruited for GC & CS by Gordon Welchman[1], who had supervised me in geometry for Part II of the Cambridge Tripos.
                                                          (Murray, 1993: 113)

There are many variations upon this theme of personal micro-networks. Roy, who was interviewed for this study, is another, slightly more indirect, but delicious, example. In 1939, the landlord of his 'digs' (accommodation) in Cambridge was a University 'bulldog'[2] who mentioned to his 'Proctor' that he had a tenant who had just graduated in languages, was very proficient in these and was currently unoccupied. The consequence, as mentioned elsewhere, was that Roy was invited to a room in the Proctor's College where he was interviewed by, as he later knew them to be, Denniston and Tiltman. They explained that they wanted him for 'confidential war work but couldn't say anything about it except that "it would be terribly boring with occasional excitement"'.

A final example of this personalization is that of William Filby, a Cambridge librarian who volunteered for the Army in June 1940 and in September was

sent to London to be interviewed by Lieutenant Colonel John
H. Tiltman who asked about my languages but seemed more
interested in my references. I gave him the name of Professor F. J. H.
Stratton, of Cambridge University, which caused Tiltman to shout
'Tubby!' and in walked Lieutenant Colonel Stratton. Stratton
commented on my dirty uniform, then turned to Tiltman and
exclaimed 'You want him, John'.   *(Filby, 1988: 272)*

This highly personalized mode of recruitment[3], in which one can trace
precise patterns of relation, subtly shaped parts of BP. In the previous
chapter I referred to how Derek Taunt of Hut 6 bemoaned not having
been recruited earlier in the war, but now I will give the rest of the
quotation which explains why this was so:

had I been at either Marlborough[4] or Sidney Sussex [College,
Cambridge], instead of the City of London School and Jesus College
[Cambridge], I might just have arrived at BP in its great pioneering
days rather than 'at the end of the beginning'.   *(Taunt, 1993: 101)*

The effect of all this is related to trust in two ways. The obvious one is
that, in terms of having a source of evidence about character and
motivations, personal acquaintance is potentially a strong basis for
this. This is summed up in shorthand by this amusing story:
'[Denniston] called on me again to ask about someone I knew: "We
know he's a communist, but is he the sort of communist who would
betray his country?" I forget whether I said "No" or "I don't know"'
(Wilkinson, 1993: 61)[5]. Perhaps less obvious is how much trust was
required on the part of those being recruited: to be told (to take an
archetypical case) to go to a railway station at a place called Bletchley
where you would be met in order to work – for the duration of the war –
on an unspecified task called for an enormous trust in those making
the approach[6].

This system of recruitment seems quaint and even bizarre to the
modern eye, and was all of a piece with the way that SIS more generally
conducted recruitment at the time (Jeffery, 2010: 318). However, the

process was by no means casual, and was accompanied by security vetting. As noted in Chapter 3 and as the post-war review explains (see also Erskine, 1986), it arose from contingency planning prior to the war which 'through contacts at the universities earmarked about 60 suitable men ... [some of whom] ... attended a course in peace time ... [a]ll joined at the outbreak or before'[7].

Alastair Denniston's papers emphasise this point. From at least 1937 it was planned to recruit staff 'of the type required' using staff from WW1 codebreaking, now in university positions, as recruiters[8]. Denniston himself recruited Gordon Welchman as part of this process, which continued after the outbreak of war, as has been shown. That it was possible rested in part on the fact that the university system was much smaller than it is now and so it was feasible to identify suitably talented individuals[9] – mathematicians and linguists in the main – relatively easily. But there was more to it than this in that it expresses a socially habituated way of recruiting within elites prevailing at the time.

An important figure in the history of recruitment at BP was C. P. Snow, later to become famous as a novelist. Prior to the war he had been a scientist at Cambridge and was brought into the Civil Service, where amongst other things he had responsibility for allocating personnel to scientific projects, including 'Tube Alloys' – the British atomic bomb project – and, to some degree, BP. I have written elsewhere of how Snow's semi-autobiographical novels have a considerable salience for understanding the nature of organization (Grey, 1996) and, in the present context, consider his alter-ego protagonist's account of how he and various other members of his Cambridge College entered the war:

within a few days [of the outbreak of war] Roy[10] had been asked for by a branch of intelligence, Francis Getliffe had become assistant director of one of the first radar establishments, I was a civil servant in Whitehall. And so with a good many of our Cambridge friends. It was slick, automatic, taken for granted. The links between the

universities and 'government' were very strong. They happened, of
course, as a residue of privilege; the official world in England was
still relatively small and compact; when in difficulties it asked who
was a useful man, and brought him in.   *(Snow, 1947: 305)*

This very nicely captures the process at work – including hints about
its gendered nature and its 'Englishness' – and is consistent with
Snow's non-fictional accounts of how the 'English Establishment'
worked at the time to recruit people (e.g. Snow, 1962: 31). It seems
fair to assume that he knew what he was talking about. His role with
respect to BP was actually to *formalize* recruitment in order to meet
the growing scale of staff needs (Lewin, 2008: 57) from 1941[11], given
which it is ironic that this role was itself facilitated by the trust
engendered by personalized networks. For Snow was not privy to the
Ultra secret, but Gordon Welchman had known him in Cambridge
before the war and recorded that '[Snow] happened to know me fairly
well and believed what I said about the importance of our work'
(Welchman, 1982: 86).

My contention, then, is that within BP, at least amongst 'the
Chiefs' and especially within the main Enigma huts, there was a network far tighter and more intimate than might initially be realized and
that this enabled not just trust but, associated with that, ways of
communicating and working together which side-stepped the confused mish-mash of different agencies and institutions in play. Of
course, by no means everyone, even within these restricted segments,
had actually known each other before BP. Indeed, the very personalization of the process meant that there were likely to be separate 'strings'
of acquaintance (e.g. contacts of Denniston, Welchman or Tiltman
etc.). But Calvocoressi, whilst stating that he met at BP only one
person whom he had known before the war, makes a very acute point
about this:

> As a consequence of the recruitment [process] nearly all of us had
> had the same sort of education and shared a common social
> background. We made, unwittingly for the most part, the same

assumptions about life and work and discipline and values.
Although we had never met before ... *we half-knew each other
already.* *(Calvocoressi 2001: 23, emphasis added)*

It is both common sense and also well established in the organization-
theory literature that commonality of background leads to high
degrees of shared social capital or 'characteristic-based' trust (Zucker,
1986; Inkpen and Tsang, 2005). In this case, both general shared background and specific pre-knowledge came together in the very tight
network of knowing and 'half-knowing' able to facilitate communication and agreement[12]. It is this, I would suggest, that explains the many
observations of BP's work such as this one, which I quoted in a different
context elsewhere:

> [In Hut 6] you might readily find a Major working under a Lieutenant
> or under a civilian, somewhat younger. Whoever was in charge was
> the person who had been judged to be more effective at doing it. It
> was meritocracy in spades ...   *(Bill Bundy, cited in Smith, 1998: 136)*

Or, to take another example that seems to disclose a similar picture,
this time from the internal history of Hut 3:

> Here [Hut 3] over five hundred and fifty individuals of widely
> differing ages, gifts, and characters, men and women, Service and
> civilian, British and American, yet formed with all their variety one
> welded whole; working – often overworking – together, year by year,
> with unpretentious skill and pertinacity, gaiety and irony, and with
> less time wasted in intrigue than one could easily have thought
> possible in this too human world. Not everyone doubtless,
> overworked. Not everyone was always angelic. This is not a fairy-
> tale. Not everyone was always content. There were grumbles ...
> [b]ut we were 'a happy ship'[13].

I will return shortly to the 'grumbles', but for now I want to give a further
illustration of how communication and co-operation worked. Crucial
to the breaking of Enigma and other ciphers were the bombes – the

electromechanical devices used to test possible solutions to Enigma – and, except for during the later stages of the war, when the Americans built large numbers of these, there was a shortage of capacity. Since the principal users of the bombes were split between different sections, notably the Naval cryptanalysts of Hut 8 and their Army and Air counterparts in Hut 6:

> There was a danger of really serious conflict of claims here, because there was no overriding intelligence authority that could balance the claims of the Admiralty against the War Office, and we had to work out our own solution[14].

The solution developed was to create a rotating bombe director (from a team of five) from one or other of these two huts with the power, during his tenure, to decide on bombe allocation. Conflict was rare 'and decisions were rarely if ever taken on what might be called party lines' with 'the decisive factor in avoiding serious conflict of opinion [being] the broadmindedness and clearheadedness of Alexander, the Head of Hut 8'[15]. This account comes from Stuart Milner-Barry, the Head of Hut 6 in succession to Gordon Welchman, but Hugh Alexander concurs that the system 'worked extremely well' and goes on to ascribe this to 'the over-whelming advantage of an inter-service organization'[16]. But this is a strange conclusion to draw in that, as Milner-Barry suggests, the problem arose rather from inter-service rivalry and the absence of a formal mechanism for resolving it. I would suggest a more plausible way of understanding the success of this arrangement is to be found in this:

> When the war broke out in 1939 I was in the Argentine, playing chess for the British team in the Olympiad. My great friend and rival, [Hugh] Alexander, was another member, as was Harry Golombek, late chess correspondent of *The Times*. We returned home immediately, and before long found ourselves at Bletchley Park, where we remained for the duration. We had been recruited by Gordon Welchman, an old friend of mine at Cambridge.
>
> (Milner-Barry, 1993: 86)

Thus it seems highly likely that the pre-existing friendship between Alexander and Milner-Barry – which began in Cambridge in the 1920s when they both played chess for the university – served as a way of patching the organizational problems caused by the competing claims of Admiralty and War Office and the shortage of resources, in this case, bombes[17]. This, indeed, is a good example of the rather neglected phenomenon in organization theory of friendship as a central part of organizing (Grey and Sturdy, 2007). One could enumerate endlessly the very dense web of friendship connections within and around BP. Another of the five bombe directors was Shaun Wylie of Hut 8, who before the war was a friend of Alan Turing's, and was recruited by him for BP. Turing preceded Alexander as Head of Hut 8, and both had been mathematics undergraduates together at King's College Cambridge, while at the same time Milner-Barry read classics at Trinity College, Cambridge[18]. Alexander before the war worked as Director of Research for John Lewis Partnership, a role filled after the war on his recommendation by Gordon Welchman. It would be time-consuming, but perfectly possible, to fill a book with the many interconnections of BP staff. As a final point, it is worth noting that, of those mentioned in the last few paragraphs, and picking up on the 'generational' point made in the previous chapter, all were born within a few years of each other, the oldest being Welchman and Milner-Barry (both born in 1906), the youngest being Wylie (born in 1913).

Thus my contention is that the way that BP worked cannot be understood without an understanding of the very fine-grained relations between some of its central players, relations which often pre-dated the war and were about personal knowledge and, in some cases, friendship rather than simply shared background. Of course, personal acquaintance and friendship do not in themselves preclude tensions and rivalries of many sorts, but they do provide a particular potential for the avoidance of institutionalized conflict. Ratcliff (2006: 76–83) discusses issues of recruitment and co-operation (including the bombe example) and draws attention to 'the pivotal importance of [a] tradition of amateurism' (2006: 77). She does not mean this term pejoratively, but rather suggests that the influx of large numbers of civilians (including those mobilized into the armed forces on a temporary basis) into BP enabled a degree of flexibility and innovation that was hidebound neither by past practices nor by enmeshment in established inter-service rivalries.

This is clearly consistent with the argument made here, but in addition my claim is that, as well as the *absence* of such rivalries, a more detailed analysis of recruitment shows a *presence* of pre-existing personal and social networks. One might say that the term amateurism codes these networks which, to use the metaphor in a different way, ran like 'DNA code' through BP's work, providing a *cultural* structure that was to some extent able to cover over the incoherent *organizational* structure of BP. The caveat 'to some extent' is important because of course there *were* very significant conflicts at BP arising from structural incoherence – the case of the Hut 3 conflicts outlined in Part I being an obvious example. Moreover, decisions about machine allocation were not always taken in the same manner as that which applied to the bombes. Another important machine resource was the Hollerith punch-card sorters, located in what was named, after its head, the Freebornery. Here a very different approach to allocation[19] was in evidence, as implied in this account:

> In several respects [Mr Freeborn] stood apart from the generality of the Park's professional staff. At my level[20] he was always known as Mr Freeborn: no Christian name, no nickname. He was a business man (borrowed from the British Tabulating Machine Company at Letchworth) and always in a business suit ... every discussion I had about work to be done for us [the JN-25 party] was with Mr Freeborn himself and he was in total command of the detail. I always went to his office in Block C, never he to mine ... it paid to ensure that the material submitted to Block C was immaculately prepared, for if it was shoddy ... Mr Freeborn would be harder to persuade to give priority next time. *(Simpson, 2011: 139)*

Thus, as ever at BP, generalization is difficult, and in particular there are two important additions and qualifications that must be made to this picture of co-ordination via trust-based personal networks. One is that making BP work also required some much more formal methods of co-operation across the different sections, services and so on. I will consider these later in this chapter. The other is that this dense social network operated amongst only some personnel – primarily the 'Chiefs' and probably more amongst the early members of that group in particular – and existed alongside other sub-cultural groups as outlined in the previous chapter. Thus there was a wide range of co-ordinative practices beyond those of personalized trust networks. Next I will focus in particular upon what might be called 'management style' and related issues of morale.

MANAGEMENT AND MORALE

In some sections it was the case, in line with what has just been said, and consistent with the suggestion in the previous chapter of Oxbridge as a cultural template, that the 'management style was that of the senior member of a common room rather than that of a director' (Simpson, 2011: 129), this with reference to the Italian Naval Section. In Hut 6, discipline

> in the sense of issuing formal orders ... hardly ever existed: orders were nearly always given in the form of requests, and accompanied by explanations ... the guiding principle all along was not to lay things down from on high, but to bring everybody into consultation, to get general agreement and to make everybody feel participants and not cogs in an unintelligible machine[21].

Newman, head of the Newmanry,

> realised that he could get the best out of us by trusting to our own good intentions and our strong motivation and he made the thing always as informal as possible ... [he] was the model of an academic administrator. *(Peter Hilton, cited in Smith, 1998: 152)*

188 MAKING BLETCHLEY PARK WORK

This is very much the received image of BP, and has probably already been written about enough both in this book and elsewhere, but it applied only in parts. Indeed, consider the Newmanry, just mentioned. The high-grade staff may have been treated as described but, as I mentioned in the previous chapter, Newman is said to have thought that the Wrens working there would have no interest in having their work explained to them, and for them work consisted of following orders and procedures. Such an approach was to be found in many other sections. The Typex[22] Room, which processed 3½ million five-letter 'groups' per week, is a good example. Here,

> Labour was 'directed'[23] and the interest nil. It became necessary to intervene and institute factory methods. This was done chiefly by keeping careful records of output per watch, per machine and per girl. This showed up weaknesses, peak hours etc., and enabled the manager to adjust numbers and skill per watch ...[24]

These examples (Newmanry Wrens and the Typex Room civilians) suggest a gendered pattern to management techniques and, whilst that is very likely to have been true, there is some complexity to it because it seems also to relate to skill and status of work. These intersect with gender because much of the lower-skill and lower-status work was indeed performed by women, but such factory methods were also used when men, or men and women together, were doing such work, with listening stations (which were not on the BP site, of course) being an obvious example. Here, as in the Typex Room, detailed Taylorist-style performance measurement was in place, with detailed breakdowns of rates of successful interception between groups, shifts and stations[25]. Similarly, detailed timings were made of bombe operations and comparative analysis performed on jobs generated from the different huts and undertaken at BP and the bombe outstations[26]. Thus, alongside the image of BP as a kind of university common room, we should hold another image, that of a factory.

Then again, in segments where the 'collegiate' style was in evidence, it was applied even where the work was unskilled and repetitious and being done by women; and the analytical point to make about this is that management systems are not solely *determined* by the type of work, but are also *shaped* by choices and cultural norms. Thus, in the Hut 6 Registration Rooms[27] the female workforce was encouraged to relieve monotony by rotating jobs in classic job-design fashion, even though this was seen to reduce efficiency, because it was more humane[28]. This is suggestive of the way that, in addition to Oxbridge collegiality, an understanding of the kind of 'Theory Y' (McGregor, 1960) management theory that had become fashionable in the 1930s (albeit not under that name) can be found at BP. Indeed, in relation to listening stations, a report on the RAF's Chicksands station bemoaned the Taylorist (or 'Theory X') approach at such stations, noting that

> Commercial firms nowadays realise the fact that the welfare of their employees is of paramount importance in the maintenance and improvement of efficiency which has a direct bearing on profits. Therefore, looked at from a purely monetary angle, it pays to study the well-being of the staff, apart altogether from any ethical concerns[29].

In fact, borrowings from commercial and industrial practice were widespread at BP (I will discuss this further in the next chapter) because it pulled together people with a wide range of such experience. Hugh Alexander, who, as mentioned, had worked at John Lewis (and perhaps the fact that this was and is a co-operative is significant) before the war, opined that

> the sort of things that make for efficiency in an operational cryptographic section are very much the same as in a business organization. The idea is to get business efficiency whilst preserving the atmosphere of a cooperative voluntarily undertaken for its own sake[30].

Understandings and experiences of industrial practice were only part of the issue, though. In Chapter 3 I discussed the 'context' of war in shaping BP, and one of the ways this manifested itself was in approaches to management. If culture is a matter of delineating 'us' and 'them', then the most significant of 'them' at the time were surely the German enemy, who were associated with autocratic management both by virtue of the Teutonic stereotype and owing to the specifically totalitarian nature of the Nazi regime. Thus, in a passage quoted in the previous chapter in a different context, the internal history of Hut 3 states that

> Ours ... was an exceptional freedom. Those who did their work well were left, within the inevitable limits, to do it their own way ... [i]t was the exact reverse of the HITLER principle of the greatest possible meddling with the greatest possible number. That trust was repaid. And if mistakes were made (as of course they were) by ignorance or negligence, the remedy was found not nearly so much in reprimands, or witch-hunts for the delinquent, as in the mortification decent persons felt at having let things down[31].

This may be taken as another example, to go with those quoted above, of the informal and collegial approach to management in some sections. But, more specifically, it is clear that it was understood specifically in contrast to that of Nazism, and a similar sentiment is found in Milner-Barry's introduction to the internal history of Hut 6, where, referring to the use of job-rotation techniques in the Registration Rooms, he writes

> I am convinced that nothing but *Prussian* methods would have succeeded; and equally clear that we had immeasurably more to lose than to gain by adopting them[32].

Whatever its motivation, there is plenty of evidence of those with managerial roles at BP giving a lot of attention to issues of morale. Welchman (e.g. 1982: 126–7) writes extensively about this, often in terms of knowledge-sharing, a matter to which I will return in the next chapter, and, interestingly, compares his management practice to that later advocated by management writer Peter Drucker (Welchman,

1982: 171). Milner-Barry provides what might almost be a definition of what is nowadays known as 'management by walking about' in stressing how important he found it to

> go round and talk, or perhaps rather to encourage other people to do the talking and to listen, so as to get the feel about what the man in the street is thinking, whether about the work or the war or billet[33] or anything else. One can learn more in this way than by any number of formal interviews ... I think one is far more likely to do too little rather than too much in the way of aimless wandering[34].

In a similar way, in Hut 8, Hugh Alexander was of the view that 'the best way of keeping up morale is by giving everyone the fullest and most current information about the results obtained from the work' and, despite the constraints of secrecy, attempted to do this with talks from distinguished visitors from amongst the military and through interaction between cryptanalysts and those doing less-skilled work[35].

I have referred elsewhere to the widely praised management skills[36] of Eric Jones in Hut 3, skills learned in manufacturing industry and, more than anything else, to do with 'handling people'. According to the interviewee Roy, another accomplished manager of a very different type from Jones was the eccentric Josh Cooper, Head of Air Section, a view borne out by another member of the section:

> as [Air Section] grew in size and importance, there were power struggles and takeover attempts behind the scenes. At first it was under Air Ministry control ... later it passed into the hands of the Foreign Office. It mattered little to us who our nominal masters were; we owed allegiance only to Josh Cooper. *(Watkins, 2006: 75)*

Here, again, it is possible to see a different way in which wider structural problems were amenable to resolution by virtue of personal relations and management style. Yet, despite these various ways in which genuine managerial attempts were made to initiate humane and co-operative ways of working at BP and to maintain morale, there was persistent discontent as well. As I mentioned in Chapter 3 one of the abiding images of Britain in WW2 is that it was characterized by a cheerful willingness of all to 'do their bit' and an uncomplaining acceptance of privations. There is surely much truth in such depictions, but it would be wrong to avoid contrary evidence. I am aware that by drawing attention to this I will offend the sensibilities of some, perhaps especially any readers who are BP veterans. Nevertheless, an honest analysis requires that it be mentioned.

One issue, which has been foreshadowed, is that much of the work at BP was of an extremely monotonous and often arduous kind. This would be true of much indexing, log reading and registration work, for example, as well as the staffing of the bombes and Hollerith machines. Physically, conditions were often poor – hot and noisy in the bombe rooms, especially – lighting levels[37] and poor ergonomic design in general were a source of health problems. Away from BP, in the Y stations, the experience of hours listening intently, often to silence whilst waiting for transmissions, followed by intense concentration when they appeared, was stressful (Clayton, 1980; Page, 2003). The fact that, very often, those involved were not aware, or only partially aware[38], of the purpose of their work added to the strain that some inevitably felt, as did the pattern of shifts. Many sections of BP worked on a three-shift system, each of 8 hours (normally 8am to 4pm, 4pm to midnight and midnight to 8am), with normal working weeks being 48 hours rising to 51 hours in changeover weeks. It is now well known that night and shift work can have significant impacts on physical and mental health[39] (Costa, 1996). Moreover, changes from day to night shifts have some particular health risks associated with them (Knuttson, 2003), something noted as the worst feature of their otherwise very different kinds of work by, for example, the interviewees Joyce, the Hut 3 analyst, and Vera, the Naval Section indexing clerk.

It is not, then, surprising to find illness amongst staff, both physical and mental, the latter usually referred to in terms of 'mental breakdown' (see Hill, 2004: 130–1 for some accounts). When interviewed for this study, administrative assistant Dora was aware of several such cases, for example, somebody quite senior who was clearly working under enormous strain and stress and had been on sick leave and was found roaming around in London ... I remember a great crisis about it, getting the police to find the man and to bring him back to us ... because he was unbalanced.

It is worth recording that, although these events had happened almost seventy years before, Dora was very uncomfortable in recalling them and, for another case she described, asked for the tape to be turned off and her account not to be quoted. How many cases of 'mental breakdown' occurred is impossible to determine, but in the section of the post-war report about the relative merits of age there is reference to different breakdown rates amongst younger and older staff[40]. This does suggest that the numbers were sufficient for such comparisons to be made, and certainly there is a large number of passing references in accounts of BP.

However, the effects of work stress were normally less dramatic, being confined perhaps to a low-level discontent, and the reasons are very easy to understand. Apart from the mundane and/or difficult nature of the work itself, there was the contrast between it and the life that some expected to be having during wartime and which was being experienced by their contemporaries. To have joined, for example, the Wrens and to be posted to HMS Pembroke V might conjure up images of 'breathing the salty air of Portsmouth Docks or Plymouth Hoe' (Wilkinson, 1993: 65). In fact, it was the Wrens' cover name for BP[41] and they found themselves in a fairly uninteresting part of the countryside, 'about the furthest place from the sea in England' (Wilkinson, 1993: 65), doing what

> was a soul-destroying job and very like being in prison, except there was no remission for good conduct. Quite the reverse: once detailed, that remained the lot of these devoted and highly intelligent girls for the duration. There were few chances for promotion, no contact with the rest of the Navy, and, due to the very necessary security restrictions, little social life when off duty.　　　*(Beesly, 2000: 70)*

Despite these privations, at least the Wrens were in uniform. Civilians faced implications, if not accusations[42], of 'dodging' against which they were unable to defend themselves.

Complaints about the mundanity of some of the work, and lack of knowledge of its purpose, sometimes openly surfaced, as in the following extracts from the Journal of the Sandridge Radio Section of the Wireless Branch of the Union of Postal Workers (UPW)[43]. The extracts are from three letters to the journal from intercept staff at the Sandridge Y station:

> [Letter 1] My personal opinion is that we are not kept sufficiently informed about the character of our work. It is obviously boring to sit on a quiet frequency for hours, but if we could be told in confidence a little more about the chaps we are intercepting and the class of work we are dealing with it would go a long way. [Letter signed 'Doc']
>
> [Letter 2 – 'reply to Doc'] He has ... only touched upon the problem ... as well as being kept in the dark about the work ... there is no incentive for that very necessary accessory – initiative. [Signature illegible]
>
> [Letter 3 – 'reply to Doc'] I ... agree ... what about allowing us to see what a few messages look like after they have been decoded? ... how about the staff being allowed to nominate 3 or 4 of their number to visit the holy of holies, 'BP'. What a thrill we would get out of hearing about, and perhaps even seeing, those mysterious figures, Mr Welchman, Mr de Grey, Mr Shiner, etc., and dear old 'Hut 5' ... if we could obtain ... just a little information about what goes on above our heads, I feel sure it would do much to stimulate that interest which is now so sadly lacking. [Letter signed 'Veteran Temp']

These extracts are interesting at several levels – the openness of communication and the fact that the operators knew the names of senior people at BP and that the messages were being successfully decoded (which was by no means generally the case amongst intercept staff).

Nevertheless, they evince discontent of the sort and for the reasons I have indicated[44].

A more insidious expression of discontent is indicated by something I have never seen any reference to in published work about BP: the circulation of a small number of anonymous letters, causing Travis to write, on 4 September 1942, a sharp rebuke to be read by all members of staff:

> I have recently received some half dozen anonymous letters ... and I wish to say immediately that I regard anonymous letter writing as despicable and futile. People who resort to this method of airing a grievance or complaining of their fellow workers are indulging in the lowest form of meanness ... I had hoped that Bletchley Park might have been free from the particular form of grubby inanity ... Anonymous letters will be placed where they belong – in the waste paper bin[45].

Whilst it is clear that these cases were rare – and what they referred to is not known – they do give a further indication that the received image of BP as a place of uniformly good spirit needs some modification. Similarly, whilst the overwhelming majority of published reminiscences speak of BP as a place of happiness and even exhilaration, for others this was not so. Hill (2004) usefully brings together a range of (anonymous) testimonies, ranging from

> What a tremendous privilege to have spent one's youth at BP – locked into this community with its extraordinary concentration of intellectual and artistic ability.   *(quoted in Hill, 2004: 136)*

to

> Nissen Huts, beastly concrete paths, ablutions with rows of lavatories and basins set side by side in a drafty concrete hut ... I loathed Bletchley.   *(quoted in Hill, 2004: 136)*

Or, to take some other examples, for Gwen Watkins

> the BP years had been an extraordinary time. We had come to BP as young, inexperienced, unfledged people and had grown up in that unbelievable atmosphere where brilliant conversation and contact with people we could never have hoped to meet in any other place had been daily occurrences. *(Watkins, 2006: 172)*

whereas Carmen Blacker says

> [I] was utterly bored with the work [and recall the] ... relief and jubilation with which I gave up my pass at the gate and for the last time walked out. *(Blacker, 1993: 304–5)*

Of course, this range of views is hardly surprising, given the many thousands of people who worked at BP and the range of work that they did. However, on the latter point, it should not be thought that the issue of boredom was confined to those undertaking the unglamorous 'minnow' roles. When the cryptanalyst Roy was told during his recruitment that the work would be 'terribly boring with occasional excitement' it was the truth. Morris (1993: 243) notes that, outside the ranks of the Turing-type geniuses, cryptanalysts' main skills were 'patience, accuracy, stamina'. Their work was 'a treadmill of routine' (Hill, 2004: 43), 'humdrum ... meticulous and often infinitely boring' (Lewin, 2008: 53), 'frustrating drudgery' (Wilkinson, 1993: 64) and 'tedious' (McKay, 2010: 70). Certainly there were moments of drama, as noted by Stuart Milner-Barry in the introduction to his internal history of Hut 6:

> I can remember most vividly the roars of excitement, the standing on chairs and the waving of order papers, which greeted the first breaking of Red [Enigma key] by hand in the middle of the battle of France. It was never surpassed, and equalled only I think by the first breaking of Brown [Enigma key] later on in the war[46].

But, as this quotation makes clear, such moments were exceptional, and memorable as a result. It really is crucial in understanding the work of BP to understand that the dominant image of it that we now have is, not entirely, but largely, wrong. Whilst I have stressed that generalizations are difficult, as a generalization the work at BP was not glamorous, it was not inspiring and, whilst underpinned by genius, did not in the main require genius even in its cryptanalytic sections. Making BP work required an intensive, and not always successful, managerial effort in the face of work which was frequently mundane, physically and mentally tiring, and sometimes appeared, to those who did not know its true purpose, to be almost meaningless.

FORMAL CO-ORDINATIVE MECHANISMS

The third and final aspect of how the work of BP was held together that I will explore is that of the various more formally constituted mechanisms which facilitated this. In a generic sense, these mechanisms might often take the form of meetings, bringing together people from different parts of 'the honeycomb', and of course such meetings took such a wide variety of forms that it would be impossible – and pointless – to enumerate them. But to this I would add the general point that there was some bias against large numbers of formally constituted meetings. This is explicit in the introduction to the internal history of Hut 6, where Stuart Milner-Barry wrote

> It [Hut 6] was . . . a very loose and informal organization with only an
> indispensible minimum of formal routine meetings. I left heads of
> departments with a very free hand in their own department . . . they
> did the same by their head of sub-sections, and heads of subsections
> by their head of shift. Each department would have its own
> meetings . . . whenever it felt like it. When major changes
> threatened, we would all get together at all levels, but avoiding as far
> as possible the monster general gatherings at which it is almost
> impossible to get anything done[47].

Consistently with this, Daphne, the interviewee who worked as an office junior in the Directorate, recalls that the senior figures at BP for whom she worked, such as Travis and de Grey, habitually spent most of their working time at their desks writing, rather than in meetings,

and indeed Birch's internal history records that Travis was 'not personally fond of meetings'[48]. One point to note about this is that it reflects
the range of management approaches in use at BP, since it is a sharp
contrast to Milner-Barry's practice of 'management by walking about',
although it is consistent with his precept of keeping formal meetings to
a minimum. However, this disavowal of meetings was not as straight-
forward as it appears. Another interviewee, Roy of the Air Section,
confirmed the general point in saying that 'meetings were not part of
the regular procedures, we didn't feel the need for it', but then continues 'we were constantly seeing each other all day, this avoided wasting
time'. In this sense, one might characterize the situation as one of
continuous meeting rather than *episodic 'meetings'*, such that the
fact of meetings taking place became invisible.

Indeed, one of the major working practices at BP was the 'watch
table', described in the case of Hut 3 thus:

> At [Hut 3's] centre was the Watch Room – in the middle a circular
> or horseshoe shaped table, to one side a rectangular table. On the
> outer rim of the circular table sat the Watch, some half-dozen people.
> The man in charge, the head of the Watch or Number 1, sat in an
> obvious directing position at the top of the table. The watchkeepers
> were a mixture of civilians, and serving officers, Army and RAF ...
> At the rectangular table sat serving officers, Army and RAF, one or
> two of each. These were the Advisers.   *(Millward, 1993: 20)*

This quotation gives a sense that what was actually occurring – on a
24-hour-shift basis – was a continuous meeting; not, to be sure, of the
sort with an agenda and minutes, but nevertheless a constant interchange between different specialisms (in this case it would be those of
emendation, translation, evaluation, commenting and signal draft-
ing[49]) and different agencies (in this case FO, Army and RAF).

Examples such as this are part of the detailed fabric of the work
of BP and may also be considered to be cases of knowledge-sharing,
something I will consider further in the next chapter. For now, I
want to draw attention to other examples of more formally

constituted co-ordinative mechanisms which spanned the broad range of BP's activities. It should already be clear that the scale and scope of these activities was vast, and no one could have a clear grasp of them all. The Directorate received daily reports from the heads of huts and sections (Lewin, 2008: 111) but, as BP grew, this in itself generated a mass of information, giving rise to two problems. One was internal co-ordination. The other was the broader and highly politicized issue of the range of different agencies, especially in Whitehall, with an interest in BP and its intelligence product.

Insofar as internal co-ordination is concerned, it is possible to discern two key types of issue. One was to do with the establishment of what were known to be necessary forms of interaction between different sections. Clearly there are numerous examples which could be provided, given the scale of operations at BP. The bombe-allocation group liaising between Huts 6 and 8 would be one example. To take another, I have referred elsewhere to the close relationship between Huts 3 and 6 (and the same would be true for the Naval dyad of Huts 4 and 8). Thus, one of the main tasks of the 'Duty Officer' in Hut 6 was to liaise with Hut 3 as to all matters of common administration and the communication of priorities between the two huts, including dealing with *ad hoc* or emergency issues as they arose and in advance of the establishment of settled routine agreements, which could be made a later date[50]. Whilst, literally, a mundane activity, the establishment of such routinized forms of liaison was especially necessary given the compartmentalization of work at BP. I will refer to other examples in the discussion of knowledge-sharing, but they are all based upon the pre-defined expectation that co-ordination is necessary.

However, a second type of issue was how to deal with situations in which it was *not* known in advance what co-ordination would be necessary. This was addressed by, amongst other things, the creation of the Cryptographic Co-ordination and Records (CCR) function under Professor Eric Vincent in November 1942[51]. The CCR created on a weekly basis a synopsis of all cryptanalytic work across different huts and sections and across the full range of codes and ciphers being tackled, whether successfully or not. To this end Vincent compiled an ongoing index derived from reports from the sections[52]. Prior to this, something similar had been attempted when, from July 1941, a record of ciphers tackled and/or solved was placed on record with the Research Section[53]. The weakness of this system was, apparently, that these reports were not summarised and became simply a huge archive of indigestible material. By contrast, the CCR mechanism seems to have functioned unproblematically – there is no evidence in the archive material of any complaint about it – and is described by Lewin (2008: 137) as largely resolving the reporting issues of the earlier period. Nevertheless, it bears saying that the application of the new system was varied. Edward Simpson, who from September 1943 headed the party working on JN-25, a Japanese Naval cipher, recalls[54] that he was not required to submit a report to the CCR and indeed was unaware at the time of its existence. Thus, this mechanism may have been less systematic than intended.

Of course, co-ordination of cryptanalytic developments was not the only cross-BP mechanism, and of the numerous examples that could be given perhaps the most important would include the W/T Co-ordination section, established under Lieutenant-Colonel H. B. Sayer in August 1942[55], the Machine Co-ordination Development Section, set up under Gordon Welchman in September 1943[56], and the committee to co-ordinate captured documents and reference books established in June 1942[57]. All of these, like CCR, may be seen as vehicles for technical co-ordination. At the same time there was an ongoing co-ordination of administration. Throughout the war a formal weekly administrative report was made by Commander Bradshaw, covering mainly staff and buildings issues. Other administrative co-ordination groupings included, at various times, the Joint Management Committee and Joint Committee of Control (these relating to the period when BP was jointly administered by SIS and GC & CS), a Communications Committee to manage the growth in telecommunications, a Buildings and Works Committee to oversee the physical fabric of the site, a Mess Committee concerned with the provision of food and the Women's Welfare Committee.

The cases mentioned here are of the establishment of permanent bodies or mechanisms operating across particular work sections – in other words, I am excluding the even larger number of more or less transient working groups set up to co-ordinate various kinds of activities at various times. One important example may serve to illustrate this. In January 1944 the German Air Force briefly introduced a modification to some Enigma machines, known in German as *Umkehrwalze* D (UKD) and referred to at BP as Uncle Dick[58]. This dramatically increased Enigma security and, had it been widely adopted, would have severely compromised the ability of BP to read Enigma ciphers. In fact, it was used only sporadically, from August 1944 (Erskine, 2001a). Nevertheless, the potential danger it posed led to the formation of the Uncle Dick Committee, chaired by Hugh Alexander. This met for the first time in April 1944, initially two or three times a week but less frequently thereafter, as the nature of the problem was understood and the danger receded, with its final meeting being in April 1945 (Marks, 2001: 123). This example is given for three reasons. Firstly, it serves as a reminder that the work at BP was subject to innumerable threats and interruptions – it is not the case, as some accounts imply, that 'Enigma' was broken and thereafter a smooth flow of decryption followed. On the contrary, the multiple variations of Enigma and the periodic developments of these made for continuing challenges. In the case of UKD, according to Milner-Barry, this led to a 'dread' which was 'one of the major preoccupations of the year [1944]'[59]. Secondly, it is illustrative of the way that co-ordinative activity within BP was a mixture of established, 'standing' arrangements and highly flexible and problem-based activity. Moreover, as the Uncle Dick Committee shows, this could be both responsive to events, such as the initial adoption of UKD, and anticipatory of events, such as how to deal with its widespread adoption were this to happen. Thirdly, whilst UKD was essentially a Hut 6 problem, the fact that the Uncle Dick Committee was chaired by the Head of Hut 8[60] shows a more formalized version of the way that Huts 6 and 8 co-operated, by contrast with the example of bombe allocation given earlier.

Turning now to issues relating to the wider external co-ordination of BP activities, these were considerably more contentious. I have already referred, in Part I, to the conflicts over control of intercept resources and the many shifting arrangements and conflicts over this at governmental level. Here the key co-ordinating entity was the Y Board and its associated committee structure. However, what was ultimately of central interest to the various ministries and services was the intelligence product of BP. Here, a wide variety of different reporting mechanisms were in operation, for example from Naval Section to the Admiralty, Air Section to the Air Ministry and Military Wing to the War Office. But this potentially meant that intelligence of interest to one ministry but routed to another would be lost. Thus, as early as May 1940[61] an Inter-Service Distribution and Reference section (D & R) was proposed, and shortly afterwards established, not as an alternative to the other distribution routes but as a 'side channel'[62] to these, so that 'any information acquired by one section or service at GC & CS will be scrutinised by an Intelligence Officer of each service, so that nothing of value may fail to be distributed to an interested quarter'[63].

These arrangements were not an unqualified success. According to Birch's internal history of sigint, this was because of a lack of shared understanding on the part of the different services as to the nature of this form of intelligence. This needs to be set in the context of the still fragile sense of BP as a sigint organization and the internal history of sigint implies, without giving details, that the D & R became an arena for this ongoing conflict[64]. In the official history, the D & R is represented as being part and parcel of the settlement of relations between GC & CS and the services, during the Y Board review of Spring 1941 (Hinsley et al., 1979: 270), although that does not tally with the fact that it had already existed for some months. At all events, from July 1941 the D & R was transformed into the Intelligence Exchange (IE) with very much the same functions[65]. By this date BP's legitimacy as a sigint organization was more assured (by virtue of the review), and an attempt by the Director of Naval Intelligence (DNI) to put in his own officer reporting to the NID was resisted. This, according to the internal history, marked 'the last of DNI's experiments aimed at safeguarding Admiralty interests at GC & CS'[66].

The IE was not universally popular. Frank Birch, Head of Naval Section, made (at the time, rather than in his later historical capacity) a series of detailed criticisms of it in the discussions through which it evolved from the D & R section[67]. Roy, the interviewee from the Air Section, was scathing:

> I thought it was totally useless. It did produce statistics but how that helped the war effort [I don't know] ... an attempt by the management to get a bit of control ... we had to send a copy of everything we produced [but] we knew who our customers were and didn't really need any help.

There are at least two interpretations of this jaundiced view, though. One is that Roy was at the time simply too junior to appreciate what purpose the IE might be serving. Against this, although it is a negative kind of evidence, I have found no reference in any of the documents or published writings on BP to any specific intelligence gain deriving from the IE. If this is so, then a second interpretation is that the IE is best understood as a political fix to deal with the concerns of, in particular, ministries deriving from the way that BP developed as an intelligence organization as outlined in Chapter 2. Meeting these concerns through assuring intelligence 'customers' that they were not losing out to other services was, perhaps, the real significance of the IE, and is consistent with the official history's account of the D & R.

What were certainly highly significant as channels for the distribution of intelligence were the Special Liaison Units (SLUs)[68]. These were one of the key organizational innovations relating to BP, and largely the responsibility of Group Captain Frederick Winterbotham, the man who, thirty years later, first brought the secrets of BP to a public audience. In essence an SLU was a small unit operating in extreme secrecy receiving Ultra and passing it to end-users. Fixed SLUs were maintained within the Admiralty, War Office, Air Ministry and RAF Fighter Command, and were fed by teleprinter. Mobile SLUs were located within the field headquarters of a military theatre and received Ultra intelligence as an enciphered radio transmission from Britain and distributed it without reference to its provenance as sigint. These mobile SLUs were not subordinate to the field commanders in the theatre of their deployment, and indeed could override these commanders if necessary to protect the security of Ultra (Ratcliff, 2006: 122). Established first in 1940, by the end of the war this was a global network of secure intelligence distribution of a sort which had never existed before. The SLU organization would be worth a book in its own right, for it was a formidable and highly complex feat (see Lewin, 2008: 138–54 for an excellent account). It should also be noted that mobile SLUs were relevant only to army and air force units. Naval units were serviced via the Admiralty by means of the Navy's W/T network (Beesly, 2000: 13). Details aside, for present purposes the point to note is, again, that the development of BP as a sigint organization entailed the development and control of a co-ordinative apparatus which extended well beyond BP itself, or even London-based government departments.

At the other end of this process, a corresponding co-ordination was needed in order to transfer intercepts to BP from the Y stations located around Britain and the world. This was achieved in two ways. Firstly, as with the fixed SLUs, it was brought about by means of the teleprinter network using telephone lines, of which by the end of the war many thousands ran into and out of BP. Whilst, at least following some early problems, it was secure and in principle fast, this method suffered from capacity constraints. Thus, the second means of intercept transfer, within Britain, was by a large team of motorbike dispatch riders – a very hard job undertaken around the clock in all weathers, from often very remote locations and in blackout conditions – work which, as Welchman (1982: 91) noted, has rarely received the recognition it deserves, something which is still true today. Indeed, there was an (unknown) number of deaths amongst the riders as a result of the difficult conditions under which they operated.

CONCLUSION
This chapter has provided an outline account of a wide assortment of ways in which the work of BP was performed – how a complex and diverse 'honeycomb' of an apparently 'anarchic' sort was co-ordinated. Clearly these ways were very varied in character, encompassing informal arrangements bred of personal friendship networks, a variety of formal and informal management styles ranging from those of the university common room to those of the mass-production factory, continuous meetings embedded in standard practices, explicitly co-ordinative procedures and institutions, transport and distribution networks and so on. Whilst varied, I do not mean to imply that the three types of co-ordination considered here proceeded in isolation from each other or were entirely unrelated. To take some examples from what has already been said, the kind of personal networks which could facilitate trust and communication can be seen as related to the deployment of a collegial style of management. This extended beyond the personal networks to inform, for instance, the more humane approach to low-skill work in the Hut 6 Registration Rooms. Similarly, it is easy to envisage how the 'continuous' meeting of the Hut 3 Watch Room, whether or not it was based upon pre-existing informal relations, would be likely to engender such relations. Or, again, the informal brokering of agreements between Hut 6 and Hut 8 over bombe allocation sits alongside the more formal Uncle Dick Committee dealing with a Hut 6 problem under the chairmanship of the head of Hut 8. Nevertheless, it does seem possible to differentiate (as is commonplace in organization theory) between more and less formal mechanisms of co-ordination and more or less directive and consultative modes of management.

My contention is that this is the very 'stuff' of organization: the practices and processes of 'organizing' that hold together diverse activities, melding them into an entity that can be called 'an organization'.

As I have stated at other points in this book, the details of this are specific to the BP case – although many are recognizable in other cases – but capturing the complexity and richness of the organizing process can only be achieved by precisely an engagement with such details.

In addition to explaining at least some key aspects of how this work of organizing – or the organizing of work – operated, I hope that I have also, as it were incidentally, captured both here and in the previous chapters something of the range of types of work undertaken at BP. Examples that have been referred to encompass cryptanalysis, translation and intelligence work, interception, Typex, Hollerith and bombe operating, dispatch riding and many others, down to a brief mention of BP's barbers! I have also shown that, for many, work at BP was arduous and stressful, and that, for some, it was demoralizing and even debilitating to health. In this and in describing the range of co-ordinative methods I hope that I have at least put to rest the image of BP as a kind of country club where a group of eccentric academic boffins lived a genteel life of elaborate crossword-solving. But if that is so, then what image or images should be substituted for it? What 'kind' of organization was this? This is the question I will address in the next chapter.

NOTES

1. Welchman was especially active in recruiting from his contacts at Cambridge and elsewhere, explicitly on the basis of friendship with those of the requisite skill (Welchman, 1982: 84–5).

2. At Cambridge, a Proctor is a University office filled by an academic nominated from the Colleges to serve a period of office, with duties including discipline. Bulldogs served as constables to Proctors, enforcing discipline which, during the period in question, was considerably more stringent than is the case nowadays.

3. A rather different kind of personalization occurred in the case of the interviewee Joyce. In 1942 she was a languages student at Girton College, Cambridge and was considering volunteering for the WRNS when she received an anonymous note in her pigeonhole suggesting that she should

join the ATS. She did, and was then called for an interview in London leading to appointment to Hut 3, where she found that staff already 'knew things about her' she had not told them. This was clearly a personalized targeting even though the actual approach was indirect.

4. An English Public (i.e. private) School. The reference to Sidney Sussex College is significant because this was Welchman's college and he, as noted above, was pivotal in early recruitment to BP.

5. It is, of course, debatable whether it is an entirely reliable basis. This 'old boy network' mode of recruitment allowed some spectacular security breaches to occur in the Cold War era, as in the famous cases of Kim Philby, Guy Burgess, Donald Maclean and Antony Blunt (Boyle, 1979). See also Andrew (1985b). On the other hand, one might say that it is remarkable how rare such cases were and, in this sense, that the 'old boy' method was fairly effective as regards trustworthiness.

6. Roy said of the then-unknown men who interviewed him 'they seemed like the real thing, these people didn't say who they were but the way they spoke, the sort of people they looked like [was convincing]'.

7. TNA HW 14/145: 4.

8. CCAC DENN 1/4: 5.

9. Sometimes things went awry. Geoffrey Tandy was recruited for his supposed knowledge of cryptograms. It turned out that his speciality was in fact 'cryptogams: mosses, ferns, and so on' (Alford, 1993: 68).

10. It is relevant to note that the character Roy (Calvert) in this passage was based upon Snow's friend Charles Allberry, an oriental linguist who, like Snow, was a Fellow of Christ's College, Cambridge, and that Allberry himself worked at BP for a period before, like Roy Calvert, volunteering for the RAF and being killed in a bombing raid on Germany. Francis Getliffe in this passage is based upon Cambridge physicist Philip Bowden. Elsewhere in his novels Snow fictionalizes, as Thomas Bevill, his real-life boss Maurice Hankey, who played a significant role in the Whitehall conflicts over control of BP and Y operations (see Chapter 1). Another character in the novels, George Passant, is based upon Snow's school teacher and mentor Bert Howard. Howard, on Snow's initiative, was also recruited to BP; in the novels Eliot recruits Passant for work in Whitehall. C. P. Snow himself is fictionalized as Lewis Eliot. Information on the figures behind Snow's characters is from (Philip) Snow (1982: 184–7) and, as regards Bert Howard's recruitment to BP, Wilkinson (1986: 120).

11. Lewin (2008: 57) gives the date as 1940, but the passage he quotes from Snow is ambiguous on this point and Welchman (1982: 86) gives 1941. The latter is more plausible because it coincides with the relative decline, although not end, of the very informal method (referred to by Welchman as 'piracy'). The development of more formal recruitment in the latter half of the war should stand as a corrective to the implication, at least, in Jeffery's magisterial history of SIS (2010: 745) that GC & CS recruitment was characterized solely by the informal, personal network method – this was primarily true only in the early stages of the war. For a recollection of being interviewed by Snow for employment at BP, see Briggs (2011: 59).

12. It does not, of course, necessarily guarantee competence. The internal history of Hut 3 records that 'haphazard methods of recruiting [meant that not] a large enough proportion of the men were of the desirable standard'. TNA HW 3/119: 45.

13. TNA HW 3/119: 4.

14. TNA HW 43/70: 8.

15. TNA HW 43/70: 9.

16. TNA HW 25/1: 38.

17. Indeed, Milner-Barry (1993: 96) implies as much. This does not, of course, mean that the agreements reached were based simply on 'good fellowship' – it was also a matter of Milner-Barry's recognition of the key importance of Naval Enigma to the battle of the Atlantic. But my point is that friendly relations enabled such 'disinterested' decision making rather than the turf wars which might otherwise have occurred.

18. Only Golombek of those mentioned in these paragraphs breaks the pattern of Cambridge connections, since he studied at King's College London (although he left before graduating), but, as noted, was associated through chess with Alexander and Milner-Barry. Wylie was an Oxford graduate but became a Fellow of Trinity Hall, Cambridge in 1938.

19. And not an uncontroversial one (see Welchman, 1982: 181–2). Roy interviewed for this study complained that, as someone working on non-Enigma low-grade GAF codes, he was rarely able to get sufficient Hollerith access because, according to him, Welchman, in his role of AD (Mechanical Devices), instructed Freeborn – with whom Roy had good relations – to prioritize Enigma.

20. Not only Simpson's level. Someone as senior as Gordon Welchman (1982) invariably refers to Freeborn as 'Mr Freeborn'. His first name was in fact Frederick (Smith, 1998: 87).

21. TNA HW 43/70: 24.

22. As noted elsewhere, Typex machines were one of the British cipher machines, themselves based upon pre-war commercial Enigma machines, and like them lacked a plugboard (see the introductory chapter for explanation of the significance of the plugboard). Thus the Typex Room was sending encoded messages from BP.

23. That is, they were civilian conscripts under Ministry of Labour directives.

24. TNA HW 14/145: 29.

25. TNA HW 14/ 154.

26. TNA HW 14/74. Time sheets were 'unpopular' with bombe operators, partly because although 'not intended to be a check on individual operators . . . naturally this was felt to be the case and they were received with misgivings'; they became 'the bugbear of the section', TNA HW 3/164.

27. These rooms sorted and registered every signal dealt with, including technical information about its source and nature, a key part of the sigint process but a very dull and mundane one when performed, as at BP, manually.

28. TNA HW 43/70: 25.

29. TNA HW 2/40. This idea of 'humane' management being justified instrumentally rather than ethically is central to the analysis – and critique – of 'Theory Y' (Roberts, 1984).

30. TNA HW 25/1: 93.

31. TNA HW3/119: 5, emphasis in original.

32. TNA HW 43/70: 25, emphasis added.

33. Compare this with my point in the previous chapter about the importance of billets to the experience at BP.

34. TNA HW 43/70: 23.

35. TNA HW 25/1: 91–2. See also Wilkinson's (1986: 16) comment on Alexander's management of morale.

36. It goes without saying that there are many different effective management styles and, as Roy said in his interview, Jones would have been poor in Cooper's role, as Cooper would have been in Jones'. The examples I have quoted here are of well-attested cases of 'good' management and there are

other, less well-known, cases such as Herbert Marchant, Deputy Head of Hut 3 (as mentioned in passing in Chapter 2), and Harold Fletcher, who, amongst other things, made a key contribution to the administration of the bombe operation as well as being Staff Officer for Hut 6. Denniston, as noted elsewhere, has been judged as lacking in management skills; unfairly, I think, as I suggested. Travis is usually seen as more effective. Of other senior people, both Bradshaw and de Grey have the reputation, deserved in my view, of being highly able managers. Alan Turing is universally described (e.g. McKay, 2010: 191) as having been unsuited to management during his period as head of Hut 8 before that role was taken by Hugh Alexander, himself apparently a highly able manager.

37. To give an extreme example, at the Chatham listening station candles in bottles were used in the early days of the war, TNA HW 14/145: 16. At BP itself, Ralph Bennett's obituary records that 'the fastidious young Cambridge don was not overly impressed by the ramshackle wooden building [i.e. Hut 3], with its nauseating fumes from leaky coke-burning stoves during the blackout' (*Daily Telegraph*, London, 23 August 2002).

38. For example, in relation to listening stations, Taunt (1993: 102) recognizes 'the tedium of receiving unintelligible messages whose importance they could only infer from our interest in them'.

39. Millward (1993: 23) states that the shift patterns were those 'allegedly recommended by the medical authorities . . . to avoid painful changes to the circadian rhythm'. He goes on to speculate that the insomnia he suffered from in later life was caused by his years of shift work at BP.

40. TNA HW 14/145: 7. In Robert Harris's (1995) BP novel *Enigma*, the hero, cryptanalyst Tom Jericho, is depicted at the beginning of the book as suffering from a nervous breakdown caused by overwork.

41. From December 1942. Prior to that date other names had been used, including HMS Pembroke III (Page, 2002: x and 5).

42. For example, 'one young man received a scathing letter from his old headmaster accusing him of being a disgrace to his school' (Welchman, 1982: 86). Speculatively, this is why BP developed so vibrant a social life in terms of concerts and clubs – amongst their own such aspersions could be avoided. I am grateful to Glenn Morgan for this suggestion.

43. TNA HW 14/19. It will be recalled that GPO staff were unionized.

44. It is worth noting in view of these expressions of discontent that in the analysis of Y station intercept results (TNA HW 14/154) referred to earlier,

in January 1944 this one, Sandridge, had an intercept rate of 35 per cent, the lowest of the five stations compared (the others, Whitchurch, Hawklaw, Brora and Denmark Hill achieved 49 per cent, 64 per cent, 59 per cent and 53 per cent, respectively). Following a complete reorganization of the station, by December 1944 the rate had gone up to 71 per cent, putting it second in the list of (now) six stations. But the report notes that 'it is still necessary for us to keep a very tight control and to check the frequent retrogressions in their early stages'. The language here is indicative of the management style in use.

45. TWA HW 14/139: Serial Order 48.
46. TNA HW 43/70: 4.
47. TNA HW 43/70: 24.
48. TNA 43/2: 465.
49. Hut 3 received from Hut 6 decrypts of signals, in German and still arranged into five-letter groups rather than into words. Emendation means the process of re-dividing the decrypt into words and trying to fill corrupt gaps (i.e. missing letters caused by incomplete or inaccurate interception). This rendered a text that could then be translated into English, evaluated for its significance, and commented on for its meaning in relation to, for example, other intelligence held. Finally, a signal was drafted to be sent to the ultimate user of the intelligence, normally via an SLU. Of these processes, the first two were performed by the Watch, the latter three by the Advisers. This explanation is a condensed summary of that given by Millward (1993: 20–3).
50. This account of the Duty Officer's work is based on an uncatalogued document written by Hut 6 Head Stuart Milner-Barry entitled 'Hut 6 Organization', dated 14 October 1943. I am grateful to Ralph Erskine for supplying me with this document. The Hut 6 Duty Officer's role appears to have been quite different from that of the Hut 3 Duty Officer (for which see Bennett, 1993).
51. TNA HW 14/59.
52. TNA HW 14/60.
53. TNA HW 14/17.
54. Personal conversation with Dr Edward Simpson.
55. TNA HW 14/48.
56. TNA HW 14/87.
57. TNA HW 14/41.

58. The *Umkehrwalze* was the reflector, or reversing wheel, on Enigma machines, a part of the mechanism for the scrambling of electrical current within the device. The standard reflector was *Umkehrwalze* B (UKB). The significance of UKD was that it was rewirable in the field and multiplied the number of possible settings. On one estimate made at BP at the time, if the standard machine had 150 million million million possible solutions for a message then UKD *multiplied* this figure by 150 million million (TNA HW 14/108). See Marks (2001) for a full technical account.

59. TNA 43/70: 14–15.

60. According to Stuart Milner-Barry, 'it was one of his [Hugh Alexander's] greatest services to Hut 6' (TNA HW 43/70: 14). *Umkehrwalze* D might, of course, have become a Hut 8 problem had its use spread to Naval Enigma, as was technically possible (Marks, 2001: 106–7).

61. TNA HW 14/5.

62. TNA WO 208/5069: 10a.

63. TNA WO 208/5069: 11a.

64. TNA HW 43/1: 194–9.

65. TNA HW 3/158.

66. TNA HW 43/1: 198.

67. Memorandum dated 15 June 1941. Catalogue number unknown – a hard copy is available on request from the author of this book.

68. Initially called Special Signals Units, a term abandoned because its abbreviation – SSU – suggested 'secret service', which might have compromised security. The term Special Communications Unit (SCU) was sometimes used to designate the communication functions of SLUs, with SLU as a generic umbrella for the two (see Lewin, 2008: 143; Ratcliff, 2006: 119). Hinsley and Stripp's (1993: xix–xx) glossary suggests a rather more precise distinction in that SCUs were primarily staffed by the army and used hand-speed Morse to transmit signals, whilst SLUs were primarily staffed by the RAF and used one-time pads and Typex to transmit signals.

6 Understanding Bletchley Park's Work

INTRODUCTION

In this chapter I will continue to examine how BP worked, but now with reference to a more evaluative set of concerns. That is to say, rather than simply exploring ways of working as in the previous chapter, I will seek to make sense of these in terms of a variety of ideas and concepts in organization studies. Both in academic writing and in everyday life organizations tend to be thought of and described in terms of categories, types or 'kinds' of organization. At its most basic, this might mean the distinction between bureaucratic and other (pre- or post-bureaucratic) types of organization. In a more developed way, this distinction gives rise to further categories such as Mintzberg's (1979) famous five-way classification of simple structures, machine bureaucracies, professional bureaucracies, divisional forms and adhoc-racies. In recent years, an array of somewhat related organizational types has been proposed under the generic label of 'post-bureaucracy' (Heckscher, 1994). These are variously described as, for example, network (Nohria and Eccles, 1992), knowledge-intensive (Alvesson, 2004) or even postmodern (Bergquist, 1993) organizations. Whilst each of these terms may carry somewhat different meanings, they form a kind of cluster of alternatives to the various forms of bureaucracy.

Another set of distinctions and categories is provided in the literature specifically concerned with 'organizational design'. Here categories such as vertical differentiation (extent of hierarchy), horizontal differentiation (extent of sub-divisionalization), spatial differentiation (geographical spread) and centralization of power and authority are amongst the most widely used (Robbins, 1990: 80–115). On this basis organizations may be categorized according to the extent to which they demonstrate these attributes. This, of course, links to the more generic typology of organizational forms in that, for example, bureaucracies are classically extensive with respect to vertical and horizontal differentiation.

It is not my intention mechanically to compare BP with each and every type or model of organization that has been proposed in the literature, which would be both wearying and sterile. Instead, I want in a more free-flowing way to explore how the 'ways of working' at BP relate to 'ways of organizing', taking as the central point of departure what remains the touchstone for organization studies: the standardization of work associated with formal bureaucracy. Following this, I will explore two particularly salient aspects of organizing work. The first is knowledge work, which suggests itself as a category because in a very obvious way the core product of BP was knowledge, specifically intelligence. It also serves as one label under which to consider issues of 'post-bureaucracy'. The second exploration is of the centralization of work, and the reasons for this may be less obvious. One is that in the only other significant academic analysis of BP's organization this is suggested as its most significant feature (Ratcliff, 2006) and so it makes sense to build upon this analysis here. The other reason is that it is in part because of centralization that such a variety of ways of working was in evidence at BP.

For it is variety that I want to stress here; the mixed modes of organizing on display. As I emphasised in the previous chapter, any image of BP as a kind of cosy university common room is misleading. But so too are the categories of organizational forms found in organization studies by encoding the messiness of organizational life under the rubric of typologies. One response to this might be to posit a 'hybrid' organization, combining different types within it, so that some parts can be characterized as, say, machine bureaucracies and others as, say, adhocracies. However, I intend to suggest something rather different, which is more about the 'twisting together' of different ways of organizing work. This distinction is subtle but significant. Hybridity leaves in place the basic typologies and simply has them operating side by side without challenging them as coherent entities. The metaphor of twisting together is intended to suggest the irredeemable interconnectedness of ways of organizing work so as to call into question their status as coherent entities.

STANDARDIZED WORK

It will be clear from what has already been said that there were many bureaucratic processes in operation at BP in the specific Weberian sense of standardized formal operating procedures based upon the application of rules. These were most evident in relation to the more factory-like operations at BP, such as the bombe rooms, the Typex room and, away from BP, the Y stations. This is clearly related to the discussion in the previous chapter of morale because, by definition, rule-based bureaucracies minimize discretion, which in turn is likely to be sapping of morale. Perhaps the dominant metaphor used in discussions of bureaucratic standardization is that it treats individuals as 'cogs in the machine'. In that respect BP was a place of contrasts. Hut 6 Head Stuart Milner-Barry, as quoted in the previous chapter, sought 'to make everybody feel participants and not cogs in an unintelligible machine'[1]. By contrast, a BP veteran who wrote with information for this study said of her highly skilled work as a translator that 'our boss ... never lost an opportunity of reminding us we were very small cogs in a very big wheel if anyone showed the slightest initiative'[2]. The importance of hierarchy and 'knowing your place' is also evident in a different, and amusing, way in the case of a young naval lieutenant who wrote an intelligence report which was critical of Admiral Dönitz, the Commander in Chief of the German Navy: 'he was told that it was most improper for a lieutenant to criticize an admiral in any way whatsoever' (Morris, 1993: 243).

Within this mixed picture, it will not serve simply to identify particular sections as having bureaucratic characteristics: the situation was considerably more complex. For example, the Hollerith-machine room, which, as previously mentioned, played a crucial role in handling and manipulating large quantities of data using a punch-card system, is in one way an exemplar of bureaucratic working. It was also an example of a case where factory-style discipline was in evidence, with, for example, records of individual efficiency of workers being posted on the walls of the machine room. Standardization in some cases, such as the processing of material for the Italian Hagelin C-38m cipher, was of an extreme sort:

> we found it necessary to lay down chalk lines on the machine room floor to ensure correct sequence movement of boxes of cards to the various machines involved[3].

This task – the creation of the Hagelin Catalogue – was a regular monthly event, and many Hollerith jobs were similarly regular, repeated events. Yet in other cases jobs were of a one-off sort and not therefore amenable to standard operating procedures. Thus, rather than envisaging the Hollerith section as bureaucratic, it is better to see it as a twisting together of bureaucratic and non-bureaucratic modes of organizing and associated ways of working.

This may be illustrated by consideration of another of the central work activities at BP, that of indexing. Indexing was crucial because it enabled the vast number of decrypted signals to be stored and cross-referenced, which in turn was the basis of deriving useable intelligence. Other indexes were concerned with listings of numerous abbreviations and specialist or technical terms. Still others related to traffic analysis, in other words indexes of messages which, whilst undecrypted, contained valuable information[4]. Brunt (2004) has made a detailed study of indexes at BP and identifies their multiple forms and uses. Just within Hut 3 these included Air, Army, Naval and Railway indexes, with each of these indexes having further sub-indexes. For example, the Air Index had five main sections (Units, Locations, Equipment, Personalities, General) and a further nine minor sections (e.g. Abbreviations, Covernames, Works Numbers of Aircraft). These indexes ran to tens of thousands of cards, and their accurate maintenance and cross-referencing called for considerable precision, yet at the same time

> Owing to the size of the operation, a large amount of *discretion* was inevitably given to indexers ... as a result it was necessary to establish quality-control measures [by means of a] 'Continuity Book', a manual of day-to-day required actions.
>
> *(Brunt, 2004: 296, emphasis added)*

Thus here again can be seen a twisting together of procedural standardization and discretion, of bureaucratic and non-bureaucratic modes of organization. Writing of the Hut 3 Air Index, the Head of the whole Hut 3 Air section noted that 'this work could be exceedingly tedious but it called for constant and thoughtful application' (Calvocoressi, 2001: 79). Something of this 'twisting together' is captured by the model of 'professional bureaucracy' elaborated by Mintzberg (1979), in which a highly skilled 'operating core' works with considerable autonomy whilst being served by a 'support structure' characterized by more standardized bureaucratic work. However, as with notions of organizational hybridity, such a model does not really capture the simultaneity of different modes of work organization. It is not just that there were various 'blocks' at BP corresponding to, say, operating core and support structure but that these 'ways of working' were interwoven so tightly as to make it all but meaningless to separate them out as components of organization.

This sense of interwoven ways of working can be taken right down to a very fine level of detail. For example, Hugh Alexander's internal history of Hut 8 remarks that

> We had quite a large number of printed forms of various kinds all of which justified their existence over and over again. It is almost impossible to have too many forms – any written work however simply done in a standard way is worth a form of its own. The total effect of labour saving devices of this kind was very great[5].

So here, in the hut where Alan Turing, whose memory so dominates received images of BP as a place of eccentric and creative genius, worked, we find a paean to that most mundane and ubiquitous of bureaucratic practices – the standard form.

Now none of this is very surprising. It is consistent with two well-established ideas within organization theory. Firstly, frequent, repeated events are likely to engender standard, formalized systems to handle them. This was the basic insight of the Aston Studies (Pugh and Hickson, 1976). Secondly, notwithstanding the ideal-type of bureaucracy as evacuating all discretion from work by virtue of standard, formalized systems, spaces for discretion persist, and, moreover, their persistence is necessary in order for those systems to operate effectively. This was one of the basic insights of the 'bureaucratic dysfunctionalist' literature of the 1950s (Blau, 1955; Gouldner, 1954). So one point to note is that these classic studies continue to have a purchase and help us to make sense of organizational phenomena.

However, what is also important is to appreciate how the bureaucratic aspects of BP undermine not only the received image of BP but also some of the analyses of its organization. Ratcliff (2006) makes much of how BP 'encouraged everyone from intercept personnel to the top cryptanalysts to collaborate and brainstorm for improvements. Initiative was assumed' (Ratcliff, 2006: 230). But this is a rather partial account[6], understating the ways that bureaucratic ways of organizing were in play, as in the case of the interviewee Dora, who, on being so bold as to send a letter without checking with her boss, was told not to 'overdo the initiative'.

There is, of course, more to bureaucracy than issues of work standardization. Going back to indexing, it is worth recalling that one shorthand definition of bureaucracy is 'domination through files', and the 'bureau' of bureaucracy can refer precisely to filed records or, more accurately, to the interaction of office holders and those records. In a broader sense, the capacity to gather, hold, search and use large quantities of filed knowledge is a central part of what constitutes modernity, something belied by the innocuous term 'information management' (Black and Brunt, 1999: 361). Whilst bound up in a myriad of ways with the development of the state, one particularly strong connection has been that between information management and intelligence operations (Black and Brunt, 1999, 2000; Black,

Muddiman and Plant, 2007). This reflects the fact that the collation and use of information lies at the heart of intelligence work and that the modern state had both the motivation and the means to invest heavily in information management.

Thus, although BP's achievements are normally thought of primarily or even solely in terms of cryptanalysis, its operations as a sigint organization, in the sense established in Chapter 2, are perhaps better thought of in terms of the way that indexes acted as a technology to make intelligible the fruits of cryptanalysis because they enabled sense to be made of the multiple fragments of information contained within individual messages sent over a period of time. Indeed, as the Head of Hut 3's Air section noted, the importance of indexes at BP 'cannot be exaggerated' (Calvocoressi, 2001: 79). In this reliance upon systematically classified knowledge BP can be understood as a form of bureaucratic organization. The fact that the indexes took the form of handwritten cards, often using shoe boxes to contain them, perhaps gives the operation a quaint, 'amateurish' air, but that should not mislead us:

> It was a most effective system. A visiting high-ranking American was nevertheless bemused: 'Goddamn, if this were the Pentagon, there would be rows and rows of shiny filing cabinets with nothing in them and you do it all in Goddamn shoeboxes'. *(Hill, 2004: 43)*

The shoeboxes reflected the general tightness of resources, but of course the use of a paper-based system of any sort reflects the necessities of a pre-computerization era. BP is well known as the place where arguably the first semi-programmable electronic computer – Colossus – was developed (Goldstine, 1993; Copeland, 2001, 2006) and in this sense stands on the cusp of the computer age, but for the most part it used pre-computer technologies. Clearly, an equivalent organization now would use computerized databases to store and retrieve the information held in indexes and almost all of the human labour of indexing would disappear (for that matter, much of the more skilled work at BP would now be readily computerized). However, the manual indexing system at BP can be regarded as a form of knowledge management and one which was crucial to BP's functioning as a sigint centre.

Whilst consistent with bureaucratic modes of organization, the centrality of knowledge to BP also evokes a sense of the widely discussed notion of knowledge work and knowledge-intensive organization (KIO), which is the subject of a large and growing literature (see Alvesson 2004). There is considerable haziness in the definition of this term (Karreman, Sveningsson and Alvesson, 2002), but key notions include the use and production of knowledge and the utilization of esoteric intellectual skills in this (Starbuck, 1992; Blackler, 1995). In these senses, it might be possible to read BP as a KIO (see Grey and Sturdy, 2009). Yet this also appears to present some paradoxes, because KIOs are typically understood as relatively new forms of organization and, moreover, forms which are associated not with bureaucracy but with 'post-bureaucracy' (Heckscher, 1994). Indeed, one can point to some obvious ways in which BP conforms to what have been identified as the definitional characteristics of post-bureaucratic organization (PBO), for example meritocratic, non-hierarchical and trust-based ways of working animated by a common commitment to an organizational mission (Heckscher, 1994: 25). That seems consistent with the account I gave in the last chapter of some of the ways that, at least, Huts 3, 4, 6 and 8 operated[7].

If this is so, then one thing it suggests is that the notion of KIOs and PBOs as a recent phenomenon is flawed, and indeed there are good reasons to think that this is so. There have been studies identifying a diverse range of very old organizations as having such characteristics, for example mediaeval monasteries (McGrath, 2005), stone-age jewellery making and the production of Renaissance Encylopaedias (Wright, 2007) and libraries (Battles, 2004). This feeds a wider critique of the inadequacy of identifying the current time as being in some unique or epochal sense an 'information age' or a 'knowledge economy' (Hobart and Schiffman, 2000; Lilley, Lightfoot and Amaral, 2004; Black, Muddiman and Plant, 2007): 'far from being a recent development linked to the appearance of what some see as a post-industrial, information society, [information management] commands a long tradition rooted in the pre-computer, industrial age' (Black and Brunt, 1999: 371). This insight is developed in detail by Black, Muddiman and Plant (2007), who do not just argue for the longstanding existence of information management but claim that in key respects the term 'information society' could be applied to Britain (and, by extension, some other countries) from the late nineteenth century. This is a good example of how historical analysis can, as I suggested in the introductory chapter, 'de-familiarize' commonsense or taken-for-granted understandings. For what these kinds of studies emphasise is how the development of modern computing tends to create a mistaken belief that this represents a kind of organizational and societal rupture with a pre-computer 'era'. In this way, it is possible to dispose of the idea that knowledge work is associated with a particular historical period, economic system or, for that matter, a determinate organizational form. How, then, was knowledge work in evidence at BP?

KNOWLEDGE WORK

The most obvious example, cryptanalysis, furnishes so many types of knowledge work that it would be impossible even to begin to do them justice here. As a 'high-level' description it is easy to see it as involving highly esoteric mathematical and linguistic skills[8]. Much of it had the character of 'pure' research work, and indeed BP had a number of research sections or sub-sections (watches), to be contrasted with operational watches. The 'fundamental distinction'[9], in Hut 6 and Hut 8, was between cipher keys which were currently breakable and which had operational urgency (with respect to military exigencies) and those which were not. The former were the responsibility of operational watches, whereas the research watches worked on keys which were not broken or which were not of sufficient importance to be broken daily. This, though, was a dynamic situation in that keys shifted between operational and research watches as and when they were broken or became important, and their importance was itself connected both to what was being yielded and to the shifting priorities of military end-users. Both operational and research watches can be seen as engaging in knowledge work, but the operational watch was in its nature a more pressured activity, calling for a temperament that could deal with that pressure[10]. Not only that, but, as Alexander's internal history of Hut 8 explains,

> Another point worth making perhaps is the desirability of good health; in a research job it probably does not matter very much if a man is C3 [i.e. unfit for military duties] physically but it matters a good deal if operational work has to be done – it is a complete fallacy to suppose that physical condition does not matter in work like this[11].

Thus one can immediately see that 'knowledge work', even within this apparently cerebral setting, is not a homogeneous entity and that it ran alongside, or was twisted together with, other kinds of work, such as the 'psychological work' implied by an ability to deal with pressure and physical work. Thus the commonplace notion that knowledge work is about 'brains not brawn' is inadequate.

The dynamic situation of the interplay between operations and research should also alert us to the way that cryptanalytic work at BP was not simply a matter of solving a cipher or cipher key and then moving on to the next problem. On the contrary, because encryption methods changed over time, keys which were at one time being read could, without warning, be 'blacked out', as happened at various times with many keys, most famously the Shark key of Naval Enigma, which became unreadable at BP for ten months from 1 February 1942 following the addition of a fourth rotor to the Enigma machines of this user group (Erskine, 2001a: 181). This was militarily crucial because it was the key used by the German U-boats in the North Atlantic which attacked Allied ship convoys. The shifting nature of Enigma use meant that there were also significant processes of 'organizational learning' in play, so that, for example, Hut 6, having failed to act on an early warning of a change in German Army Enigma encipherment methods on one occasion, developed processes to act on such warnings in the future and thereby minimized future blackouts[12].

This kind of learning, which is usually understood as a key aspect of knowledge work (see Starbuck, 1992), did not just take the form of developing organizational protocols as a result of past mistakes. It is also evident in a variety of everyday interactions. A few examples may be useful to illustrate the nature of such interactions. The interviewee Ron recalls how, in the Newmanry, where machines including the Colossus computer were used to attack Fish ciphers,

> A lot of the university people had informal meetings[13] and would write ideas on a blackboard and leave them there so that other people could pick them up and write something else ... if they had ideas about how Colossus could be used to break other parts ofthe message that it wasn't designed to do they began to put their ideas on to the blackboard. Later the blackboard stuff got transcribed into a book.

In a similar way, again in the Newmanry, 'tea parties were started; anyone could call one, ideas were bandied about, you came if you could and brought your own tea. Tea parties didn't decide things but they led to action on all fronts' (Wylie, 2001: 339).

The sense here is very much of the kind of Oxbridge College cultural template I referred to in Chapter 3. If it conveys an image of rather genteel interactions, elsewhere in BP such get togethers had a more ebullient feel. The context for this example was a change made to some Army Enigma machines in July 1944, giving rise to a new and initially puzzling version called 'Enigma Uhr' (for technical details see Ulbricht, 1999). This was another case, then, of the ongoing challenges faced by cryptanalysts, as with the 'Uncle Dick' threat discussed in the previous chapter. As a solution began to be found,

> For about 48 hours, the Qwatch[14], where the operations were being conducted, presented an appearance reminiscent of a rugger scrum, or alternatively an assembly of chess masters conducting a

post-mortem after an important game. Most of the participants (who included a strong contingent from Hut 8) appeared to play non-stop throughout the period[15].

Whilst this was a response to a particular set of events, similar practices – and the image of them as having a 'playful' character – were more routinely embedded in Hut 6:

> I urged the people who were having the fun of breaking enigma keys or decoding messages signed by Adolf Hitler to miss no chance of reporting that some particular success had resulted from something done [in Hut 6] ... I also requested feedback from Hut 3 ... All this was aimed not only at boosting morale throughout Hut 6, but also at making sure that each part of the activity would know how its output was going to be used, so that it could itself devise methods that would increase the value of that output. *(Welchman, 1982: 127)*

Learning and knowledge-sharing operated in many other ways too. One of the most basic tools of cryptanalysis is a 'crib'. This refers to a message which has been decrypted in one cipher or cipher key but which has also been transmitted in an as yet unbroken cipher or key and can therefore be used as a way of deciphering both that message and others in the second cipher or key[16]. The possibility of a crib meant that it was vital to apply knowledge gained in working on one cipher or cipher key to the analysis of another. This was indeed a very common method at BP, because identical messages were often transmitted in a variety of different Enigma keys and/or in different ciphers. Thus, if one of these keys or ciphers was broken then it became possible, or at least easier, to break another. This also meant that success against so-called low-grade ciphers could be vital to breaking high-grade ciphers such as Enigma.

In particular, breaking weather ciphers was of critical importance (see e.g. Erskine, 1988; Ratcliff, 2006: 94–5). Weather reports were transmitted in various ciphers and keys and, moreover, often used standardized language, making guesses of possible cribs easier[17].

If a weather report was broken then it could be used as a crib to break another encipherment of the same report. Indeed, it was precisely this method which allowed Hut 8 to end the Shark blackout, as noted in the diary of George McVittie, head of the Meteorological section:

> 13 December 1942. Big day today for the [Meteorological section]. After many months the naval Enigma with four wheels solved (broken) today by our DAN cribs. Congratulations all round from [Shaun] Wylie and from Travis who remarked that this would never have been achieved if we had worked in separate compartments like the Americans[18].

This quotation also points to the core issue of facilitating knowledge-sharing between different sections in the face of secrecy. I indicated in the previous chapter some of the co-ordinative mechanisms at BP that sought to achieve this, but there were also more detailed and specific sets of interconnections. Examples include the sharing of cryptanalytic techniques between Huts 6 and 8 and also the complex of Hut 6, Hut 3 and SIXTA. The Hut 6–Hut 3 connection has been alluded to several times already – the intermingling of the cryptanalytic and intelligence operations relating to Army/Air Enigma[19]. SIXTA, by contrast, was concerned with analysis of Army and Air traffic that was not decrypted but analysed for its volume, source and other technical characteristics. The significance of this traffic analysis (TA) might be to reveal, for example, the build up of military units in a particular place. Central to TA was the activity known as log reading, which consisted of laborious searches for patterns in Morse traffic passing within very large numbers of different transmission networks (for fuller accounts, see Thirsk, 2008; Pearson, 2011). Reports on this analysis were then passed to the 'fusion room', where they could be studied alongside the fruits of decrypted messages in order to create, in due course, a very complete picture of enemy signals activity to be used both by Hut 6 in its ongoing cryptanalytic efforts and by Hut 3 in its ongoing intelligence work. For this purpose the fusion room produced a weekly report for the two huts.

I am using the Hut 6–Hut 3–SIXTA example because it is both an important and a well-documented one, but similar interconnections could be identified in other parts of BP. The overall point here is to give a flavour of the kinds of knowledge work being conducted at BP but, perhaps more importantly, to show that this involved much more than individual esoteric expertise: it required the creation of patterns of working and co-operation between individuals and groups. Nor was this knowledge work simply that of cryptanalysis and traffic analysis, it also encompassed translation and intelligence-analysis work. As has been mentioned elsewhere, translation work required much more than a knowledge of the relevant language, be it German, Italian or Japanese: decrypts typically contained highly technical and abstruse military terms and abbreviations which translators had to become familiar with and which were stored in specialist indexes so that a detailed knowledge of them was organizationally available. Intelligence analysis was perhaps even more dependent not just upon specialist knowledge but also upon judgment in order to make sense of the myriad of small pieces of information which could, collectively, yield useable intelligence.

Finally, mention should be made of a different but perhaps more obvious form of learning and knowledge-sharing, that of training. The picture here was very mixed. In many cases it took the form of on-the-job training, described by a number of interviewees in the phrase 'sitting with Nellie' – the expectation was that staff would pick up the necessary skills. This kind of informal knowledge-sharing would seem to be all of a piece with the kinds of informal social networks I discussed in the previous chapter. However, according to the post-war review this became less common as the war progressed and formal training was initiated both for low-skill work, such as, from 1942, Typex operating and, at the other end of the skill spectrum, from 1941, for cryptanalysis. Particular needs such as, for example and in particular, the need to train translators and others in Japanese also resulted in the establishment of formal training courses, in some cases in conjunction with the School of Oriental and African Studies.

Individual sections at BP established their own training systems, with the Hollerith room having a formalized course for new entrants, for example[20]. This picture of a shift towards formalization of training is evident in the internal history of Hut 3, which from 1942 established, as did other huts, a 'training watch' to supplant previous on-the-job approaches[21].

Yet there is a sense in which the more highly skilled forms of knowledge work remained in the final analysis something which could not be codified and trained. Ron, the interviewee who maintained Fish machines, arrived at BP in 1944, well into the period when more formalized training systems were in place. Yet neither did he receive training nor were there any manuals for the machines: 'we did it by instinct, the machines were so complicated and we just hoped and prayed they would never go wrong [in ways we could not fix]'. Similarly, in the post-war review a key ability for linguists over and above knowledge of the language *per se* was the 'power to apply knowledge as a basis for guess work'[22]. Simpson's (2010) account of work on the JN-25 explains how 'means had to be found of enabling [staff] to make the judgments quickly and objectively, of standardising the judgments across the team and of initiating new recruits (for the team was expanding rapidly) without the least delay' (Simpson, 2010: 77). But at the same time, he goes on to suggest that 'in cryptanalysis, the imaginative hunch grounded in experience could sometimes make the most important contribution of all' (Simpson, 2010: 78). In a similar way, but relating to intelligence analysis rather than cryptanalysis, Harry Hinsley's 'powers as an interpreter of decrypts were unrivalled and were based on an ability to sense that something unusual was afoot from the tiniest clues'[23].

Thus here it is possible to see how 'instinct', 'guesswork' and the 'imaginative hunch', all of which gesture towards the uncodifiable parts of work, are twisted together with the standardization of knowledge and work processes. Hinsley's 'ability to sense something unusual' was inter-woven with the more prosaic tool of the intelligent analyst, the index. But that indexing was not merely mechanical and itself required judgment and constant thoughtfulness, just as the JN-25 party combined guesswork with standardization of judgments. Or, to take a different example, the 'brainwork' of cryptanalysis also required physical and emotional resilience. It is this intermingling which I have sought to stress throughout this chapter. Now, though, I turn to one particular reason why so many different kinds of working were evident at BP: the way in which it had been constituted.

CENTRALIZATION OF WORK

I have referred on numerous occasions to the hitherto most extensive academic treatment of BP's organization (Ratcliff, 2006). At the heart of that analysis is the claim that

> [T]he Allied sigint success rested on the British development of a centralized signals intelligence organization.   *(Ratcliff, 2006: 74)*

On this view, it was the bringing together of expertise on a single site and under the umbrella of GC & CS which enabled, in particular, the kind of knowledge work just sketched to occur. To continue with the SIXTA example from the previous section, it is significant that from May 1942[24] it moved from Beaumanor, a WO site, to BP and that, from January 1943 but not before, the log readers were enwised to the Enigma secret, enabling much more effective co-ordination of their work with that of cryptanalysis (Smith, 1998: 94–5). It is precisely these kinds of developments which Ratcliff is referring to in her analysis of centralization (e.g. Ratcliff, 2006: 86). There are some caveats to be made, though. I have remarked elsewhere that the emphasis on centralization somewhat underplays the various organizational fissures discussed in Chapter 1, and somewhat over-states the extent of knowledge-sharing. Moreover, as the SIXTA case shows, this centralization was achieved processually, over time[25], and so is perhaps better thought of as a direction of travel, rather than as an accomplished state – something which itself had to be 'worked on'.

Nor was this direction of travel uniform. For example, as noted elsewhere, following the 1942 reorganization, diplomatic and commercial decoding moved to London with Denniston, and hence was not on the BP site and to a large degree was separately organized. More significantly, with the Japanese attack on Pearl Harbour and the entry of the USA into the war, the locus of operations necessarily shifted eastwards. This was partly for logistical reasons – the delay in receiving Japanese intercepts at BP (Simpson 2011: 141–3). It was also partly because American resources in staff, machines and communications were so much greater. Moreover, the politics of UK–US relations were fraught because of the different military and strategic priorities of the two countries and, more particularly, because of British fears about the security of Ultra (Gladwin, 1999)[26]. This was not the only source of pressure to decentralize. The global nature of the war and of sigint, combined with the technicalities of where interception could take place and how intercepts could be transported, meant that there were also patterns of regionalization. For example, some traffic could be intercepted only in the Middle East, with cryptanalysis taking place in Cairo under the aegis of the Combined Bureau Middle East (CBME) (Hinsley, 1993c: 62). In the Pacific, GC & CS maintained outposts in Singapore (prior to its capture by the Japanese in 1942), Hong Kong (which fell at the end of 1941), India and Ceylon (modern-day Sri Lanka) and these, alongside combined operations with Australian sigint, fell under the Far East Combined Bureau (FECB) (Cain, 1999)[27]. Thus, both geographically and organizationally GC & CS was considerably more dispersed than might be thought[28] (see also Aldrich, 2000: 234–60).

With all of the caveats made, the centralization thesis clearly has some purchase, especially when compared with the sigint operations in the USA and, even more so, Germany (Ratcliff, 2006: 56–71 and 180–97). One remarkable consequence of it is that, as Calvocoressi (2001: 80) amongst others noted, the people in the world with the most profound overall knowledge of German military operations were to be found not in Germany but in Britain, and more specifically at BP. Of course, very few at BP had such knowledge and so once again it must be emphasised that alongside the kinds of knowledge-sharing and centralization of expertise I have described there was also compartmentalization. As should by now be clear, this combination and the associated ways in which different parts of BP exhibited different ways of working are what makes its organization especially complicated.

So far as compartmentalization is concerned, this was largely to do with secrecy and, as has already been explained, was central to the way that BP worked. The tension between this and the need to share knowledge was an ongoing organizational task. As George McVittie noted, in the earlier quotation about the interaction of work on weather codes and on Enigma, by some standards, such as those of the USA, compartmentalization at BP was relatively limited. Others, such as Dilly Knox, lamented the effects of excessive internal secrecy (Erskine, 2010: xii). There are certainly examples of this, and Ratcliff (2006: 107) surely over-states the case in saying that 'from the directors on down, Bletchley's staff applied the "need to know" restriction neither rigidly nor narrowly'. For example, Edward Simpson headed the JN-25 working party at BP yet did not know, either at the time or for many years thereafter, that another group, under Hugh Foss and subsequently Geoffrey Wall in Hut 7, was working on JN-25 variants. Similarly, Simpson had no interchange with the party working on JN-11, a cipher presenting related problems to those of JN-25, even though it was based in the same corridor at BP, whilst he had no direct communication with the GC & CS outstation in Colombo, Ceylon, which was also working on Japanese Naval ciphers. In fact, by virtue of routine exchanges on some technical matters, Washington felt closer than GC & CS Colombo to Simpson[29].

Another example comes from Hugh Alexander's internal history of Hut 8, where he describes 'an episode in the history of the section over which even the least sensitive of us would gladly draw a veil of considerable opacity'. In 1942, a group in Hut 8 working on a particular form of Mediterranean Naval traffic was having no success 'until someone from Hut 6 ... having a casual look round pointed out' that it was an old system the solution to which was already known. Alexander records that, had they had this information earlier, 'we could certainly have been reading it for some months, possibly since 1941'[30]. Such examples all seem to be unintended consequences of the encultured, default position of secrecy. This point is taken up by Erskine (2010: xii–xiii) in articulating the key paradox of 'need to know' as a basis for security: how can you know in advance who needs to know what? Although the CCR (discussed in the previous chapter) attempted to address this issue, its essentially paradoxical nature meant that no ultimate resolution is possible[31]. In this respect, whilst one can kind find all kinds of knowledge work at BP, these depart from at least ideal-type understandings of KIOs in which full and transparent sharing of knowledge across organizations is aimed for (Heckscher, 1994: 27). Instead, in its valorization of secrecy BP was more obviously akin to bureaucracy, for, as Max Weber noted, 'the concept of the "official secret" is the specific invention of bureaucracy, and nothing is so fanatically defended by the bureaucracy' (Gerth and Mills, 1991: 233).

I will return later to the ways in which we might make sense of this complexity, but for now will consider a further aspect of centralization. The development of a sigint organization centred on BP, coupled with its rapid growth via a staff mainly mobilized for wartime service, had many effects. The principal effect was to draw together a disparate range of organizations and people with a variety of prior experiences. I am not here thinking of the structural and cultural matters arising from this, but rather the importation of organizational techniques from elsewhere and their deployment within BP. This has been touched on already in cases ranging from the importation of Oxbridge College management styles and GPO working methods through to the way that Hugh Alexander brought into Hut 8 understandings of organization derived from his experience of the John Lewis co-operative. In this way, a kind of *smörgåsbord* of organizational techniques came together according to the vagaries of personality as well as the consequences of the range of organizations and activity types brought into play by virtue of centralization.

One important example is the way that the crucial indexing function developed at BP. The procedures used 'were homegrown, and it might be said that their development was based on reaction to problems as they arose' (Brunt, 2004: 299), but this was not a haphazard or random process. The first index at BP was the Hut 3 Air Index (Lewin, 2008: 121), which was the creation of Flying Officer (later Wing Commander) Reginald 'Cully' Cullingham. Cullingham had, before the war, been the Hamburg representative of Kelly's Directories and, although recruited to BP for his knowledge of the German language, utilized their indexing methods when building the Air Index (Brunt, 2004: 295). Although he is not named, it is Cullingham who is being referred to here:

> From first to last the Air Index was designed and nurtured by a strange genius, a man of everyday appearance and attainments who had, and knew he had, a particular gift for that very thing: indexing. He was a triangular peg in a triangular hole.   *(Calvocoressi, 2001: 79)*

Whilst Cullingham was not directly responsible for building other indexes, the success of the Air Index and the fact that new indexes were built using staff seconded from the Air Index meant that the basic procedures spread out and were adopted elsewhere. Thus in this example can be seen precisely a blend of chance appointments and adoption of organizational techniques from elsewhere. Had Cullingham not worked at BP, no doubt there would still have been indexes developed; had these not been based on Kelly's Directories, they would presumably have been based on something else. The same basic process of adaptation would probably have been in play, but the precise way it was inflected would have been different. Moreover, it would no doubt be possible to trace how Kelly's itself developed its indexing system, making, perhaps, borrowings from elsewhere, for indexing itself has a wider history encompassing libraries, businesses and, indeed, military intelligence (Black and Brunt, 1999).

A second example, of a rather different kind, concerns the many inter-relations between the British Tabulating Machine Company (BTMC) and BP. One strand of this was the Hollerith Room, which, as has been mentioned, was run by a manager, Mr Freeborn, on secondment from BTMC, using its machines and procedures and some of its staff. So here there is a direct importation of organizational techniques into BP. This is not, however, the same as the Cullingham case in that there it was only chance that he happened to bring a knowledge of indexing with him. Freeborn was not first recruited to BP only then serendipitously to make use of his knowledge of data-processing techniques; rather, it was BTMC's expertise in this field which led to a relationship with BP, which in turn led to Freeborn's appointment.

In any case, Hollerith data-processing systems were not the only aspect of the BP–BTMC relationship: BTMC was also responsible for building the British bombes at their factory at Letchworth in Hertfordshire, and this required a very intensive set of contacts with BP. Senior staff at BTMC visited Hut 6 and were enwised to the Ultra secret, although the assembly-line workers at BTMC were not[32]. Liaison was for a period undertaken by Commander Malcolm Saunders and by Gordon Welchman, whilst on the BTMC side Harold 'Doc' Keen masterminded the engineering of the bombes. This in turn entailed a further web of organizational arrangements, since components for the bombes were assembled not at the Letchworth factory but via a 'putting out' system to part-time workers in village halls around Hertfordshire and beyond (Welchman, 1982: 140). One point to make about this is that, whereas it was a process of centralization which brought BP into contact with BTMC, it itself entailed a decentralization to these village-hall sub-assembly units. This is a further, albeit perhaps minor, illustration of the indeterminacy of the notion of centralization and the way that detailed examination undercuts the broad characterization of BP as 'centralized'.

The BTMC example also sheds light on the complexity of a way of organizing that brought together so many different agencies and entities. There are several dimensions to this. One is related to interservice issues. The original bombe contracts were paid for by SIS funds, but, as the building programme expanded, payment came from the Admiralty, causing a temporary interruption to the work schedule

(Welchman, 1982: 140). A second issue was that, since BTMC itself had to source raw materials from other companies, most of which were engaged in various forms of war-related production, but could not reveal the importance of its requirements because of secrecy, this required intervention from BP to secure supplies. For this purpose, in contrast to the 'non-hierarchical' way of working in some parts of BP, 'Saunders was brought in, attired in his Navy uniform, to apply Admiralty pressure on suppliers and Government departments' (Welchman, 1982: 141). Thirdly, BTMC was not the only source of machines at BP. The GPO also had a role, and this led to disputes involving BP, BTMC and the GPO – more particularly its Dollis Hill experimental research centre – over the design of electronic components and, more broadly, control of decisions relating to machine-building (McKay, 2010: 367).

It is necessary, then, to be wary of too readily concluding that BP's organization can be thought about in terms of the centralization of work. Or perhaps it would be better to say that it is necessary to be aware of the limitations of categories such as centralization – like bureaucracy, knowledge work or other such terms – to speak adequately to the messy complexities of organizational life.

CONCLUSION

What sense, then, are we to make of the work of BP? In this and the previous chapter I have drawn attention to the wide variety of kinds of work being done at BP and, I hope, conveyed at least a sense of what it was 'about'. This is worthwhile in itself, both because it 'decodes' the dominant received image of BP and because it makes concrete the work done, which, as suggested at the outset of this part of the book, can sometimes be lost in the abstractions of organization theory. It is also worthwhile because it moves beyond the 'honeycomb' model of BP (Lewin, 2008: 137), which perhaps conjures up images of regular, identical cells and a homogeneous force of worker bees.

This variety of work is, of course, inseparable from the way in which BP brought together a range of organizations and functions and, in this sense, centralized sigint. Clearly many of the issues which have been sketched are inter-related in that the variety of work forms is linked to the variety of management styles, the presence or absence of bureaucratic features and so on. One way to consider this would be in terms of the variety of control methods in play. In broad terms, these encompass forms of direct, hierarchical and bureaucratic control associated with the military and with factories – as evidenced in, say, the bombe rooms and outstations and the Hollerith room – and forms of normative control based upon shared values and trust rather than hierarchy – as evidenced in, say, Huts 3 and 6. It might further be said that these forms of control map onto the extent to which the work involved was of a highly skilled, knowledge-based sort or of a more routine, manual sort.

An analysis of this sort would be compatible both with contingency theory (Burns and Stalker, 1961) and with labour-process analysis (Friedman, 1977), so that what BP exhibits is, on the one hand, a combination of mechanical and organic organization depending primarily upon the predictability of work and, on the other, a combination of direct control and responsible autonomy depending primarily upon the skill level of work. Such accounts have a certain amount of purchase and should not be entirely discounted. Nevertheless, they do not do justice to the complexities which emerge from a detailed examination. To take some specific examples from the preceding chapters, the routine and low-skill work of the Hut 6 Registration Room was managed through normative rather than direct control; yet elsewhere translators doing highly skilled work were told not to show initiative. The highly skilled work of cryptanalysts was also frequently mundane and routine; the routine work of indexing and log reading called for and allowed discretion and judgment. I have tried to suggest that what we find at BP is a twisting together of a huge variety of different kinds of organizing, working and managing in a complex way which is 'encoded' by categories such as 'mechanical', 'organic', 'direct control', 'normative control' and so on. This may be seen as part of the more general problem in organization theory of over-polarizing organizational forms, for example and in particular those of bureauc-racy and post-bureaucracy, as others have pointed out (Karreman, Sveningsson and Alvesson, 2002; Courpasson, 2000).

Nor will it serve simply to see BP as a 'hybrid' of different ways of working, or some combination of Mintzbergian 'structure in fives', for this tells us little about how these ways relate and interact. Instead, the implicit assumption is that these different ways are discrete entities rather than being always and everywhere intermingled. Similarly, stressing centralization by itself fails to draw out the heterogeneity and complexity of what was entailed for two related reasons. On the one hand, the suggestion that BP 'brought together' disparate elements implies a greater homogenization than was the case. On the other, in so doing, it occludes the way in which heterogeneity was itself a conse-quence of centralization. In other words, to answer the question 'how was BP organized?' either by saying 'in a hybrid way' or 'in a centralized way' does not take us very far in understanding its complexity.

What perhaps better captures this complexity is the growing stream of literature in organization studies growing out of March's (1991) examination of 'exploration' and 'exploitation' in organizations and organizational learning in particular. This has led to formulations of the 'ambidextrous organization' (e.g. He and Wong, 2004; Raisch *et al.*, 2009) which seek to understand the co-existence of and 'balance' between proceduralism and innovation, and in this sense are a re-visiting of the perennial autonomy versus control debate which, as suggested at the outset of this part of the book, lies at the heart of many of the issues discussed here. At times this literature resembles traditional understandings of hybrid structures in associating 'exploi-tation' with mechanical organizational forms and 'exploration' with organic forms, but it often seeks to go beyond this by showing how, as with the BP case, these can be intertwined (e.g. Gupta, Smith and Shalley, 2006). In particular, Adler and Borys (1996) suggest that in some circumstances creativity can be fostered by organizational rules rather than being antithetical to them and in this way, too, move beyond the binary logic of more conventional literature.

Another illuminating parallel is with Pitsis *et al.*'s (2003) account of the 2000 Sydney Olympics. Here a wide variety of different organizations linked by collaborative networks and alliances was brought into play in a way that precluded any definition of 'an organization' having this or that characteristic. Rather, its characteristic *was* precisely that of the heterogeneous network. Pitsis *et al.* (2003) explain the working of such a network in terms of a 'future perfect strategy' in which projections of an imagined future animated by a shared sense of purpose created competent semi-autonomous project teams which together delivered a successful Olympic event. There are some affinities here with the work of BP. In particular, Welchman's establishment of organizational protocols in anticipation of Enigma being broken resembles future perfect strategy. Similarly, particular sections at BP exhibit the kind of competent semi-autonomy of the Olympics case. The principal differences would be, firstly, that the requirements of secrecy cut across a fully developed sense of shared purpose – although, as noted in Chapter 3, the context of war could to an extent supply this – and, secondly, that unlike with the Olympics there was no temporally defined end point known in advance in that no one at BP could know the timetable for the war as a whole. On the other hand, the defined timescales of, for example, daily key changes, could be seen as a very compressed example of a similar thing. At all events, the sense of organization defined by its heterogeneous networks seems a more helpful one in explaining BP than that of contingent hybridity of ideal-type organizational models[33].

Another useful way of approaching BP is via the concept of 'bricolage', which has been used within organization theory to explore how makeshift improvisations of diverse materials are set to work within organizational settings (e.g. Weick, 1993)[34]. The notion is also taken up by Gabriel (2002) to examine how managers and others draw selectively upon a variety of theories to inform their practice. The result is not a coherent, classifiable whole but rather a series of pragmatic adaptations, rather like the adaptations of recipe books in cookery (Gabriel, 2002: 143) or, as others have it, the improvisations of jazz

(Meyer, Frost and Weick, 1998). It makes little sense to seek to understand these 'paragrammatic' (Gabriel, 2002) practices by reference to classical cookery books or, for that matter, classical music scores. In the same way, it makes little sense to try to understand organization in terms of models or typologies: what is at stake is a less rational and more situationally embedded sense of organizing work. Something similar is entailed by the ways that management and organization ideas can be seen to 'travel' and get 'translated' as they are applied and re-applied in new settings (Czarniawska and Sevon, 1996). In terms of BP, the purchase of these notions is evident in terms of the bringing together of, *inter alia*, friendship networks rooted in Oxbridge Colleges; of drawing on understandings and experiences of how organizations work, whether as general as invocations of humanism ('Theory Y', so to speak) as a template for industrial practice or as precise as the transfer of indexing techniques from Kelly's to BP; or simply of inventing *ad hoc* pragmatic mechanisms such as the CCR and the IE to meet particular functional or political demands.

It should not be thought, however, that what is being suggested here is a kind of chaotic free for all in which any and every notion of organizing gets lumped together, and no further sense can be made of it. For one thing, the question of what ways of organizing are legitimate within any given context will be defined and limited by prevailing norms and understandings. For example, the way that the Hut 6 Registration Room was managed meritocratically seems to have grown out of the wider norm within Hut 6 deriving from Oxbridge College styles – the more factory-like style of organizing which applied to similar work in other parts of BP was illegitimate or less legitimate within that context. Within the Hollerith Room, by contrast, the prevailing mode of organizing deriving from BTMC made an informal, relaxed and collegiate way of organizing far less legitimate but permitted factory discipline. At the risk of pretentiousness, one way of conceptualizing this might be in terms of 'strings of inter-organizationality' stretching from, *inter alia*, the FO, the GPO, Oxbridge Colleges, BTMC and the armed services, all – to continue the metaphor – knotted together at the particular place and time that was BP. I will return to this metaphor, and others I have used in this book, in the next, concluding, chapter.

In these ways, the sense of BP as a place of 'creative anarchy' (Hinsley *et al.*, 1979: 273) or, as organization theorists might put it, 'organized anarchy' (Cohen, March and Olsen, 1972) can be 'decoded' to bring to light the variety of situated practices through which BP worked. It is this which I hope I have done in this section of the book. What I have not done, however, is make any judgment about whether it 'worked' in the sense of being effective, as opposed to considering how it 'worked' in the sense of operating. There is an old joke, sometimes attributed to an apocryphal graduate of one of the French *Ecoles Normales Supérieures*, which might be taken to apply rather well to BP's organization: 'that is fine in practice, but it couldn't possibly work in theory'. For BP did work in the sense that it successfully broke a large number of codes and ciphers, including many variations of Enigma, which had been thought to be unbreakable and, moreover, it identified and disseminated useable intelligence which in turn contributed to Allied military success. It had its failures, too. One high-profile, although contentious, example is the failure to predict the 1944 German counter-offensive in Western Europe known as the Ardennes Offensive or the Battle of the Bulge (see Bennett, 1994: 268–73 for details). Nevertheless, few would doubt that BP's successes outweighed its failures. But was this because of or despite the ways in which it was organized? That is, strictly speaking, an unanswerable question – there is no counterfactual.

Ratcliff (2006) addresses this by comparing BP with German sigint and argues that the centralized nature of BP was decisive by comparison, pointing to the fragmented nature of German sigint organization and also the way that the failure to integrate cryptanalysis and intelligence functions led, even when cryptanalysis was successful, to a failure to translate this into useable intelligence. In a similar way, and in the face of similar kinds of inter-service territorial disputes to those experienced at BP, the US case is instructive. Prior to the Pearl Harbour attacks US sigint responsibility was divided between army and navy, so that each took charge on alternate days in 'an absurd bureaucratic compromise' (Andrew, 2001: 10). It was precisely the avoidance of such clumsy fragmentations which, for Ratcliff, explains BP's success. This argument has some mileage, but has one important limitation for, as so often in the study of organizations, causality is difficult to establish. Thus it could equally be argued that BP's centralization was a consequence rather than a cause of its success. In particular, had Enigma ciphers not been broken on a large scale then the likelihood of developing a more or less unified sigint complex would have been very much lower. Perhaps in the end an evaluation of this sort is not possible: BP was what it was and did what it did and all that can be done is to show, as has been attempted here, *how* it worked.

NOTES
1. TNA HW 43/70: 24.
2. At the request of the correspondent I have divulged neither the name of the 'boss' in question nor the section, since this would allow the identity of the boss to be deduced.
3. TNA HW 25/22: 23.
4. It will be obvious from this, as is not always clear in accounts of BP, that there was not a single 'index'.
5. TNA HW 25/1: 93.
6. It appears to rest primarily on the case of Hut 6.
7. Of course, it can also be said that BP exhibited some distinctly pre-bureaucratic modes of organizing. This is particularly evident in terms of those kinds of informal, personalized recruiting methods described in the previous chapter and their consequences in terms of friendship as a mode of organizing. One of the core features of a Weberian bureaucracy is impersonality in recruitment and organizational practice and the ways in which these supplanted nepotism, patronage and idiosyncracy.
8. It should not, however, be forgotten that breaking ciphers was not a purely intellectual achievement. Key breakthroughs were also associated with the capture by the military of enemy codebooks and machines which greatly aided cryptanalysis, as explained and emphasised by Kahn (1991) and Sebag-Montefiore (2000).

9. The distinction is described as being 'fundamental' to understanding the organization of Hut 6 according to the Hut Head Stuart Milner-Barry in an uncatalogued document entitled 'Hut 6 Organization', dated 14 October 1943. I am grateful to Ralph Erskine for supplying me with this document.
10. TNA HW 43/70: 13.
11. TNA HW 25/1: 91.
12. TNA HW 43/70: 13–15.
13. Cf. discussion of meetings 'culture' in the previous chapter.
14. Since Enigma Uhr produced (from the cryptanalysts' point of view) a stream of nonsense, the group looking at it took the name Qwatch, from 'Quatsch', the German word for nonsense, and 'watch', the term often used at BP for a work group/shift. Note that the Qwatch had a wider existence and set of responsibilities beyond the Enigma Uhr episode; see the internal history of Hut 6, HW 43/70: 169.
15. TNA HW 14/108.
16. To give a very simple illustration, imagine a basic substitution cipher in which A = B, B = C, C = D through to Z = A. In this cipher the word 'hello' would be rendered 'ifmmp'. Then imagine another cipher in which A = C, B = D etc. In this cipher the word 'hello' would be rendered 'jgnnq'. If you solve the first cipher and discover that the first word of the message is 'hello', you can then look at the same message in the second cipher and work backwards to discover that A = C is that cipher. Another version of the same process would be if a message were transmitted on one network in plaintext – with no encipherment at all – which again gives an easy crib if the same message is transmitted on another network in enciphered form. Another variant would be if you guessed (perhaps by reasoning, perhaps because it had always been the case in the past) that a message begins with the word 'hello' – you can then use this guess to see whether it yields the solution. For example, the message reads 'ifmmp kpio'. You guess it might begin with the word 'hello' and if so that the cipher is A = B. If that is so, then the rest of the message will yield a meaningful plaintext word. It does: 'John'. Whilst, of course, this example is ludicrously simplified to illustrate the principle, something of this sort provided some of the best-known breakthroughs at BP, for example the fact that many messages routinely ended with the stereotypical words 'Heil Hitler', or even consisted simply of 'nothing to report', provided an important source of cribs. A more elaborate method of achieving a similar result was to try to provoke the

Germans into sending a message the content of which was known in advance. This could be done by having mines laid at known co-ordinates in the expectation that the Germans would then transmit a message reporting their own mine-clearing activities around these co-ordinates. Since BP already knew what the co-ordinates were, they had a ready-made crib (so-called 'gardening cribs'). Sending lone reconnaissance planes to remote locations was also a way of generating such cribs.

17. For this reason, where a station was transmitting a weather report in a breakable cipher BP sometimes sought to ensure that the RAF did not bomb it and thus deprive the cryptanalysts of a reliable crib.

18. CCAC RLEW 5.

19. One, literal, conduit for this during the early days of the war was a wooden tray, propelled by string and a broom handle which passed decrypts from Hut 6 to Hut 3 (Welchman, 1982: 129). As with index cards in shoeboxes, this rather quaint system should not lead to the view, sometimes heard, that this was an 'amateurish' operation.

20. All information in the paragraph to this point is based upon TNA HW 14/145: 11–13.

21. TNA HW 3/119: 44. See HW 43/70: 112 for the analogous development of formalized training in Hut 6. The timing of this move to formalized training can be read as an aspect of the more general move to formalization associated with the 'making' of BP's organization, but it also coincided with similar developments within SIS (Jeffery, 2010: 479) and hence may have a wider explanation.

22. TNA HW 14/145: 6.

23. From his entry in the Oxford Dictionary of National Biography.

24. Strictly speaking, it was not entitled SIXTA until February 1944, when it merged with another TA group at BP.

25. As noted in Chapter 2, Denniston resisted bringing MI8 TA (i.e. what became SIXTA) into BP.

26. The issue of Anglo-US sigint relations and co-operation is an enormously complex one and is well beyond the scope of this book. A series of agreements was brokered – the Holden Agreement in October 1942 to share Naval sigint, and the parallel Travis–Strong Agreement (sometimes informally called the BRUSA agreement) of May 1943 to share Army–Air and secret-service sigint – culminating after the war in the UKUSA agreement which has been the foundation of sigint co-operation between

the two countries to the present day. Indeed the text of the initial, 1946, agreement was only declassified in June 2010 (TNA HW 80/4). For more detailed discussion and explanation of this issue see Gladwin (1999) and Budiansky (2000, 2001). As regards post-war issues, see Aldrich (2002, 2010).

27. Additionally, there were combined US and Australian sigint operations (Cain, 1999). It is also worth noting that there was extensive sigint cooperation between the UK and Canada and between the USA and Canada (see e.g. Hinsley, 1993: 308n). See also the special issue on American–British–Canadian intelligence relations 1939–2000 of *Intelligence and National Security*, Volume 15, Issue 2, 2000.

28. And, as noted in several places elsewhere, the interception service was both organizationally and geographically dispersed, albeit increasingly under the influence, control and direction of BP.

29. Personal conversation and correspondence with Dr Edward Simpson.

30. All quotations in the preceding sentences are from TNA HW 25/1: 38–9.

31. And although the CCR did not exist at the time of the Hut 8 example, it did at the time of the JN-25 one.

32. Or supposedly not: McKay (2010: 223–224) refers to a case in which security may have been breached, at least to the extent of an unauthorized leakage of the fact that BTMC was building decoding machines.

33. This should not be taken to imply that BP was 'a network organization', of course – again, it had elements of such organization interwoven with other, for example hierarchical, forms.

34. In fact, a similar notion may be applied not just to organization but also to the way in which we analyse organization, a point taken up in the next chapter.

Conclusion: Reviving Organization Studies

I began this book by stating that my twin aims were to explicate the way that Bletchley Park was organized and to develop a particular approach to organization studies. The result has been the first social-scientific account of BP, as opposed to accounts provided by historians of intelligence, journalists or its former employees. That in itself is perhaps unusual since, by and large, it is relatively rare for organization studies to venture out of its own domain in an attempt to show what it, as a discipline, can say about the social world that cannot be, or is not, said by others. So this has been an attempt at turning outwards a discipline which has on many accounts become increasingly inward-looking (Starbuck, 2003).

Of course, what has been provided is only one kind of social-scientific account, not least because of its organizational focus and, within that, only one kind of organizational account because of its particular form of analysis. What 'form of analysis' is it? That is not, I hope, an easy question to answer. I have deliberately avoided positioning it as a study rooted in any particular literature or 'school' of organization studies because it seems to me that the elaboration of more and more sub-literatures has contributed to making the discipline esoteric and inward-looking. But, of course, in a more general way there are some clear analytical preferences on display. At the very broadest level, this book stands in a tradition of interpretative analysis traceable, like organization studies itself, back to Max Weber, in which 'Verstehen' or understanding, rather than positivist explanation, is sought. Within that broad frame I have also sought to emphasise processual aspects of organization, the sense of organization as a verb denoting actions over time which create and re-create the entity or noun of organization.

In keeping with such an approach, I have attempted to do more than pay lip service to the duality of social structure and human agency, by showing how there is a constant interlinkage between human beings and the collectivities of various groups, sub-groups and institutions; and among these groups, sub-groups and institutions. As regards structure, this has entailed demonstrating how the organization of BP was not determined by, for example, the culture of British wartime society or the technological imperatives of codebreaking. Such things were real and relevant, but were both moderated and mediated by the contradictions, complexities and choices of human agency. As regards agency, this entails more than simply noting the roles of individuals (Willmott, 2011: 69), because these individuals are themselves enmeshed within and produced through structures. Thus, to give but one example, the organizational practices enacted at BP by people brought there from Oxbridge colleges can hardly be understood in isolation from their enculturation within those institutions. So my account has attempted to capture agency and structure not as two 'blocs' or poles but as inseparable and mutually implicated in the production of organization.

Again at a general level, I have attempted to do what all social science should do, namely to 'de-familiarize' that which seems commonsensical or obvious by providing an 'understanding' which is challenging to these views (Bauman, 1990). My main strategy in this respect has been to use historical distance as a way of standing somewhat outside of what is being examined (Tosh, 2006: 32). This is perhaps particularly helpful when trying to grasp organizational process, the contours of which are quite difficult to see in the here and now. But distance is only one aspect of providing an interpretative understanding; what is also required is closeness (Merton, 1972). This paradoxical combination of distance and closeness has been widely discussed within, in particular, ethnographic studies of organization, which are perhaps the archetype of interpretative research. There, the dyad of observation and participation, for all that it is complex in practice, provides an answer in principle to this paradox (Neyland, 2008: 1). In a historical study, participation is impossible. Instead, 'closeness' may be achieved by a very detailed engagement with sources.

Throughout this book, I have sought such an engagement by going into rather more empirical detail than is common within organization studies. This detail has in places been extremely fine-grained (although drawing on only a small sub-set of the available material), reflecting my view that for interpretative work to be convincing it needs to be able to dig right down to the very smallest detail as well as to speak of and to broad themes of organizational and social analysis. Much of this detail has been derived from the archive sources identified in the introductory chapter, but I hope that I have avoided the empiricist trap of 'archivism' both by virtue of the analytical way that these sources have been handled and also by counterposing them with other kinds of material, such as various secondary sources, published reminiscences and research interviews. The interviews, which I have used in part to personalize and certainly in order to achieve 'closeness', were possible because the BP case, whilst historical, is of a particular sort: close enough in time to allow at least limited oral history methods to be used.

So this has been a study of a particular sort, defined by the precepts I have summarised here, but within those general precepts I have been quite cavalier in my use of theories and literatures which are more usually treated discretely. In organization studies there has been some attention paid to organizational improvisations (Meyer, Frost and Weick, 1998; Weick, 1998) but less to what might be their counterpart, namely 'theoretical improvisations'. Such improvisations would be less concerned with the straitjacket of form and more attentive to the pragmatics of understanding. For the messy complexities of organization rarely fit the neat categories and concepts of narrowly defined literatures. So, just as we can use the notion of 'bricolage' (Gabriel, 2002) to understand the ways in which organizational practice occurs – as, indeed, I did in relation to BP in Chapter 6 – so too can we engage in the practice of bricolage when theorizing organizations. This is a different kind of response to the paradigmatic fracturing of organization studies from that of sequentially deploying different approaches to a particular case (e.g. Hassard, 1993). Instead it is a more free-flowing 'raid' upon different approaches as and when they seem useful.

An inevitable consequence of this is that the organization-studies literature has been treated with a 'light touch', referring to some of its main contours and headlines in order to make particular points as well as to position the text in relation to these contours. I am aware that for some readers this will be unsatisfying, but it is part of the attempt to find a different way of doing organization studies. As a field, this seems to have elevated 'the literature' to a fetish, so that nowadays most *papers* in 'good' journals typically carry about a hundred references – and often many more. A generation ago, authors of whole *books* did not find it necessary to reference so frenetically. A classic work like Selznick (1949), for example, got by with just sixty. Now, of course, this partly reflects the massive growth in the volume of published work in the intervening period, and I am not suggesting that referencing in quantity is a problem in itself (and I have hardly stinted myself in this regard). But what it seems to go hand in hand with is an ever narrower apprehension of the questions and issues to be addressed by organization studies, with each contribution almost strangled by a kind of *faux* professionalism in the struggle to locate itself within highly specialized sub-literatures and according to uninspiring formulae (Grey, 2010). This has also led to a situation in which 'it is doubtful that an organization studies researcher has the time for even minimally adequate processing of the information generated by the large volume of sharply differentiated research studies in the field' (Mone and McKinlay, 1993: 290). Indeed, it has been suggested that the strictures of academic journals in particular may be one 'reason why there are no new and exciting theories' in organization studies and that 'we need books to provide a space within which we can be novel and where we do not have to pay such expansive homage to those who have gone before' (Suddaby, Hardy and Huy, 2011: 245).

Certainly the consequence of the dominant norms of academic journals is that writing on a broad canvas about organization has become extremely rare, and the many interconnections and overlaps between different sub-literatures have been occluded.

By contrast, in the course of the book I have made mention of a wider variety of different kinds of theories of organization – for example those relating to trust, leadership, culture, organizational structure, organizational forms, management styles, institutions and organizational politics. That is not to say that all these are compatible or that there are no substantive differences and debates within organization theory. On the contrary, I have at points indicated the problems, limitations and inconsistencies of different kinds of theory. At the same time, the emergence of so many isolated sub-literatures within the field often means that what are at root very similar insights are artificially separated for reasons as trivial as differences in terminology or simply authors' ignorance of each other, but also fed by an institutionalized valorization of 'uniqueness' in published work (Mone and McKinley, 1993).

So my general approach has been to treat the accumulated body of organization studies as a resource for my primary purpose of providing an understanding of Bletchley Park and in the process to address some very broad issues – at the most generic level, that of how organization is accomplished over time. The organization-studies literature is enrolled to enable me to pursue these issues, rather than letting this literature get in the way of doing so. In a way, the aim is a more 'self-confident' form of organization studies, willing to draw upon and showcase its rich heritage to demonstrate what it can say about organization, rather than fiddling around endlessly with internal discussions about this or that sub-literature. In this sense, it should be stressed that this book is *not*, and does not aspire to be, a work of organizational theory in any normal sense of that term: it is rather an attempt at a certain kind of analysis.

Of course, I am not the only person attempting to provide broad-based understandings of organization which are attentive to de-familiarization, distance and closeness to empirical material and are pragmatic with respect to theoretical resources. For that matter, such attempts are not confined to organization studies. In cultural studies, for example, Calhoun and Sennett (2007: 1–12) are at pains to eschew theoretical tribalism and to use detailed empirical study to illuminate the processes of 'practicing culture' rather than the static products of this practice. Going back to organization studies, Watson's (2011) case for a Pragmatist ethnography has some similarities to my approach, as in particular does Czarniawska's (2008) development of the notion of action nets. The latter offers an interpretative, process-orientated way of analysing the complex and messy web of connections between practices or activities, the actors and institutions produced through this web, and the ways in which this in turn reproduces legitimate social orders in general and organizations and organization fields in particular. This approach itself draws upon and modifies a range of literatures in organization studies, including institutional theory, sensemaking, actor-network theory and narrative analysis, enabling Czarniawska and others to illuminate diverse empirical sites ranging from city management (Czarniawska, 2002) to man-made and natural disasters (Czarniawska, 2009).

Whilst the details of this approach are different from those of that adopted here, what they share beyond some broad affinities is a certain style or strategy of analysis – not a method, but an approach or orientation which, like Watson's (2011), is ultimately concerned with 'how things work in organizations'. This is certainly not to posit those of us who research and write about organizations as having some god-like access to the truth of organizational life but, more humbly, to suggest that, with a degree of assiduity, sensitivity, insight and good faith, we can gain greater insights into organizations by virtue of our research and writing than without. In particular, the attempt to understand how things work in organizations entails the making of interpretations of the evidence available, interpretations which, again, are not infallible but, if we show our 'workings', should be intelligible and, one hopes, plausible to others.

DECODING BLETCHLEY PARK

In this book, the metaphorical term I have used for the making of such interpretations is 'decoding'. I will shortly review some of the 'decodings' that have been made, but first want to emphasise what was said about this term in the introductory chapter. Of course, its use was suggested by the fact that BP was a 'decoding organization', but there is more at stake here than a play on words. Instead, I found the term expressive because it speaks to the twin aims of the book. Firstly, it suggests, precisely, an interpretation of BP's organization. Here I should stress again that it does not suggest a discovery of a single or objective truth. Thinking of cryptanalysis at BP, the decoding of a single message might perhaps be thought of in this way, in that it would either be an accurate decryption of the message originally sent or not (I say 'might perhaps' because processes of translation themselves entail interpretation). But the production of intelligence derived from multiple messages was most certainly an interpretative act, requiring judgment in the face of ambiguity and incomplete knowledge. These kinds of judgements are also at stake in my attempts at 'decoding organization', which are fundamentally attempts to ask and answer the question 'What does this mean?'.

Secondly, the term 'decoding' resonates with the other aim of the book, namely to approach organization studies in a certain way. And here my contention has been that much, although by no means all, of organization studies 'encodes' organization both by the deployment of arcane vocabulary and also through the straitjacket of typologies, ideal types, concepts and constructs which do not necessarily assist the understanding of 'how things work in organizations'. Thus decoding also refers to the process of moving away from, over, beneath or behind (I am not quite sure which spatial metaphor is the right one) the encodements of organization theory, of which perhaps the foremost is precisely to encode the verb of organization as the noun organization (Weick, 1979). That is not to say that this analysis dispenses with concepts, constructs and so on. Indeed, it is hard to see how it would be possible to write anything intelligible which did so. But the intention has been to do so in a 'light' rather than a 'heavy' way, being alive to the ways in which such constructs are partial and heuristic, orientating us towards a world which is never captured by them.

These meanings aside, there has been another, particular, kind of decoding going on in this book, which is related to the goal of de-familiarization and arises from the specific empirical focus. For the historical case of BP also brings with it a set of public and popular images. One of the ways in which this book uses organization studies to illuminate BP is to problematize these images. In particular, I have been at pains to show that the image of BP as a place where a small number of eccentric male mathematicians broke the Enigma code with a combination of genius and prototype computers is highly misleading. On the contrary, there were very many people, most of them women, not men, at BP. Most of what they did there involved not genius but a mixture of hard physical work and routine procedural work, and the latter was the case even for the cryptanalysts. So far as those cryptanalysts were concerned, only a few were geniuses, although most were certainly highly intelligent, by no means all were mathematicians and very few were eccentric. So far as Enigma is concerned, it was not in fact a code but a cipher, or, rather, it was not a single cipher but a cipher system with a broad set of variants; and the prototype electronic computer – Colossus – was used not for Enigma but for the Fish cipher, more specifically Tunny. Furthermore, BP's work was not just concerned with Enigma but involved a wide variety of other codes and ciphers, including not just Fish but also, for example, JN-25 and Hagelin C-38m as well as many 'low-grade' ciphers and (in London, rather than at BP) diplomatic and commercial ciphers.

However, it is important to say that there is more at stake here than counterposing this fuller picture of BP with the more restricted public image, an image which is increasingly tied to the person of Alan Turing. That image itself requires understanding and explanation. One point to make is that it is not an absolutely false picture of BP – it has just enough verisimilitude for it to be viable and not wholly ridiculous.

Moreover, there are other reasons why this image has achieved such prominence. These are partly to do with more general apprehensions of Britain at war, which tend to emphasise amateurishness, ingenuity and triumph in the face of overwhelming odds. The received image of BP fits such apprehensions, as does the somewhat related idea of it as a place of unity of purpose, harmony and high morale. Again this is an image with some truth, although, as I have suggested, a partial one. In particular, I showed in Part I of the book that there were a great many high-level conflicts within and around BP, conflicts over what kind of organization it should be and over who should control it. I also showed in Chapter 5 that morale was not uniformly high, and in Chapter 3 that narratives of shared wartime spirit conceal some significant variations and entail some mythologization.

There may also be some narrower reasons why, when the story of BP began to become public knowledge in 1974, it became understood in the way it did. These relate to the issue of the ubiquity of the war within British public consciousness – I referred in the introductory chapter to how this was true for me in my childhood – but also to the then-prominent sense that Britain was in political and economic crisis, moral decline and a permanent 'state of emergency' (Sandbrook, 2010). Against this background, the BP story, appearing when it did, could be taken up as a contrast to decline, but also as an indicator of what had been lost. For here was a story of extraordinary success and one, more-over, that was ethically pristine[1] and quintessentially British, or perhaps even English. Some of this is nicely summed up in a review of Aldrich's (2010) study of GCHQ:

> GCHQ grew out of the Government Code and Cypher School at Bletchley Park, now famous for its contribution to the breaking of German military codes, which no one saw as a 'threat to personal liberty' – rather the reverse. It also acquired something of a cuddly image, which may have disarmed people later on. The early code-breakers were eccentric, untidy individualists, usually Oxbridge mathematicians, chess champions and expert crossword-puzzle

> solvers, assisted by bevies of debutantes whose tedious job it was to
> transcribe their data ... The image is important, because it was
> supposed to say something about Britain's essential superiority over
> the Germans, who could muster more regiments than we could,
> but were far too regimented to make the best use of them. What
> Britain lacked in brute strength it made up for in ingenuity and wit.
>
> *(Porter, 2010: 20)*

So one limited, but important, task in this book has been to provide a
more nuanced account of BP than that which has permeated popular
consciousness. That task is in one way entirely specific to BP. But it does
carry wider implications for organization studies to the extent that it
points to some of the complexities of doing historical research on
organizations which are well known and which are not located so far
in the past as to have no resonance in contemporary culture. Moreover,
it is suggestive of the way that one thing which such research can do is to
give voice to those who are otherwise marginalized by received accounts
and in this way resonates with recent interest in subaltern experience –
the experience of non-elite groups – in organization studies. In this way,
calling into question the account of BP which foregrounds its elite
carries a wider implication for the study of organizations. I will now
turn to the other broad arguments that have been made.

MAKING ORGANIZATION

The chapters of this book have provided a kind of interlocking and
overlapping set of accounts of BP which, although categorized in terms
of the themes of structures, cultures and work, are not intended to
suggest that these themes are distinct. This is perhaps especially
important to flag up in an analysis which purports to show the messy
complexity of organization, since such an ambition is rather contra-
dicted by employing such a categorization. As suggested earlier, I think
some categorization is unavoidable if a comprehensible narrative is to
be provided, but it is as well to acknowledge the irony. What runs
across the three sections is an attempt to demonstrate how BP was
'made' over time: made from and within a tangle of different

organizations encompassing most obviously the Foreign Office, SIS, the War Office, the Admiralty, the Air Ministry (and associated sections of these such as NID, OIC, MI8 etc.), the army, the navy and the air force (and both male and female branches of these services); and including less obviously the GPO, BTMC, the Ministry of Works and others. One point which I should stress is that it is easy to write as if these various organizations were themselves in some way entities because the focus is on the making of BP. But, of course, it would be equally possible, were one to look at any one of them, to show that each was, in its own way, made: the details would be different, but the fact of 'madeness' would still be there.

This sense of organizational structure-as-process (Strati, 2000; 2008) moves beyond seeing structure simply as a rational organizational response to various contingencies such as organizational size, technology or customer demand not because these contingencies are irrelevant – they are not – but because the way in which they are understood and acted upon is not contained within them. Instead, political processes and choices (Child, 1972; Pfeffer and Salancik, 1978) but also non-rational and chance factors all come into play. In this sense I suggested that there is a 'contingency to contingency', and structural outcomes are necessarily under-determined: they could have been different.

As well as its assembly as 'an organization', BP also in large part constructed signals intelligence as a defined and socially legitimate 'organizational field'. This point is an important one for historians of intelligence, since it was shown in some detail how and why this particular category of intelligence was constituted at BP. But it is also an important point for organization studies since what it denotes is the way in which an organization (so to say) can construct its own environment rather than simply responding to, or seeking a fit with, it. Such an analysis is referred to by Barley (2010: 778) as 'the path not taken' in organization studies, although of course that is not to say that it has been entirely ignored (e.g. Pfeffer and Salancik, 1978; Perrow, 1986; Weick, 2001). However, there is more at stake in this than showing two-way interactions between organization and environment. The more profound point is that the *boundary* between what is inside and what is outside organization is constantly socially negotiated and in that way different from the relationship between a biological organism and its environment, which has been the standard anchor of such metaphors in organization studies.

Thus in the BP case what is in evidence is not a set of interactions between discrete spheres of organization and environment. To take but one example, the ways in which those working at BP were an amalgam of FO and service personnel means that it makes little sense to treat the FO and the services and service ministries as an 'external environment'. At the same time, precisely because of this amalgam, BP can hardly be said to have existed as a self-contained 'organization'. Instead, what can be seen is an ongoing negotiation over what this 'organization' was and who controlled it. In particular, through a highly political and conflicted process, signals intelligence in the sense of the drawing together of interception, cryptanalysis and intelligence amounted to a construction – in the face of competing claims and institutions – of the 'business' that BP was in. The consequences were far reaching in that from then on sigint, not just in the UK but globally, was understood in those terms (Taylor, 2007). Thus sigint now seems like a self-evident, natural and 'familiar' category because the social and organizational conditions of its construction at BP have disappeared from view. Note that this is not an example of the mimetic isomorphism identified by neo-institutional theory (DiMaggio and Powell, 1991). Bletchley Park did not emulate legitimate forms of sigint organization but rather such a form was created there.

I suggested briefly in Chapter 2 that the construction of sigint has some resonance with another development in neo-institutionalism, that of institutional entrepreneurship (DiMaggio, 1988). In one way this concept is a response to a 'problem' which is no more than an artefact of neo-institutionalism itself, namely that it cannot easily explain change and innovation. More specifically, it attempts to explain how 'organizational fields' come to exist in the first place and the role of agency within institutions. The BP case is illustrative of what might be called institutional entrepreneurship, most obviously in the role of Gordon Welchman in developing the new organizational processes to handle Enigma, and indeed this is very much how his role is described in accounts of BP, his own included. However, to do so is to fall into the trap intrinsic to the concept, which 'presents actors as incredibly rational, opportunistic, strategic and seemingly unconstrained by institutional arrangements and other actors. A more balanced and realistic approach to embedded agency within a context of collective action is called for' (Maguire, 2008: 678). Approached in this more critical way, institutional entrepreneurship can be used to open up political processes of institution-making (e.g. Maguire and Hardy, 2006) which have affinities to the discussion here of the way that BP and sigint were constructed, which does not make the actions and decisions of individuals irrelevant, but locates them within a wider social and organizational setting.

This 'setting' should also be understood within the more general historical process through which, throughout the twentieth century, state and society became interconnected in ways both new and more extensive than in the past, especially as a result of the world wars (Cronin, 1991; Edgerton, 2011). Bletchley Park is a case in point, with a predominantly civilian organization becoming intimately enmeshed with the military, and as a result processes of conflict and negotiation occurred as this new set of relations was shaped and re-shaped over time, such as those relating to defining what sigint was and who had legitimate ownership of it. In a more general way, BP is an example of the mobilization of the population in line with an intensive and well-orchestrated mobilization of sentiment, for example through the kinds of propaganda films discussed in Chapter 3. For all its fractures (Calder, 1969), this served to forge a significant – if perhaps these days somewhat sentimentalized – sense of wartime national purpose. Thus the making of BP is in part recognizably an aspect of the making of, at least, British society during WW2 through a bringing together of people and institutions that would otherwise have been separate. That cannot be ignored in understanding BP's organization, but nor should it be over-stated: wartime culture does not provide anything like a complete account of BP. Clearly, distinct organizations during the war differed markedly in character and, although wartime culture may well have been relevant to all of them, this difference suggests that other issues must be considered.

Closely related to this is the fact that BP's organization was made through an assembly of cultural materials. I say 'closely related' because to an extent these materials were linked to the organizations brought together at BP. Again, then, the notion of an 'inside' and an 'outside' of organizational culture is chimerical. In Part II, following Parker's (2000) approach of apprehending culture as 'unity and difference', I suggested that there were a wide array of what I called the pillars and splinters of culture, that is to say, the more homogeneous and more heterogeneous elements. With the many caveats made in those chapters, the pillars were connected with the war itself, with the secrecy that was so defining a feature of BP and with the recruitment strategy which, whilst changing over time, retained the imprint of its early basis within Oxbridge Colleges and carried their culture into BP[2]. However, just as wartime national culture was itself more heterogeneous than its received image suggests, so too was BP culture. The many 'splinters' I identified included those of gender, educational level and discipline, age, service or civilian affiliation, 'Chiefs and Indians', indoctrination into different secrets and several others.

This analysis was intended to convey something more than the existence of 'sub-cultures'. Rather, the point was that culture almost endlessly divides and re-divides, with each 'distinction' being susceptible to further splintering. But culture also almost endlessly re-combines, so that these various distinctions intersect and interact with each other rather than being fixed or static categories. So again BP was 'made' from a complex tangle, neither reducible to something which can simply be called 'BP culture' nor understandable in terms of typologies of organizational culture which encode culture by flattening or erasing altogether its complexity. This 'tangle' was shown to be a dynamic one, simultaneously integrating and differentiating, in the way suggested by Martin (1992, 2002), something I attempted to capture through the metaphor of a kaleidoscope that holds together a picture which is nevertheless ever-changing.

Related again was the material presented in Part III, where I sought to explain how BP worked, in part as a response to the call to 'bring work back in' to organization studies (Barley and Kunda, 2001). Here too can be seen processes of making organization, whether through personal networks of trust; through management in general and the management of morale in particular; through meetings, committees and other devices of co-ordination; through practices of knowledge-sharing and learning; or by the borrowing of work and organizational techniques from elsewhere. Many of these practices are mundane in the extreme and yet are crucial to the production and reproduction of organization by creating a 'web of workable arrangements' (Dalton, 1959). Such mundanity is easily overlooked or discounted as uninteresting, but it is the 'stuff' of organizing.

Yet again, as with the discussion of structures and cultures, what was central here was diversity and indeterminacy. Thus attempts to make BP's work fit into standard categories of organizational analysis such as bureaucracy, post-bureaucracy or centralization were shown to be inadequate to the mess and complexity which constantly eludes such categories. In particular, in Chapter 6 I gave consideration to the category of knowledge work. In one way, BP can be seen as exemplifying dominant understandings of knowledge work as consisting of esoteric, specialized knowledge deployed with considerable discretion in non-hierarchical settings (Starbuck, 1992). Yet closer examination suggested a more complex situation, rendering knowledge work a more fragile category than might be thought (see also Grey and Sturdy, 2009). Thus even the most obvious exemplar of knowledge work, cryptanalysis, entailed much that was routine and mundane, whilst the routine clerical work of indexing, for example, required discretion. So for BP to 'work' there were multiple, intertwining interactions between different kinds of work, all of which were necessary to its operations, in ways similar to those suggested by the concept of 'organizational ambidexterity' (Raisch *et al.*, 2009).

This 'twisting together' of standardization and judgment, or 'exploration and exploitation' (March, 1991), suggests that decoding work in organizations entails beginning from the complexities of the work itself, rather than encoding these complexities by imposing abstract models of organization upon them. This in a way is a variant on the theme of showing how BP entailed more than the received image of the 'genius codebreaker', being instead a much more varied and interdependent set of activities. One reason why this was obvious at BP was that it existed at the cusp of computerization and so many work processes which are nowadays largely invisible could be discerned. For example, the modern-day 'knowledge worker' might be imagined tapping away at a laptop computer, but the tasks being performed might be understood as no more than the mundane filing and clerical work which at BP was performed by human labour (cf. Lilley, Lightfoot and Amaral, 2004: 141).

Not just this last point but all of the insights summarised in this section are aided by the fact that this is an historical study. The visibility of organizational processes and of the societal context of organization and work is made easier by historical distance. That is not to say that similar insights cannot be, and have not been, achieved through the study of present-day organizations. But historical distance can enable a distinctive perspective on what most of this book has been about, namely organization as 'an accomplishment' rather than as a thing which just 'exists'. One reason, perhaps unusual, why BP offers a vehicle for an analysis of 'organization-making' is the way that it came together in a particular geographical space for a particular and defined period of time, and that site and period were characterized by rapid growth. In a sense[3], the BP story is one with a beginning, a middle and an end in a way which is rarely the case when studying organization in the present.

That may suggest that the wider significance of what I have said about it is rather limited. In many senses BP is a unique case, as, indeed, must ultimately be true of any case study. However, it is possible to see many resonances, at least, between BP and other organizations, including those of the present day. For example, the management of the Typex room, described in Chapter 5, with its intensive monitoring of individual output levels does not seem very far removed from current systems for managing call centres (Bain *et al.*, 2002). Again, the enclosed, secretive community of BP might bear some comparison with the self-contained 'Googleplex' campus of the Google corporation (Stiernstedt and Jakobsson, 2009). Another instance would be the parallels between the 'instinctive' ability of an intelligence analyst or cryptanalyst to spot tiny hints – as discussed in Chapter 6 – and Weick and Roberts' (1993) observation of the way that flight crews need to be alert to small things which might have large consequences. Or, to give a final example, Stuart Milner-Barry's stress on 'listening' as central to his management of Hut 6, again described in Chapter 5, is echoed in contemporary practices of the management of knowledge workers as outlined by Alvesson and Svengisson (2003).

No doubt many such parallels could be enumerated. They require careful handling, of course, because they carry the danger of anachronism. Equally, there are many aspects of BP which are highly unusual and will have very limited resonance, if any at all. In particular, the extreme secrecy, both internal and external, is hardly commonplace. This may indeed be a point of interest in that, by definition, studies of secret organizations are extremely rare and really feasible only when conducted historically (cf. Davies, 2004). To understand BP would surely be impossible without appreciating how central secrecy was, and this analysis has been able to flesh out the suggestive remarks made by Herman (1996) about the way in which the cultures of secret organizations operate. For example, secrecy has an impact in the creation of insider and outsider groups and also has a tendency to become an end in itself, so that secret-keeping is the default and ingrained position. Yet even on this point BP may be merely an extreme example of something more widespread in that various forms of formal and informal secrecy can be found in other settings (Costas and Grey, 2011).

But, in any case, I have not sought to emphasise these kinds of parallels in this book. For I am not claiming that BP is representative of organization in general so much as that it is illustrative of organization-making. The illustration is particular in its detail, but that organizations need to be 'made' in some sense is definitional to them: they do not emerge spontaneously but through processes of, at a minimum, the hiring and co-ordination of staff, but also growth, acquisition, merger, diversification and so on. In this way, analysing the process of organization-making has a purchase beyond the case of BP[4]. If that is so, then the 'style' of analysis pursued here may also have a wider purchase. At the very least it is a reminder that organization is an 'achievement', not a given, and this is important because it is the reason why speaking of 'an organization' as a thing is not enough, for that thing is a moment, or a succession of constantly crystallizing and re-crystallizing moments, sustained by work – not so much the ostensible work of the organization (although that as well) but rather the work of organizing the organization.

REPRESENTING BLETCHLEY PARK

In this respect the archive material used in this study is fascinating. On the one hand, through the maze of memos, reports, notes of meetings and so on it is possible to glimpse aspects – certainly not the entirety, not least because by definition it captures only that which was recorded and preserved – of the work of 'organizing the organization' unfolding over time. On the other hand, in the numerous internal histories prepared at the end of the war it is possible to see retrospective representations of that work. These are typically neater, more shaped, more comprehensible than was the process itself. And, of course, this book is another kind of retrospective representation, itself seeking to give comprehensible shape to this process. But it is different from those internal histories as well. Most obviously, it is different because also included in the account it offers are the internal histories themselves. It is also more remote in time, shaped by my particular knowledge of organization studies and also – partly as a result – a little more open about the conditions and limitations of its own production. Nevertheless, in a sense which I do not think is altogether fanciful, this book is itself now a part – a very minor part – of an ongoing stream of textual representation of BP.

It is, of course, a partial representation and could be nothing but that. There can in general be no definitive and exhaustive accounts of organization, which will always run beyond anything that can be said about it, even if one had unlimited space. Apart from that general limitation of principle, there are some specific, empirical ways in which this account of BP is partial. It has focussed far more on Enigma than on other ciphers and, within that, more on Hut 3 and Hut 6 than on anything else. This is partly because these matters are by far the best documented but also because, at least organizationally, they are illustrative of some key themes. There is hardly anything in this book about the processes inside government ministries and other agencies which interacted with BP, and what there is comes mainly from a 'BP perspective' because of the kinds of data used. There is also very little on the relationship with the USA in general and its sigint agencies in particular, and only very slightly more on intelligence distribution. I have not made anything but passing mention of comparisons between BP and the sigint organizations of other countries such as the USA and Germany. Perhaps the biggest omission of all is that I have not discussed that area of BP's work concerned not with breaking enemy ciphers but with protecting the security of British ciphers. All of these omissions are mainly for reasons of space, and also manageability. Even with these limitations of scope the documentary basis for this book in terms of archive sources has been vast, running to many thousands of documents, leaving aside the many secondary sources utilized. These pragmatic concerns are real and, I hope, understandable. However, it is also the case that, in what is already a very detailed empirical study, to have extended it into these other areas would have made it still more difficult to convey the analytical themes I have pursued.

In addition to those analytical themes, or rather as a further illustration of them, I have throughout this book used a series of metaphorical
images in the attempt to capture BP. Accounts of organization have
almost always had recourse to such images in one way or another,
common examples being envisaging organization as a machine, an
organism, a brain or a computer. These and other metaphors were identified in Morgan's (1986) influential work and, at least since its publication, organization studies has been extensively attentive to their role
both within organizations and within its own accounts of organizations
(e.g. Grant and Oswick, 1996). Metaphors are, of course, never 'innocent'
or neutral: they selectively highlight particular features of organization
and thereby assert their primacy, with potentially corresponding effects.
To take an obvious example, machine metaphors highlight the predict-
able, designed and inhuman, rendering marginal and perhaps illegitimate
the chaotic, uncontrollable and emotional. Yet metaphors are also ines-
capable since organization is intangible and ungraspable directly: perhaps in this sense the very term 'organization' is a metaphor.

The kinds of metaphors I have used in this book are all variants on
a theme. Thus I have variously written of BP as a cityscape in flux, as a
jigsaw or as a kaleidoscope. Elsewhere I have referred to splinters and
crystals. On many occasions the metaphor has been of threads, strings,
twine and knots. None of them in itself quite captures the image I want
to convey, and for that reason I have not stuck with just one. But, taken
together, perhaps these metaphors express some sense of complexity
and of movement that coalesces at moments to make a meaningful
picture and then shifts again. That sense is closer to showing the
combination of the dynamic process of organization as a verb with the
instantiation of this process that is organization as a noun, the combination which the book as a whole suggests as a way of understanding BP
but also organization more generally. Similarly, the irreducible simul-
taneities of action and structure and of organization and environment
are at least partially captured by these images.

Such metaphors are clearly related to those found in the many
descriptions of the organization of BP that use the metaphor of anarchy

in some way or other, as, to take a particular example, in the official history (Hinsley *et al.*, 1979: 273). A related metaphor in Birch's internal history is of 'a patchwork of extemporised expedients'[5]. This is a telling phrase, in that extemporization compares well with the jazz metaphor of improvization (Weick, 1998), whilst the image of a 'patchwork' is not dissimilar to that of a jigsaw. It also very much implies the kind of 'twisting together of different threads' and the 'strings of inter-organizationality' which in Chapter 6 I referred to as characterizing the ways that BP worked. That is, the idea that an array of borrowings from and relationships between organizations coalesced at BP, and made it in the particular form it took. However, there is an important difference. When these and similar expressions occur, both in official documents and in commentaries on BP, they seem invariably to imply 'deficiency' – that this was in some way an 'improper' or, as Birch has it, 'freakish' way of organizing, with the associated implication that there is a proper or normal way that is to be preferred. I have not wanted to make such implications and have used a different set of metaphors as a result. For it is not clear to me that there is a template for proper organizing: rather, I would suggest that organizing often and perhaps always has a 'messy' or 'extemporized' character. Again, it can be said that this is particularly obvious in the case of BP because of the circumstances of its making but, if so, then again my point would be that it is nevertheless illustrative of what with entirely different details and in entirely different contexts can be found elsewhere.

It is this messiness and complexity which makes organization so interesting and elusive. It is not always well captured by the encodements of organization studies, which are typically concerned with tidying and simplification. Thus, in making organization comprehensible, it is also made less rich and more familiar. The process of 'decoding organization' in the way that I have attempted here also aims for comprehensibility, but with perhaps a little less sacrifice of richness, by remaining alert to the strangeness of the ways in which human beings work together. An element of that remains indecipherable, like the missing elements of an intercepted Enigma message.

PARADOXICAL CHALLENGES

Earlier, I sought to explain what 'kind of analysis' is provided in this book by positioning it in terms of a particular way of using empirical detail, historical analysis and organizational theory, and implied that in this way it stood in some relation to the work of others who seem to be seeking similar ways. In particular, I summarised the way that one of the world's leading organization theorists, Barbara Czarniawska (2008), has provided her own response to the present state of organization studies in propounding 'a theory of organizing'. At the end of that work, she itemizes some ten 'wishes, pleas or simply memoranda' (Czarniawska, 2008: 132) for the renewal of organization theory which – reading them after the bulk of this book had been written – have a considerable resonance for me. They are, as she says, paradoxical and yet, paradoxically, should be strived for at the same time (Czarniawska, 2008: 133). In the light of what I have now said about the nature of this book, in this section I will extend the attempt to position it by considering how it relates to these precepts. This is not, I should stress, intended as a way of evaluating its merit but as a way of recapitulating its intentions.

Czarniawska's first precept is 'to be close to the practice of organizing while keeping enough distance to be able to problematise it' (Czarniawska, 2008: 133). This precisely describes the position I outlined above, in which closeness and distance were cardinal principles of the analysis. Her second is 'to represent organizational practices in a way that will demystify them while revealing their everyday dramatism' (Czarniawska, 2008: 133). This speaks to my emphasis on de-familiarization allied to a strong focus on specific detail of mundane practices, conflicts and so on. As I noted in the introductory chapter, the BP story is one of considerable dramatic possibilities, and its enduring interest to the public is testament to this. But there is a more 'low-key' drama to be found as well in, say, the administrative conflicts over control of sigint or, in a very different way, the swirl of cultural splinters brought into daily contact at BP.

The third injunction is 'to be of help to employees in shaking free from absurdities not of their making, and in justifying the seeming absurdities of their making' (Czarniawska, 2008: 134). This seems to speak to the concerns within critical management studies (CMS) about emancipation. Whilst much of my work has been located within this tradition, the present book is not primarily 'critical' in this sense and, of course, any absurdities there may have been are long in the past, so that it would seem itself absurd to bemoan the work practices at BP. That said, as I suggested earlier in this chapter, what this analysis has done is to devote attention to what might otherwise have been the marginalized experiences and voices at BP, those of the men and, especially, women undertaking unglamorous jobs, largely unrecognized in the received image of BP. The notion of de-familiarization is again relevant here as it links to that of de-naturalization, which is a core concern of CMS (Fournier and Grey, 2000) – the idea of seeking to identify how that which seems to be objectively given and so 'just the way things are' is constructed. In broad terms this apprehension of received wisdom is present in, for example, the suggestion that dominant narratives of British wartime society need to be problematized in the ways indicated in Chapter 3. Relatedly, the discussion of morale in Chapter 5 was an attempt to interrogate such dominant narratives as they apply to BP.

Czarniawska's fourth plea is 'to maintain plurivocality of the field, and to develop a clear voice to speak for theory' (Czarniawska, 2008: 134). This is partly to do with preserving organizational voices and here the attempt to ensure that the full range of experiences at BP was represented in this book is again relevant. But I hope that my own voice has also been present – more insistently, I suppose, in the 'wraparounds' such as this conclusion, the introductory chapter, and the introductions and conclusions to each part of the book; but also, in more muted form, throughout the text. Whether that voice speaks 'for theory' is less clear. In many ways I have sought to speak 'across theory', and this has some affinity with the suggestion that organization studies should 'poach freely from many sources, disciplines and domains and . . . become more conscious of a specificity of organization theory as a genre' (Czarniawska, 2008: 135). In a similar spirit I have ranged around history, intelligence history, cultural history and various social sciences, as well as within different traditions of organization studies; and I have used sources ranging from public information films screened during WW2 through oral history interviews to archive material. These piratical raids are not, of course, unproblematic, and to some they may be quite unacceptable, whether in principle or just as practiced here.

I have made some play of the case for drawing upon older and perhaps more unfashionable parts of the organization-studies literature, whilst also seeking to provide an alternative to established ways of studying organizations, and in this way attempted something similar to the suggestion of the need to maintain 'close ties with the past of organization theory, and to re-invent this field of theory constantly anew' (Czarniawska, 2008: 136). Czarniawska's next challenge is that of the need 'to keep plurality and tensions whilst continuing translations and communication within and across the borders of the genre' (Czarniawska, 2008: 136). Here she is concerned with the dispute between those who would want organization studies to become more integrated and those who would want it to celebrate its schismatic character. I suppose I would see this book as located within this tension. On the one hand, I see possibilities in selectively and eclectically drawing upon a wide range of approaches; on the other hand, I have not sought, and would not think it possible to achieve, an integration of these.

The final injunctions in Czarniawska's list are more difficult to respond to. She urges a striving 'for beauty and utility' (Czarniawska, 2008:136) as a contrast to 'rigour', which she sees as 'rigid, stiff and severe'. I take the contrast here to be between the stifling orthodoxies of the journals in the organization-studies field, orthodoxies which have exsanguinated the capacity of 'the literature' to say much that is interesting, let alone beautiful or useful, and a more vibrant and engaged scholarship. It will be clear from what I have said already that I agree, although I would not presume to pronounce on whether this book meets the requirement. Finally, she advocates that we 'draw advantages from globalization while preserving the local treasures'. This perhaps applies to an historical study less than it would to others. That said, BP was part of a global conflict between tyranny and freedom and within that it drew on highly localized ways of organizing to make a decisive impact upon the conflict.

So this book might be read as one kind of attempt to address the rather demanding challenge Czarniawska has posed for organization studies. But it was not conceived of or intended in that way, but rather in more personal terms, as I will now explain.

FINAL THOUGHTS

I mentioned in the introductory chapter that this book has been a labour of love. That is so, because of my intense fascination with its subject, but it has also been something else: an attempt at a new direction not just for organization studies but for myself as someone working within that field. At least some of my writing in the past has taken the form of critiques of what is wrong with organization studies (e.g. Grey, 2009, 2010). Here I have sought to do something different by providing an example of how I think organization studies might better proceed. In a way, it is an extended answer to a question which, both socially and professionally, when talking to academics in other disciplines, I am often asked when I mention my subject: so what is that? I have always struggled to find an answer which is neither embarrassingly trivial nor absurdly over-complicated. As I have been working on BP I have used the study in such conversations to explain what I do and have always been rewarded with responses expressing both comprehension as to its value and interest as regards its content. Of course, that is in part because of the public visibility of BP, which in itself is perhaps no bad thing: why shouldn't organization studies be concerned with things of public interest?

At all events this book is an attempt at a positive response to my longstanding – and growing – dissatisfaction with much of the work in the field for being, indeed, either embarrassingly trivial or absurdly over-complicated. In this way it is an experiment intended to see whether there is a middle ground between these things through which a revived form of organization studies could emerge. This experiment is in large part a matter of the adoption of a certain style of analysis, as indicated earlier, especially in terms of the manner of the use of organization theory. It is also a matter of methodology, in that it uses a historical case and, finally, of extending the normal range of the kinds of organizations considered by organization studies. This range is normally quite limited, with banks, consultancy firms, airlines, manufacturing companies, call centres and so on featuring promi- nently and repetitively (Rehn, 2008). Breaking with this established repertoire may also be a way of reviving organization studies. Of course, some may feel that this is an entirely misplaced exercise, that organization studies is proceeding perfectly well and is in no need of any such reviving. On such a view, the experiment will necessarily be a failure, and an ill-conceived one at that. But for those who also worry about the state of organization studies, I offer it as one way to respond positively to that worry.

In the end what that response amounts to is an approach to organization studies which is both intensive and expansive. It is intensive in that it entails a detailed, even laborious, engagement with fine-grained empirical material. Complex organizations are just that, and organization studies needs to do justice to this complexity. In this case, much of the detail has been drawn from archival study, but clearly this is only one way that a similar effect could be achieved. For that matter, it has its own limitations in terms of its ability to convey the more embodied and experiential sense of organizational life that might be achieved by an ethnography, for example. This can be partly com- pensated for by the use of other materials – memoirs and oral history interviews, in this case – but, like any other method, it has its own partialities. Alongside this intensiveness runs an expansive approach to analysis in which the insights of organization studies broadly conceived are mobilized in order to make sense of empirical detail. It is important that the two go hand in hand: intensive detail lapses into empiricism if not held within a broad analytic frame; an expansive analysis lapses into abstraction if detached from empirical detail.

Above all, perhaps, is the need to find a way of writing that can integrate such an intensive and expansive undertaking and which can represent organization as both entity and process, both action and structure, both inside and outside. Of that I will not write further. Those familiar with them will have noticed that in the previous section I did not mention the fifth of Czarniawska's precepts, namely 'to shape organization theory texts more deliberately, while hiding the makings of them more skilfully' (Czarniawska, 2008: 135). What a challenging and enchanting notion that is. But part of its challenge is not one of what to write, but of what not to write, for

> A text will not become better because the author explained to the readers why they ought to see it as good ... as to what is good organization theory, tastes differ, and so do times and places. The proof of the pudding is most certainly in its eating: it is worthwhile experimenting with new forms and voices, but it is also necessary to remember that many experiments fail. *(Czarniawska, 2008: 135)*

I have said that this book is an experiment of sorts. Its success or failure is for its readers to judge. If it is a failure then it will at least serve as warning to others. If it is successful then it may prove useful to those seeking to develop their own ways of reviving organization studies.

NOTES

1. Subsequently, some ethical questions about BP's work have been raised of which the most controversial is undoubtedly whether and to what extent it possessed knowledge of the Holocaust, as Breitman (1998) claims. That some decrypted material related to the Holocaust is not in doubt (see within the TNA HW 19/ISOSICLE sub-series). Whether this amounted to knowledge of the Holocaust and its extent cannot be said with certainty. The most comprehensive overview and discussion of the relevant available evidence is Hanyok (2011). It may be that further declassification of documents will shed more light on this in the future. Another controversy relates to whether BP had advance knowledge of

the devastating air raid on Coventry on 14 November 1940. However, despite the persistence of claims to this effect (see e.g. McKay, 2010: 111–117), the exhaustive examination in the official history (Hinsley *et al.*, 1979, Appendix 9: 528–48) leaves room for little doubt that they are misplaced.

2. Again one could be more fine-grained than this. Some would undoubtedly have said then, as they do now, that different Oxford and Cambridge Colleges have different cultures and so to speak of Oxbridge College culture in the singular is a misnomer. Others might say that any such differences are trivial: but to those involved that might not be so. This is another example of what I said in Chapter 4 about culture constantly re-dividing.

3. But only in a sense – although the time and place of BP means that there is a beginning and an end, it was located in a longer history going backwards in time – and I have partly examined this in relation to GC & CS in the inter-war period – and forward into the post-war period, something I have said hardly anything about (but see Aldrich, 2010).

4. There are some organizational cases which might be particularly close in various respects to that of BP. An obvious example is the Manhattan Project to develop the US atomic bomb during WW2. Here, too, to stereotype both it and BP, a group of often young, often highly educated staff worked in a secret and compartmentalized organization in a remote location (or locations), doing a wide variety of work tasks and doing so in concert with a range of military and commercial agencies. One significant difference, perhaps, is that the Manhattan Project occurred within the organizational infrastructure of the US Army Corps of Engineers. See Rhodes (1986) for an account of the project and Norris (2008) for some comments on, specifically, organizational aspects.

5. TNA HW 43/1: 145.

Appendix A. Timeline 1919–2011

Date	GC & CS/Bletchley Park/Interviewees	War events
1919	GC & CS formed from Admiralty Room 40 (NID 25) and MI1b, under control of the Admiralty. Commander Alastair Denniston appointed as its first operational Head.	Treaty of Versailles between Germany and Allied Powers signed following WW1.
1922	GC & CS moved to FO Control.	Mussolini came to power in Italy.
1923	GC & CS moved to SIS Control within FO.	
1924	Naval Section of GC & CS established.	
1930	Military (Army) Section of GC & CS established.	
1933		Hitler came to power in Germany.
1936	Air Section of GC & CS established.	Italy and Germany allied to form 'Axis'. German military forces entered the Rhineland in defiance of Treaty of Versailles.
1937	Italian Naval Enigma broken by Dilly Knox of GC & CS.	
1938	BP site purchased for GC & CS. Trial mobilization of GC & CS. Denniston recruited Gordon Welchman.	Munich agreement. Germany occupied Czech Sudetenland.
July 1939	Polish cryptanalysts reveal their knowledge of Enigma decryption methods to GC & CS staff.	
August 1939	Mobilization of GC&CS staff to BP.	Molotov–Ribbentrop Pact between Germany and the USSR

Date		
September 1939	BP staff numbered approximately 200.	Germany invades Poland. Britain and France declare war on Germany; WW2 begins.
January 1940	*Roy recruited to BP Air Section as cryptanalyst.* First break of a wartime Enigma cipher – Army Green key, followed by GAF Red key.	
April 1940		German invasion of Denmark and Norway
May 1940	First SLUs established. Most Army and Air Enigma became unreadable on 1 May. Red re-broken from 20 May.	Churchill became Prime Minister. Battle of France.
May–June 1940	Some SLUs in operation and Ultra was being used under 'Source Boniface' cover by the army. First breaks of Naval Enigma Dolphin key.	Dunkirk evacuation of British forces (Operation Dynamo). German defeat of France. Battle of Britain.
August 1940– December 1940	Some GAF low-grade ciphers, but probably not Enigma, yielded useful intelligence.	
January 1941	*Dora joined BP as administrative assistant.*	
February 1941	Breaking of tactical ciphers and, to a limited extent, Ultra, contributed.	British defeat of Italians in North Africa.
March 1941	Ultra intelligence crucial for first time in a military engagement. Y Board establishes new structures for relationship between services and GC & CS.	Battle of Matapan.
April 1941	Ultra had disclosed German intentions from January, and aided British withdrawal.	German invasion of Yugoslavia and Greece (Operation Marita).

Date		World events
May 1941	Ultra revealed plans. *Daphne joined BP as office junior.*	German invasion of Crete (Operation Mercury).
June 1941	First break of Army Enigma Vulture (Eastern Front key).	German invasion of the USSR (Operation Barbarossa). USSR allied with Britain.
September 1941	Naval Enigma Dolphin key broken every day for the rest of the war from this date.	
October 1941	Alan Turing, Gordon Welchman, Hugh Alexander and Stuart Milner-Barry wrote to Churchill asking for more resources and he agrees. Naval Enigma Shark key broken.	
December 1941	Approximately 2,500 people employed at BP. Brigadier van Cutsem's inquiry into GC & CS organization begins.	Japanese attack on Pearl Harbour. USA entered WW2. USSR, USA and Britain (and Empire, Commonwealth and Dominions) formed 'Allies'.
January 1942	Brigadier van Cutsem's report on GC & CS organization.	
Early February 1942	Major reorganization of GC & CS. Commander Edward Travis installed as operational head at BP (formally, Deputy Director, Service). Joint administrative control of BP site between GC & CS and SIS ended. Naval Enigma Shark key became unreadable on 1 February. *Vera joined BP as WRNS clerical worker.*	Singapore captured by Japanese.
October 1942	Holden Agreement between UK and USA to share Naval Sigint. *Joyce joined BP Hut 3 as intelligence assessor.*	

Date		
October–November 1942	Ultra made an important contribution to British victory.	Second Battle of El Alamein (Operation Supercharge).
December 1942	Naval Enigma Shark key re-broken.	
February 1943		German defeat at Stalingrad.
May 1943	Ultra played role in causing U-Boat withdrawal. Travis–Strong agreement (often referred to as BRUSA 1943) between UK and USA to share Army, Air and secret-service sigint.	Withdrawal of many German U-boats from North Atlantic.
September 1943	Approximately 5,500 people employed at BP.	Allied invasion of mainland Italy. Italian surrender to Allies.
Early 1944	Colossus Mark 1 operational. *Ron joined BP Testery as engineer.*	
March 1944	Second wartime reorganization of GC & CS. Commander Sir Edward Travis retitled as Director.	
June 1944	Peak size of BP staff (8,700–10,000, depending on how counted). Continuous supply of Ultra to forces contributed to success of operation.	Allied landings in Normandy (Operation Overlord).
July 1944	Ultra made crucial contribution.	Allied mobile offensive within Normandy Campaign (Operation Cobra).

Date	Event
December 1944–January 1945	Battle of the Bulge arising from German counter-offensive (Operation Watch on the Rhine). Alleged main failure of Ultra.
May 1945	German unconditional surrender to Allies. VE Day celebrated. BP read signal of German surrender.
August 1945	Atomic bombs dropped on Japan. Japanese unconditional surrender to Allies. VJ Day celebrated.
1946	GC & CS moved from Bletchley Park to Eastcote and (on most accounts) formally changed its name to GCHQ.
1968–74	Various limited public references to the wartime work of GC & CS and to Ultra began to appear in Polish, French and English.
1974	Publication of Winterbotham's book *The Ultra Secret* and beginning of widespread revelation of the BP story.
1979	Publication of first volume of the Official History of British Intelligence in the Second World War, with considerable detail on the first two years of BP's work.
1987	GCHQ ceased to use BP for training courses.
1992	Formation of Bletchley Park Trust to preserve the BP site and communicate the work that had occurred there. Most BP documents declassified by this date.

1995	Publication of Robert Harris's novel *Enigma* contributed to upsurge of public interest in BP.	
1999	Channel 4 screened documentary 'Station X'. Sixtieth anniversary of the main BP mobilization.	Sixtieth anniversary of the outbreak of WW2.
2001	Release of the film *Enigma* based on Harris's novel sparked further public interest.	
2004–2008	*Daphne, Dora, Joyce, Ron, Roy and Vera interviewed for this book.*	
2009	Ninetieth anniversary of formation of GC & CS. British government announced that surviving BP veterans would be awarded a 'commemorative badge' to honour their work.	Seventieth anniversary of the outbreak of WW2.
2011	Memorial to those who worked at Bletchley Park unveiled by Her Majesty Queen Elizabeth II.	

Main source of information on link of Ultra to military events: Hinsley (1993a); on size of BP staff Nigel de Grey's post-war review, TNA HW 14/145.

Appendix B. Table of Interviewees

	Daphne	Ron	Vera
Role	Office Junior	Engineer	Indexing Clerk
Section or unit	Directorate	Testery	Naval Section
Main location	Mansion	Testery	Block A
Employing organization	Foreign Office	GPO	WRNS
Manager	Nigel de Grey (via intermediary), second in command of GC & CS	Captain Gil Hayward	Watch Officer
Main duties	Clerical tasks	Maintaining teleprinters and other Fish-related mechanical and electrical devices	Maintaining records of Naval Enigma decrypts
Education	Left school at 14. No formal qualifications.	City and Guilds technical qualifications	School Certificate
Date joined BP	May 1941	Early 1944	February 1942
Indoctrination	No	Fish	No
Gender	F	M	F
Approximate age on joining BP	14	19	20
Approximate age at time of interview	77	79	82

	Joyce	Dora	Roy
Role	Intelligence Assessor/Analyst	Administrative Assistant	Cryptanalyst
Section or unit	Military Section	Administration	Air Section
Main location	Hut 3	Hut 9	Hut 10
Employing organization	ATS	Foreign Office	Foreign Office
Manager	Watch Officer	Commander Alan Bradshaw, Head of GC & CS Administration	Josh Cooper, Head of Air Section
Main duties	Specialized identification of wireless information in Army and Air Enigma transmissions	Secretarial and administrative tasks	Breaking 'low-grade' GAF codes
Education	Completed first year of Cambridge degree in Modern Languages	Secretarial College	Cambridge graduate in Modern Languages
Date joined BP	October 1942	January 1941	September 1939
Indoctrination	Enigma	No	Enigma
Gender	F	F	M
Approximate age on joining BP	19	20	22
Approximate age at time of interview	82	83	89

Appendix C. Brief Profiles of Key Figures

Only those frequently or significantly mentioned are listed.

Alexander, Hugh: Head of Hut 8 from 1942, Head of Naval Section IIJ (Japanese Naval codes) from October 1944.

Birch, Frank: Head of Naval Section at GC & CS from 1940 and of the historical section at GCHQ after the war. Author of the post-war internal 'History of British Signals Intelligence 1914–1945'.

Bradshaw, Alan, Acting Paymaster-Captain (RN): Under various titles, head of administration at BP. Seconded from NID.

Butler, J. D. A, Colonel: Head of MI8 until June 1941.

Calvocoressi, Peter, Wing Commander (RAF): Head of Air Section (3A) of Hut 3 from 1942. Author of *Top Secret Ultra* (Calvocoressi, 2001).

Clarke, William E. Francis 'Nobby': Head of Naval Section at GC & CS until 1940.

Cooper, Josh: Head of Air Section at GC & CS.

Cullingham, Reginald, Wing Commander (RAF): Head of Air Index in Hut 3.

Davidson, Francis Henry Norman, Major-General: Director of Military Intelligence (DMI) at the War Office, 1940–44.

Denniston, Alastair, Commander (RN): Deputy Director (meaning operational Head) of GC & CS from 1919 until February 1942, thereafter Deputy Director of GC & CS (Civil Section), based in London until retirement in 1945.

De Grey, Nigel: Senior manager at GC & CS (formal title, if any, unknown) until 1942. Under various titles, second in command at BP from 1942. Senior Deputy Director of GCHQ 1946–51. Author of the post-war (1949) review of GC & CS operations.

Freeborn, Frederick: Senior manager at BTMC, seconded to BP as Head of the Hollerith section (or 'Freebornery').

Godfrey, John, Rear-Admiral (RN): Director of Naval Intelligence (DNI) at the Admiralty 1939–42.

Hankey, Maurice, Lord: As Minister without Portfolio (1939–41) and Paymaster-General (1941–2) was perhaps the most important politician as regards BP's organization, playing a key role in Y policy.

Hinsley, Harry: Hut 4 Naval intelligence analyst with many other roles, including, from 1943, Head of NS V (Naval traffic analysis). Later he held the important post of intelligence staff officer. After the war, as Professor Sir Harry Hinsley, the lead author of the official history of British Intelligence in the Second World War (e.g. Hinsley, 1993c).

Humphreys, Robert, Group Captain (RAF): Head of Air Section (3A) in Hut 3 until February 1942.

Jones, Eric, Group Captain (RAF): Head of Hut 3 from July 1942, and also Assistant Director, GC & CS from March 1944. Later, Director of GCHQ, 1952–60.

Knox, Dillwyn (Dilly): Cryptanalyst engaged in various specialized research activities and Head of ISK at BP until his death in 1943. A key contributor to the breaking of Enigma ciphers.

Menzies, Stewart, Major-General Sir: Chief of SIS ('C') from November 1939 and Director of GC & CS, 1939–44, thereafter Director-General.

Milner-Barry, Stuart: Head of Hut 6 from 1943. Author of the introduction to the internal history of Hut 6.

Newman, Max, Professor: Head of the 'Newmanry' at BP, leading machine attacks on Fish.

Saunders, Malcolm, Commander (RN): Initially Head of NID8G, the liaison party between OIC and BP NS. Later Head of Hut 3 until February 1942, thereafter in charge of bombe production until April 1943, when he was posted to Eastern Fleets, Y posts.

Simpson, Edward: Head of JN-25 party at BP from September 1943.

Sinclair, Hugh, Admiral (RN): Chief of SIS ('C') and Director of GC & CS until his death in November 1939.

Snow, Percy, Dr: Director of Scientific and Mathematical Manpower for the Civil Service, involved in allocating staff to BP from 1941. Better known as the novelist C. P. Snow.

Tester, Ralph, Major: Head of the 'Testery' at BP, leading 'hand' (i.e. non-machine) attacks on Fish.

Tiltman, John, Brigadier: Head of Military Section at GC & CS until 1944. Chief Cryptographer from 1942.

Travis, Edward, Commander (RN) Sir: Second in command at BP until 1942. Deputy Director of GC & CS (Service) from 1942 (meaning Head of BP), entitled Director of GC & CS from 1944. Remained as Director of GCHQ until 1952.

Turing, Alan: Head of Hut 8 until approximately November 1942, but more noted as an outstanding cryptanalyst who worked principally on Naval Enigma and Fish. Had a key role in the design both of the bombes and of Colossus.

Van Cutsem, W. E., Brigadier: Deputy Director of Military Intelligence at the War Office. Author of an important review of BP's organization in early 1942.

Vincent, Eric, Professor: Amongst other things, Head of the Cryptographic Co-ordination and Records (CCR) section.

Welchman, Gordon: Head of Hut 6 until 1943, Assistant Director (Mechanical Devices) from 1943. Architect of many organizational processes at BP as well as making important contributions to cryptanalysis and to bombe design. Author of *The Hut Six Story* (Welchman, 1982).

NOTES

(i) Military ranks and other titles shown are the highest achieved during WW2 according to the *Oxford Dictionary of National Biography* (DNB).

(ii) In some cases only major roles are shown and job titles have been simplified.

Appendix D. Organization Charts 1940–46

In the charts, only individuals named in the text of the book appear, with first names shown only on first mention.

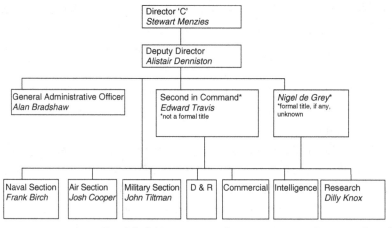

FIGURE I. Simplified Organization Chart, 23 May 1940 (Source: adapted from TNA HW 14/5).

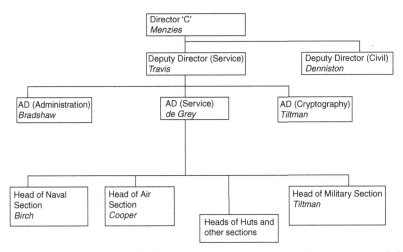

FIGURE 2. Simplified Organization Chart, February 1942 (Source: compiled from various TNA documents).

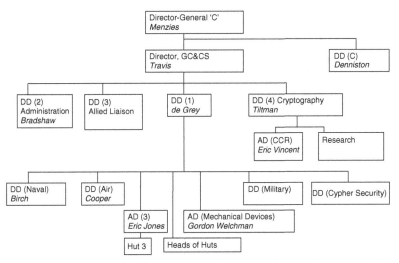

FIGURE 3. Simplified Organization Chart, November 1944 (Source: compiled from various TNA documents).

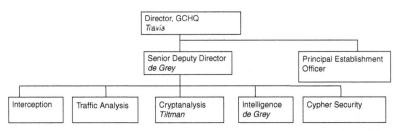

FIGURE 4. Simplified Organization Chart, 1946 (Source: adapted from Aldrich, 2010: 563).

Glossary of Terms

*Terms in **bold** cross-reference to listings in this glossary. The glossary should be read in conjunction with the list of abbreviations at the beginning of this book.*

Abwehr: German military intelligence organization, using various versions of **Enigma** and also **hand ciphers**, attacked at BP mainly by **ISK** and **ISOS**.

Admiralty: British government ministry with responsibility for the navy and naval operations.

Air Ministry: British government ministry with responsibility for the RAF.

Air Section: Section at BP concerned with air force **signals intelligence**.

Bigoted: The cover name for people at BP who had been **enwised** to the D-Day landing plans.

Billet: A place of accommodation, usually a private house whose occupants had a member of BP staff placed with them, sometimes also used to refer to accommodation in a military camp or hostel.

Block: A concrete structure (cf. **hut**) built at BP to house work sections.

Bombe: A fast electromechanical device used to test possible solutions to a **cipher key** (most especially of **Enigma**). The word derives from the Polish word *bomba* for earlier Polish versions these machines, and has no relation to the English word 'bomb'. Effective use of the bombes was reliant upon the prior identification, by **cryptanalysts** using manual means, of relatively more likely solutions, called 'menus'. Thus successful and timely decryption entailed both manual and electromechanical operations. The bombes themselves were operated by Wrens and were located both at BP and at a number of outstations.

Boniface or Source Boniface or Agent Boniface: The cover name for a fictitious human agent used extensively until late 1941 for **Ultra** intelligence. The term was still used informally, including by Churchill, until 1945, but was officially supplanted by the term Ultra.

Cipher (sometimes cypher): Technically 'any system, other than a **code**, of substituting letters or numbers for the letters of a message, or of transposing them' (Hinsley and Stripp, 1993: xiv). In practice many ciphers substitute *and* transpose message letters. Compare with 'a **cryptographic** system in which letters or numbers represent **plaintext** units (generally single letters) in accordance with agreed rules' (Smith and Erskine, 2001: 522).

Code: Technically, 'a system of substituting groups of two or more letters or numbers for the words, phrases, sentences, punctuation, etc., of a message' (Hinsley and Stripp, 1993: xv). Compare with 'a cryptographic system, generally set out in a codebook, in which groups of letters or numbers represent **plaintext** units of varying lengths' (Smith and Erskine, 2001: 522).

Codebreaker: Generic term for **cryptanalyst**. Sometimes used nowadays, highly misleadingly, to refer to anyone who worked at BP.

Colossus: A semi-programmable electronic device (in many senses an electronic computer and arguably the world's first such), several versions of which were developed at BP to solve **Fish**, especially **Tunny**.

Commercial traffic: **Encrypted** signals of a commercial rather than a **diplomatic** or **military** nature.

Corrupt: Missing or misheard text within an **intercept**.

Crib: In a generic sense, an evidential clue used in cryptanalysis. For example, if a message were sent in one Enigma **key**, and that was successfully decrypted, then it would provide a crib for the same message sent in another thus far unread key. Similarly, cribs might be available between **low grade** and **high grade** ciphers, or they might be found in the repetition of stereotypical phrases (e.g. 'Heil Hitler' or 'nothing to report'). Occasionally a crib might come from a **plaintext** message which could then be compared if the same message were transmitted in **cipher**.

Cryptanalyst: One engaged in **cryptanalysis**.

Cryptanalysis: The analysis of **codes** and **ciphers**, primarily with a view to deciphering the content of the messages they contain.

Cryptography: Literally, the writing of codes and ciphers, but commonly used at BP to mean **cryptanalysis**.

Decrypt: As a noun, a deciphered message. As a verb, the act of deciphering an **enciphered** message, also known as decryption.

Diplomatic traffic: **Encrypted** signals of a diplomatic rather than a **military** or **commercial** nature.

Direction finding: Determining the direction of a received wireless signal. By combining information from two or more receivers its source may be 'fixed' by triangulation. Closely related to both **interception** and **traffic analysis**.

Directorate: The term used at BP to denote those senior managers with Director, Deputy Director or Assistant Director status.

Encipher: To transform a message into **cipher**.

Encode: To transform a message into **code**.

Encrypt: Generic term meaning to **encipher** or **encode** text.

Emendment: The allied processes of transforming a decrypt from transmitted letter groups into normal language (e.g. HEILH ITLER becomes HEIL HITLER) and inserting letters missing as a result of a **corrupt** intercept (e.g. HE?LH I?LER becomes HEILH ITLER becomes HEIL HITLER). The emended text can then be translated.

Enigma: A **cipher machine** used by German (and other) military forces and intelligence agencies, which had been developed (and enhanced) from a system first used in the pre-war period for commercial purposes, in particular by the addition of a **plugboard**. It was not a single machine but rather one with multiple variants, each of which employed different **keys**. Hence Army or *Heer* Enigma, with keys such as 'Vulture'; Air or GAF or *Luftwaffe* Enigma with keys such as 'Red'; Naval or *Kriegsmarine* Enigma with keys such as' Dolphin'. Other important users of Enigma were the **Abwehr** and the *Reichsbahn* (railways). Various modifications to different machines were made throughout the war. The key point to note is that Enigma is an over-arching term for a multiplicity of machines, services, user groups and daily set ups, and that these changed over time.

Enwised: The British term used to mean being told of a particular secret, e.g. the breaking of Enigma (so – 'Enigma-enwised'). Later supplanted by the US term **indoctrinated**.

Fish: BP cover name, derived from the German covername *Sägefisch* (sawfish), for high-grade non-Morse traffic used by Nazi Germany for strategic communications. It had three main variants, according to the encryption machine used, called Tunny, Sturgeon and Thrasher at BP (each of which had several **keys**). Some **Tunny** was broken at BP, very little Sturgeon and no Thrasher.

Freebornery: The BP section utilizing **Hollerith** machines, named after its head, Frederick Freeborn of the British Tabulating Machine Company.

Fusion room: Section at BP comparing/integrating **decrypted** material from **Hut 6** with **traffic analysis** findings from **SIXTA**.

Hagelin: Cipher machines invented by Boris Hagelin, of which the C-38m used by the Italian Navy, and broken in **Hut 4**, was the most important variant from a BP perspective.

Hand cipher: A message **enciphered** by hand rather than by machine (cf. **machine cipher**).

Heath-Robinson machines: Pre-cursors of **Colossus**, developed to attack **Fish** and named after fantastic cartoon machines drawn by William Heath-Robinson (and hence generic term for any bizarre mechanical device).

High grade: A cipher designed to provide a high level of security – not necessarily denoting that the information carried by the cipher was of intrinsic importance.

Enigma, Fish, Hagelin C-38m and JN-25 were all high-grade ciphers. The intelligence derived from these ciphers was dubbed Ultra.

HMS Pembroke V: The cover name used by the WRNS for BP from December 1942.

Hollerith machines: Punch-card data-handling machines invented by Herman Hollerith to process US census data in the 1890s and used in the Freebornery at BP for data-processing and -management tasks.

Human intelligence (HUMINT or humint): Intelligence derived from human agents, in contrast to signals intelligence.

Hut: Prefabricated temporary wooden structures to house BP working sections, which then gave their name to those sections (even, in some cases, when no longer or only partially located there).

Hut 3: Section translating, emending and analysing decrypted material from Hut 6 and distributing the resulting intelligence to military commands and government ministries via Special Liaison Units.

Hut 4: Section responsible for non-Enigma naval cryptanalysis and translating and analysing the results of this plus decrypted Naval Enigma material from Hut 8 and distributing the resulting intelligence to the Admiralty.

Hut 6: Section breaking Army (Heer), Air (Luftwaffe or GAF) and Railway (Reichsbahn) Enigma.

Hut 8: Section breaking Naval (Kriegsmarine) Enigma.

Index: Card-based systems to store, cross-reference and retrieve information, extensively used at BP to handle enormous quantities of material from, for example, decrypts.

Indoctrinated: The US term for enrolment into a particular secret or level of classified information, which as the war progressed became increasingly used at BP and supplanted the term enwised.

Intercept: As a verb, to engage in interception. As a noun, the message heard as a result.

Interception: Listening to transmissions via Y stations, the precondition for cryptanalysis, traffic analysis and signals intelligence.

ISK: Illicit or Intelligence Services Knox, the designation given both to the section that deciphered German intelligence service Enigma and to the resulting decrypts.

ISOS: Illicit or Intelligence Services Oliver Strachey, the designation given both to the section that deciphered German intelligence-service hand ciphers and to the resulting decrypts.

JN-25: The Japanese Navy's principal super-enciphered code.

Key: A term used in various ways, of which, as regards Enigma, the principal are (i) the Enigma used by a particular user group, giving rise to assigned names at BP, e.g. 'Red', 'Kestrel' or 'Shark'; (ii) the unique daily machine set up of a key in the first sense. Thus each Enigma key in the first sense had a daily key in the second sense. Note that ciphers other than Enigma also had keys.

Listening posts or stations: **Interception** or **intercept** stations, also known as **Y stations**.

Log reading: The process of reading and analysing the characteristics (e.g. point of origin and receipt, frequencies) of **traffic** and thus an aspect of **traffic analysis**.

Low grade: A **cipher** designed to provide a lower level of security – not necessarily denoting that the information carried by the cipher is of low importance or that the cipher is easily broken.

Machine cipher: **Cipher** utilizing machines (e.g. **Enigma**) to **encipher** text (cf. **hand cipher**).

Mansion, the: The term used for the main mansion house at BP, rather than the **huts** and **blocks** built subsequently.

Meteorological Section: Section at BP concerned with **weather codes** and **ciphers**.

Military Wing: Section at BP concerned with army **signals intelligence**.

Military traffic: **Encrypted** signals of a military rather than a **diplomatic** or **commercial** nature. From 1942 BP itself was concerned exclusively with military traffic, but GC & CS in London dealt with diplomatic and commercial **traffic**.

Naval Section: Section at BP concerned with naval **signals intelligence**.

Newmanry: Section (headed by Professor Max Newman) developing machine attacks (e.g. **Colossus**) on **Fish** rather than the hand attacks of the **Testery**.

Park, the: Term often used at the time by its staff for Bletchley Park.

Party: Term often used at BP for a work group undertaking a particular task (cf. **Hut** and **Watch**).

Plaintext or plain text: A message (or part thereof) transmitted without **encipherment**, or the text resulting from the **decryption** of an enciphered message.

Plugboard: An electrical (re-cabling) modification of pre-war commercial **Enigma** machines, made to military Enigma machines, very significantly increasing their security. Hence, 'plugboard Enigma' to describe such machines.

Room 40: Cryptanalytic section of the Admiralty during WW1 (formally, NID 25), which merged with MI1b to form GC & CS in 1919.

Signals intelligence (SIGINT or sigint): Intelligence derived from wireless transmissions, including that from **cryptanalysis**, **traffic analysis** and **direction finding**. Increasingly used in WW2 to denote the entire process from **interception** through cryptanalysis and intelligence analysis to distribution.

SIXTA: **Traffic analysis** section for Army and Air traffic (Naval traffic analysis was undertaken separately, in Section V of Naval Section, although the title of this section varied).

Special Communications Unit (SCU): A variant of **Special Liaison Units**, and some-times embedded within them, for the distribution of **Ultra** to military commands.

Special intelligence: A term for **signals intelligence**, used before and at the start of WW2 but mainly obsolete by the end at BP, although still used by the OIC.

Special Liaison Unit (SLU): Units responsible for **Ultra** distribution to military com-mands (via encoded transmissions to 'mobile' SLUs) or government ministries (via teleprinter lines to 'fixed' SLUs).

Station X: A name for BP deriving from its initial status as the tenth war station of SIS.

Testery: Section (headed by Major Ralph Tester) developing hand (i.e. purely linguistic and mathematical) attacks on **Fish** rather than the machine attacks of the **Newmanry**.

Traffic: Generally, signals, more specifically those with some particular shared char-acteristic (e.g. point of origin, cipher used).

Traffic analysis: Principally, the gathering of intelligence from the fact, volume, source and technical characteristics of signals without their having been **decrypted**.

Tunny: Version of **Fish** enciphered on the Lorenz SZ 40/42 machine, read at BP using **Colossus**.

Typex: British **high-grade machine cipher**, based upon the pre-war commercial Enigma machine and in that sense simpler than the **plugboard** version used by German military forces, but never broken.

Ultra: A reduction of 'Top Secret Ultra'. Cover name for **signals intelligence** derived from **cryptanalysis** of **high-grade** ciphers such as **Enigma** and **Fish**. Supplanted the earlier term **Boniface** from late 1941.

Umkehrwalze: Reversing wheel (or reflector) on **Enigma** machines. The standard version was Umkehrwalze B. A field-rewireable version, Umkehrwalze D (known at BP as Uncle Dick), which massively increased security, was intro-duced to a limited extent in 1944.

War Office: British government ministry with responsibility for the army.

Watch: Used imprecisely to denote some functional work groups or sections at BP, or a particular shift of a work group. Presumably derived from naval usage but not confined to **Naval Section** at BP.

Weather codes or ciphers: **Encrypted** transmission of weather conditions. These were made ubiquitously by German forces and provided an important source of **cribs** as well as specific weather intelligence of use to e.g. allied air forces flying over Europe.

Whitehall: Generic term for the British government, and more especially its permanent civil service as opposed to politicians and parliament (derived from the street in London where many government buildings are located).

Wireless telegraphy intelligence: A term used in various ways, usually to mean **traffic analysis**. Largely obsolete as a term from 1943.

Y: In origin, possibly a diminutive of 'wireless'. Sometimes used as a generic term for what came to be called **signals intelligence** but increasingly came to refer primarily to the **interception** of transmissions and **direction finding**.

Y Board: Main committee overseeing and co-ordinating **signals intelligence** policy, with a series of sub-committees dealing with various aspects thereof.

Y stations: **Interception** stations, also known as **listening posts or stations**.

References

Abrams, P. 1982. *Historical Sociology*. Shepton Mallet, Somerset: Open Books.

Addison, P. and Crang, J. (eds.) 2010. *Listening to Britain. Home Intelligence Reports on Britain's Finest Hour – May to September 1940*. London: The Bodley Head.

Adler, P. and Borys B. 1996. 'Two types of bureaucracy: Enabling and coercive', *Administrative Science Quarterly* **41**: 61–89.

Aldrich, H. 1979. *Organizations and Environments*. Englewood Cliffs, NJ: Prentice-Hall.

Aldrich, R. J. 2000. *Intelligence and the War against Japan: Britain, America and the Politics of Secret Service*. Cambridge: Cambridge University Press.

Aldrich, R. J. 2002. *The Hidden Hand. Britain, America and Cold War Secret Intelligence*. New York: Overlook Press.

Aldrich, R. J. 2010. *GCHQ. The Uncensored Story of Britain's Most Secret Intelligence Agency*. London: HarperPress.

Alford, V. 1993. 'Naval Section VI' in Hinsley, H. and Stripp, A. (eds.), *Codebreakers. The Inside Story of Bletchley Park*. Oxford: Oxford University Press, pp. 68–70.

Alvesson, M. 2004. *Knowledge Work and Knowledge Intensive Firms*. Oxford: Oxford University Press.

Alvesson, M. and Deetz, S. 2000. *Doing Critical Management Research*. London: Sage.

Alvesson, M. and Skoldberg, K. 2009. *Reflexive Methodology. New Vistas for Qualitative Research*. 2nd edn. London: Sage.

Alvesson, M. and Svengisson, S. 2003. 'Managers doing leadership: The extraordinarization of the mundane', *Human Relations* **56**: 1435–59.

Anand, V. and Rosen, C. 2008. 'The ethics of organizational secrets', *Journal of Management Inquiry* **17**: 97–101.

Andrew, C. 1985a. *Secret Service. The Making of the British Intelligence Community*. London: Heinemann.

Andrew, C. 1985b. 'F. H. Hinsley and the Cambridge moles: Two patterns of intelligence recruitment', in Langhorne, T. B. (ed.), *Diplomacy and Intelligence in the Second World War: Essays in Honour of F. H. Hinsley*. Cambridge: Cambridge University Press, pp. 22–40.

Andrew, C. 2001. 'Bletchley Park in pre-war perspective', in Smith, M. and Erskine, R. (eds.), *Action This Day*. London: Bantam, pp. 1–14.

Appleby, J., Hunt, L. and Jacob, M. 1995. *Telling the Truth about History*. New York: W. W. Norton and Company.

Bakken, T. and Hernes, T. 2006. 'Organization is both a noun and a verb: Weick meets Whitehead', *Organization Studies* 27: 1599–616.

Bain, P., Watson, A., Mulvey, G., Taylor, P. and Gall, G. 2002. 'Taylorism, targets and the pursuit of quantity and quality by call centre management', *New Technology, Work and Employment* 17: 170–85

Barley, S. 2010. 'Building an institutional field to corral a government: A case to set an agenda for organization studies', *Organization Studies* 31: 777–805

Barley, S. and Kunda, G. 2001. 'Bringing work back in', *Organization Science* 12: 76–95

Batey, M. 2010. *Dilly. The Man Who Broke Enigmas*. London: Biteback Publishing.

Battles, M. 2004. *Libraries: An Unquiet History*. New York: W. W. Norton.

Bauman, Z. 1990. *Thinking Sociologically*. Oxford: Blackwell.

Beer, M and Nohria, N. 2000. *Breaking the Code of Change*. Boston, MA: Harvard Business Publishing.

Beesly, P. 2000. *Very Special Intelligence. The Story of the Admiralty's Operational Intelligence Centre 1939–45*. Reissued edition (orig. 1977). London: Greenhill Books.

Bendix, R. 1956. *Work and Authority in Industry*. New York: John Wiley.

Bennett, R. 1993. 'The Duty Officer, Hut 3', in Hinsley, H. and Stripp, A. (eds.), *Codebreakers. The Inside Story of Bletchley Park*. Oxford: Oxford University Press, pp. 30–40.

Bennett, R. 1994. *Behind the Battle: Intelligence in the War with Germany, 1939–1945*. London: Sinclair-Stevenson Ltd.

Bergquist, W. H. 1993. *The Postmodern Organization: Mastering the Art of Irreversible Change*. San Francisco, CA: Jossey-Bass.

Biggart, N. W. and Hamilton, G. G. 1987. 'An institutional theory of leadership', *Journal of Applied Behavioural Science* 23: 429–41.

Black, A. and Brunt, R. 1999. 'Information management in businesses, libraries and British military intelligence: Towards a history of information management', *The Journal of Documentation* 55: 361–74.

Black, A. and Brunt, R. 2000. 'MI5 1909–1945: An information management perspective', *Journal of Information Science* 26: 185–97.

Black, A., Muddiman, D. and Plant, H. 2007. *The Early Information Society. Information Management in Britain Before the Computer*. Aldershot, Surrey: Ashgate.

Blacker, C. 1993. 'Recollections of *temps perdu* at Bletchley Park', in Hinsley, H. and Stripp, A. (eds.), *Codebreakers. The Inside Story of Bletchley Park*. Oxford: Oxford University Press, pp. 300–5.

Blackler, F. 1995. 'Knowledge, knowledge work and organizations: An overview and interpretation', *Organization Studies* **16**: 1021–46.

Blau, P. 1955. *The Dynamics of Bureaucracy*. Chicago, IL: Chicago University Press.

Bok, S. 1984. *Secrets: On the Ethics of Concealment and Revelation*. New York: Vantage Books.

Bonsall, A. 2008. 'Bletchley Park and the RAF Y service: Some recollections', *Intelligence and National Security* **23**: 827–41.

Booth, C. and Rowlinson, M. 2006. 'Management and organizational history: Prospects', *Management and Organizational History* 1: 5–30.

Bourdieu, P. 1986. *Distinction. A Social Critique of the Judgment of Taste*. London: Routledge.

Boyle, A. 1979. *The Climate of Treason*. London: Hutchinson.

Breitman, R. 1998. *Official Secrets. What the Nazis Planned, what the British and Americans Knew*. New York: Hill and Wang.

Briggs, A. 2011. *Secret Days. Code-breaking in Bletchley Park*. Barnsley, Yorks.: Pen & Sword/Frontline.

Brown, C. 2005. *1966 and All That*. London: Hodder.

Brunt, R. 2004. 'Indexes at the Government Code and Cypher School, Bletchley Park, 1940–1945', in Rayward, W. B. and Bowden, M. E. (eds.), *The History and Heritage of Scientific and Technological Information Systems*. Silver Spring, MD: American Society for Information Science and Technology, pp. 291–9.

Budiansky, S. 2000. *Battle of Wits. The Complete Story of Codebreaking in World War II*. London: Viking.

Budiansky, S. 2001. 'Bletchley Park and the birth of the very special relationship', in Smith, M. and Erskine, R. (eds.), *Action This Day*. London: Bantam, pp. 211–36.

Burke, C. 2010. 'A lady codebreaker speaks: Joan Murray, the bombes and the perils of writing crypto-history from participants' accounts', *Cryptologia* **34**: 359–70.

Burns, T. and Stalker, G. 1961. *The Management of Innovation*. London: Tavistock.

Cain, F. 1999. 'Signals intelligence in Australia during the Pacific War', in Alvarez, D. (ed.) *Allied and Axis Signals Intelligence in World War II*. London: Frank Cass, pp. 40–51.

Calder, A. 1969. *The People's War: Britain 1939–1945*. London: Jonathan Cape.

Calder, A. 1990. *The Myth of the Blitz*. London: Jonathan Cape.

Calhoun, C. and Sennett, R. 2007. 'Introduction', in Calhoun, C. and Sennett, R. (eds.), *Practicing Cultures*. London: Routledge, pp. 1–12.

Calvocoressi, P. 2001. *Top Secret Ultra*. 2nd edn. Kidderminster, Oxon.: Baldwin.

Carr, E. H. 1987. *What Is History?* 2nd edn. London: Penguin.

Carter, F. 2010. 'The Turing bombe', *The Rutherford Journal* 3, www.rutherford-journal.org/article030108.html.

Child, J. 1972. 'Organizational structure, environment and performance: The role of strategic choice', *Sociology* **6**: 1–22.

Clayton, A. 1980. *The Enemy is Listening: The Story of the Y Service.* London: Hutchinson.

Copeland, B. J. 2001. 'Colossus and the dawning of the computer age' in Smith, M. and Erskine, R. (eds.), *Action This Day*. London: Bantam, pp. 342–69.

Copeland, B. J. (ed.) 2004. *The Essential Turing*. Oxford: Oxford University Press.

Copeland, B. J. 2006. *Colossus. The Secrets of Bletchley Park's Codebreaking Computers*. Oxford: Oxford University Press.

Clark, P. and Rowlinson, M. 2004. 'The treatment of history in organization studies: Towards an "historic turn"?' *Business History* **46**: 331–52.

Cohen, M. D., March, J. G. and Olsen, J. P. 1972. 'A garbage can model of organizational choice', *Administrative Science Quarterly* **17**: 1–25.

Costa, G. 1996. 'The impact of shift and night work on health', *Applied Ergonomics* **27**: 9–16.

Costas, J. and Grey, C. 2011. 'The Hidden Architecture of Organizations. Exploring Varieties of Secrecy'. Unpublished Working Paper.

Courpasson, D. 2000. 'Managerial strategies of domination. Power in soft bureaucracies', *Organization Studies* **21**: 141–61.

Cronin, J. 1991. *The Politics of State Expansion: War, State and Society in Twentieth Century Britain*. London: Routledge.

Crouch, C. 1994. *Industrial Relations and European State Traditions*. Oxford: Oxford University Press.

Croucher, R. 1982. *Engineers at War 1939–1945*. London: Merlin Press.

Czarniawska, B. 2002. *A Tale of Three Cities, or the Glocalization of City Management*. Oxford: Oxford University Press.

Czarniawska, B. 2008. *A Theory of Organizing*. Cheltenham, Gloucs.: Edward Elgar.

Czarniawska, B. (ed.) 2009. *Organizing in the Face of Risk and Threat*. Cheltenham, Gloucs.: Edward Elgar.

Czarniawska, B. and Sevon, G. (eds.) 1996. *Translating Organizational Change*. Berlin: De Gruyter.

Dakin, A. 1993. 'The Z watch in Hut 4, part I', in Hinsley, H. and Stripp, A. (eds.), *Codebreakers. The Inside Story of Bletchley Park*. Oxford: Oxford University Press, pp. 50–6.

Dalton, M. 1959. *Men Who Manage*. New York: John Wiley and Sons.

Davies, P. 2001. 'From amateurs to professionals: GC and CS and institution-building in sigint', in Smith, M. and Erskine, R. (eds.), *Action This Day*. London: Bantam, pp. 386–402.

Davies, P. 2004. *MI6 and the Machinery of Spying*. London: Frank Cass.

Deal, T. E. and Kennedy, A. A. 1988. *Corporate Cultures: The Rites and Rituals of Corporate Life*. London: Penguin.

Denniston, R. 2007. *Thirty Secret Years. A. G. Denniston's Work in Signals Intelligence 1914–1944*. Clifton-upon-Teme, Worcs.: Polperro Heritage Press.

Dietz, G., Gillespie, N. and Chao, G. 2010. 'Unravelling the complexities of trust', in Saunders, M., Skinner, D., Dietz, G., Gillespie, N. and Lewicki R. (eds.), *Organizational Trust. A Cultural Perspective*. Cambridge: Cambridge University Press, pp. 3–41.

DiMaggio, P. 1988. 'Interest and agency in institutional theory', in Zucker, L. (ed.), *Institutional Patterns and Organizations: Culture and Environment*. Cambridge, MA: Ballinger, pp. 3–22.

DiMaggio, P. and Powell, W. 1991. 'Introduction', in Powell, W. and DiMaggio, P. (eds.) *The New Institutionalism in Organizational Analysis*. Chicago, IL: University of Chicago Press, pp. 1–38.

Donaldson, L. 2001. *The Contingency Theory of Organizations*. Thousand Oaks, CA: Sage.

Donaldson, L. 2003. 'Organization theory as a positive science', in Tsoukas, H. and Knudsen, C. (eds.), *The Oxford Handbook of Organization Theory*. Oxford: Oxford University Press, pp. 39–62.

Dufresne, R. and Offstein, E. 2008. 'On the virtues of secrecy in organizations', *Journal of Management Inquiry* 17: 102–6.

Dupuis, J.-P. 2008. 'Organizational culture', in Clegg, S. and Bailey, J. (eds.), *International Encyclopedia of Organization Studies Vol. III*. Thousand Oaks, CA: Sage, pp. 1035–9.

Edgerton, D. 2011. *Britain's War Machine: Weapons, Resources and Experts in the Second World War*. London: Allen Lane.

Edwards, R. 1979. *Contested Terrain*. London: Heinemann.

Elton, G. R. 1969. *The Practice of History*. London: Fontana.

Enever, T. 1999. *Britain's Best Kept Secret. Ultra's Base at Bletchley Park*. 3rd edn. Stroud, Gloucs.: Sutton Publishing Limited.

Erskine, R. 1986. 'GC and CS mobilises "men of the professor type"', *Cryptologia* 10: 50–9.

Erskine, R. 1988. 'Naval Enigma: The breaking of Heimish and Triton', *Intelligence and National Security* 3: 162–83.

Erskine, R. 2000. 'Afterword: Codebreaking in the Battle of the Atlantic', in Beesly, P., *Very Special Intelligence. The Story of the Admiralty's Operational Intelligence Centre 1939–45.* Reissued edition (orig. 1977). London: Greenhill Books, pp. 263–84.

Erskine, R. 2001a. 'Breaking German naval enigma on both sides of the Atlantic', in Smith, M. and Erskine, R. (eds.), *Action This Day.* London: Bantam, pp. 174–96.

Erskine, R. 2001b. 'Enigma's security: What the Germans knew', in Smith, M. and Erskine, R. (eds.), *Action This Day.* London: Bantam, pp. 370–85.

Erskine, R. 2010. 'Foreword', in Batey, M. 2010. Dilly. The Man Who Broke Enigmas. London: Biteback Publishing, pp ix–xviii.

Erskine, R. and Weierud, F. 1987. 'Naval enigma: M4 and its rotors', *Cryptologia* **11**: 235–44.

Evans, D. 2003. *BP: The Development and Historical Function of the Fabric.* Bletchley Park Trust (bound mimeo, 150 pp.). Available at Bletchley Park Trust Archive or from the author of this book.

Evans, R. 2000. *In Defence of History.* London: Granta Books.

Eytan, W. 1993. 'The Z watch in Hut 4, part II', in Hinsley, H. and Stripp, A. (eds.), *Codebreakers. The Inside Story of Bletchley Park.* Oxford: Oxford University Press, pp. 57–60.

Ferris, J. 2005. *Intelligence and Strategy: Selected Essays.* London: Routledge.

Fetterman, D. 1998. *Ethnography Step by Step.* 2nd edn. Thousand Oaks, CA: Sage.

Filby, W. 1988. 'Bletchley Park and Berkley Street', *Intelligence and National Security* **3**: 272–84.

Fournier, V. and Grey, C. 2000. 'At the critical moment: Conditions and prospects for critical management studies', *Human Relations* **53**: 7–32.

Freedman, M. 2000. *Unravelling Enigma: Winning the Code War at Station X.* Barnsley, Yorks.: Pen and Sword Military.

Friedman, A. 1977. 'Responsible autonomy versus direct control over the labour process' *Capital and Class* **1**: 43–57.

Gabriel, Y. 2002. 'On paragrammatic uses of organizational theory – a provocation', *Organization Studies* **23**: 133–51.

Gabriel, Y. 2010. 'Organization studies: A space for ideas, identities and agonies', *Organization Studies* **31**: 757–75.

Garfield, S. 2005. *We Are at War. The Diaries of Five Ordinary People in Extraordinary Times.* London: Random House.

Gerth, H. H. and Mills, C. W. (eds.) 1991. *From Max Weber: Essays in Sociology.* London: Routledge.

Giddens, A. 1984. *The Constitution of Society. Outline of the Theory of Structuration.* Cambridge: Polity Press.

Gladwin, L. 1999. 'Cautious collaborators: The struggle for Anglo-American crypt-analytic co-operation 1940–43', in Alvarez, D. (ed.) *Allied and Axis Signals Intelligence in World War II*. London: Frank Cass, pp. 119–45.

Golden, B. 1992. 'The past is the past – or is it? The use of retrospective accounts as indicators of past strategy', *Academy of Management Journal*, **35**: 848–60.

Goldstine, H. 1993. *The Computer from Pascal to von Neumann*. Princeton, NJ: Princeton University Press.

Gouldner, A. 1954. *Patterns of Industrial Bureaucracy*. New York: Free Press.

Grant, D. and Oswick, C. 1996. *Metaphor and Organization*. London: Sage.

Greenwood, R. and Hinings, C. R. 2002. 'Disconnects and consequences in organ-ization theory', *Administrative Science Quarterly* **47**: 411–21.

Grey, C. 1996. 'C. P. Snow's fictional sociology of management and organizations', *Organization* **3**: 61–83.

Grey, C. 2009. *A Very Short, Fairly Interesting and Reasonably Cheap Book about Studying Organizations*. 2nd edn. London: Sage.

Grey, C. 2010. 'Organizing studies: publications, politics and polemic', *Organization Studies* **31**: 677–94.

Grey, C. and Sinclair, A. 2006. 'Writing differently', *Organization* **13**: 443–53.

Grey, C. and Sturdy, A. 2007. 'Friendship and organizational analysis: Towards a research agenda', *Journal of Management Inquiry* **16**: 157–72.

Grey, C. and Sturdy, A. 2008. 'The 1942 re-organization of GC and CS', *Cryptologia* **32**: 311–33.

Grey, C. and Sturdy, A. 2009. 'Historicising knowledge-intensive organizations: The case of Bletchley Park', *Management and Organizational History* **4**: 131–50.

Grey, C. and Sturdy, A. 2010. 'A chaos that worked. Organizing Bletchley Park', *Public Policy and Administration* **25**: 47–66.

Gupta, A., Smith, K. and Shalley, C. 2006. 'The interplay between exploration and exploitation', *Academy of Management Journal* **49**: 693–706.

Hamer, D., Sullivan, G. and Weierud, F. 1998. 'Enigma variations: An extended family of machines', *Cryptologia* **22**: 211–29.

Handy, C. 1985. *Understanding Organizations*. 3rd edn. London: Penguin.

Hanson, N. 2008. *Priestley's Wars*. Ilkley, Yorks.: Great Northern Books.

Hanyok, R. 2011. *Eavesdropping on hell: Historical Guide to Western Communi-cations Intelligence and the Holocaust, 1939–1945*. Mineola, NY: Dover Books. Also available (2005 version) at www.nsa.gov/about/_files/cryptologic_heritage/publications/wwii/eavesdropping.pdf.

Harris, R. 1995. *Enigma*. London: Hutchinson.

Hassard, J. 1993. *Sociology and Organization Theory*. Cambridge: Cambridge University Press.

Hassard, J. and Parker, M. (eds.) 1993. *Postmodernism and Organizations*. London: Sage.

Hayes, N. and Hill, J. (eds.) 1999. *Millions Like Us? British Culture in the Second World War*. Liverpool: Liverpool University Press.

Hayward, G. 1993. 'Operation Tunny', in Hinsley, H. and Stripp, A. (eds.), *Codebreakers. The Inside Story of Bletchley Park*. Oxford: Oxford University Press, pp. 175–92.

He, Z-L. and Wong, P-K. 2004. 'Exploration vs. exploitation: An empirical text of the ambidexterity hypothesis', *Organization Science* **15**: 481–94.

Heckscher, C., 1994. 'Defining the post-bureaucratic type', in Heckscher, C. and Donnelon, A. (eds.), *The Post-Bureaucratic Organization. New Perspectives on Organizational Change*. Thousand Oaks, CA: Sage, pp. 14–62.

Herman, M. 1996. *Intelligence Power in Peace and War*. Cambridge: Cambridge University Press.

Herman M. 2001. *Intelligence Services in the Information Age*. New York: Frank Cass.

Herman M. 2007. 'Secret intelligence in an open society'. Unpublished text of talk given to 'Friends in Council Society', Cheltenham, Gloucs., 6 November. Referred to by kind permission of the author.

Hernes, T. and Weik, E. 2007. 'Organization as process: Drawing a line between endogenous and exogenous views', *Scandinavian Journal of Management* **23**: 251–64.

Hersey, P. and Blanchard, K. H. 1993. *Management of Organizational Behaviour: Utilizing Human Resources*. 6th edn. Englewood Cliffs, NJ: Prentice Hall.

Hill, M. 2004. *Bletchley Park People*. Stroud, Gloucs.: Sutton Publishing Limited.

Hinsley, H. 1993a. 'Introduction: The influence of Ultra in the Second World War' in Hinsley, H. and Stripp, A. (eds.), *Codebreakers. The Inside Story of Bletchley Park*. Oxford: Oxford University Press, pp. 1–13.

Hinsley, H. 1993b. 'The influence of Ultra'. Talk to the Computer Laboratory, Cambridge University, 19 October. www.cl.cam.ac.uk/research/security/Historical/hinsley.html.

Hinsley, H. 1993c. *British Intelligence in the Second World War* (abridged edn). London: HMSO.

Hinsley, H. and Stripp, A. (eds.) 1993. *Codebreakers. The Inside Story of Bletchley Park*. Oxford: Oxford University Press.

Hinsley, H., Thomas, E., Ransom, C. and Knight R. 1979. *British Intelligence in the Second World War* (Volume 1). London: HMSO.

Hinton, J. 2010. *Nine Wartime Lives*. Oxford: Oxford University Press.

Hobart, M. and Schiffman, S. 2000. *Information Ages: Literacy, Numeracy and the Computer Revolution*. Baltimore, MD: Johns Hopkins University Press.

Hodges, A. 1982. *Alan Turing: The Enigma*. London: Random House.

Hofstede, G. 2001. *Culture's Consequences: Comparing Values, Behaviors, Institutions and Organizations across Nations*. 2nd edn. Thousand Oaks, CA: Sage.

Hogarth J. 2008. *An Extraordinary Mixture: Bletchley Park in Wartime*. Glasgow: Mansion Field, Zeticula.

Hough, P. 2004. *Understanding Global Security*. London: Routledge.

Inkpen, A. and Tsang, E. 2005. 'Social capital, networks, and knowledge transfer', *Academy of Management Review* **30**: 146–65.

Jackall, R. 1988. *Moral Mazes. The World of Corporate Managers*. New York: Oxford University Press.

Jacques, R. 1996. *Manufacturing the Employee. Management Knowledge from the 19th to the 21st Centuries*. Thousand Oaks, CA: Sage

Jeffery, K. 2010. *MI6. The History of the Secret Intelligence Service 1909–1949*. London: Bloomsbury.

Jenks, C. 2005. *Culture*. 2nd edn. London: Routledge.

Jones, C. 2008. 'Editor's introduction' (to special issue on secrecy in organizations), *Journal of Management Inquiry* **17**: 95–6.

Kahn, D. 1991. *Seizing the Enigma*. Boston, MA: Houghton Mifflin.

Kahn, D. 1996. *The Codebreakers. The Story of Secret Writing*. Revised edition. New York: Scribner.

Kahn, D. 2010. 'How the Allies suppressed the second greatest secret of World War II', *The Journal of Military History* **74**: 1229–41.

Kanter, R. M. 1977. *Men and Women of the Corporation*. New York: Basic Books.

Karreman, D., Sveningsson, S. and Alvesson, M. 2002. 'The return of the machine bureaucracy? Management control in the work settings of professionals', *International Studies of Management and Organization* **32**: 70–93.

Kieser, A. 1994. 'Why organization theory needs historical analyses – and how this should be performed', *Organization Science* **5**: 608–20.

Kilduff, M. and Brass, D. 2010. 'Organizational social network research: Core ideas and key debates', *Academy of Management Annals* **4**: 317–57.

Kilduff, M. and Tsai, W. 2003. *Social Networks and Organizations*. London: Sage.

Kipping, M. and Usdiken, B. 2008. 'Business history and management studies', in Jones, G. and Zeitlin, J. (eds.), *The Oxford Handbook of Business History*. Oxford: Oxford University Press, pp. 96–119.

Knowles, M. and Knowles, H. 1972. *Introduction to Group Dynamics*. Chicago, IL: Follett.

Knuttson, A. 2003. 'Health disorders of shift workers', *Occupational Medicine* **53**: 103–8.

Kunda, G. 1992. *Engineering Culture*. Philadelphia, PA: Temple University Press.

Legge, K. 1995. *Human Resource Management. Rhetorics and Realities*. Basingstoke, Hants.: Macmillan.

Lewin, R. 2008. *Ultra Goes to War*. Reissued edition (orig. 1978). Barnsley, Yorks.: Pen and Sword Military.

Lilley, S., Lightfoot, G. and Amaral, P. (2004). *Representing Organization: Knowledge, Management, and the Information Age*. Oxford: Oxford University Press.

Littler, C. 1982. *The Development of the Labour Process in Capitalist Societies*. London: Heinemann.

Luke, D. 2005. *My Road to Bletchley Park*. Cleobury Mortimer, Salop.: M. and M. Baldwin.

Lummis, T. 1987. *Listening to History. The Authenticity of Oral Evidence*. London: Hutchinson Education.

Maguire, S. 2008. 'Institutional entrpreneurship' in Clegg, S. and Bailey, J. (eds.) *International Encyclopedia of Organization Studies Vol. II*. Thousand Oaks, CA: Sage, pp. 674–8.

Maguire, S. and Hardy, C. 2006. 'The emergence of new global institutions: A discursive perspective', *Organization Studies* **27**: 7–29.

March, J. 1991. 'Exploration and exploitation in organizational learning', *Organization Science* **2**: 71–87.

Marks, P. 2001. 'Umkehrwalze D: Enigma's rewirable reflector, part I', *Cryptologia* **25**: 101–41.

Marwick, A. (ed.) 1988. *Total War and Social Change*. Basingstoke, Hants.: Macmillan.

Marwick, A. 1995. 'Two approaches to historical study: The metaphysical (including "postmodernism") and the historical', *Journal of Contemporary History*, **10**: 5–35.

Martin, J. 1992. *Culture in Organizations. Three Perspectives*. Oxford: Oxford University Press.

Martin, J. 2002. *Organizational Culture: Mapping the Terrain*. Thousand Oaks, CA: Sage.

McGrath, P. 2005. 'Thinking differently about knowledge-intensive firms: Insights from early medieval Irish monasticism', *Organization*, **12**: 549–66.

McGregor, D. 1960. *The Human Side of the Enterprise*. New York: McGraw-Hill.

McKay, S. 2010. *The Secret Life of Bletchley Park*. London: Aurum Press.

Merton, R. K. 1972. 'Insiders and outsiders: A chapter in the sociology of knowledge', *American Journal of Sociology*, **78**: 9–47.

Meyer, A., Frost, P. and Weick, K. 1998. 'The organization science jazz festival: Improvisation as a metaphor for organizing: Overture', *Organization Science* **9**: 540–2.

Meyer, J. and Rowan, B. 1977. 'Institutionalized organizations: Formal structure as myth and ceremony', *American Journal of Sociology*, **83**, 2: 340–63.

McLaine, I. 1979. *Ministry of Morale: Home Front Morale and the Ministry of Information in World War Two*. London: George Allen and Unwin.

Middlemas, K. 1979. *Politics in Industrial Society. The Experience of the British System since 1911*. London: Andre Deutsch.

Miller, P. and Rose, N. 2008. *Governing the Present*. Cambridge: Polity.

Millward, W. 1993. 'Life in and out of Hut 3' in Hinsley, H. and Stripp, A. (eds.), *Codebreakers. The Inside Story of Bletchley Park*. Oxford: Oxford University Press, pp. 17–29.

Milner-Barry, P. S. 1986. 'In memoriam W. Gordon Welchman', *Intelligence and National Security* **1**: 141.

Milner-Barry, S. 1993. 'Hut 6: Early days' in Hinsley, H. and Stripp, A. (eds.), *Codebreakers. The Inside Story of Bletchley Park*. Oxford: Oxford University Press, pp. 89–99.

Mintzberg, H. 1979. *The Structuring of Organizations*. Englewood Cliffs, NJ: Prentice-Hall International.

Mone, M. and McKinlay, W. 1993. 'The uniqueness value and its consequences for organization studies', *Journal of Management Inquiry* **2**: 284–96.

Moran, C. 2012. *Classified: Secrecy and the State in Postwar Britain*. Cambridge: Cambridge University Press.

Morgan, G. 1986. *Images of Organization*. London: Sage.

Morris, C. 1993. 'Navy Ultra's poor relations' in Hinsley, H. and Stripp, A. (eds.), *Codebreakers. The Inside Story of Bletchley Park*. Oxford: Oxford University Press, pp. 231–45.

Morrison, K. Undated. '"A maudlin and monstrous pile": The mansion at Bletchley Park, Buckinghamshire', www.english-heritage.org.uk/content/imported-docs/ p-t/thehistoryofthemansionbletchleypark.pdf.

Munir, K. 2005. 'The social construction of events: A study of institutional change in the photographic field', *Organization Studies* **26**: 93–112.

Murray, J. 1993. 'Hut 8 and Naval Enigma, part I' in Hinsley, H. and Stripp, A. (eds.), *Codebreakers. The Inside Story of Bletchley Park*. Oxford: Oxford University Press, pp. 113–18.

Neyland, D. 2008. *Organizational Ethnography*. London: Sage.

Nohria, N. N. and Eccles, R. G. 1992. *Networks and Organizations: Structure, Form and Action*. Boston, MA: Harvard Business School Press.

Norris, R. 2008. 'Lessons of the Manhattan Project', presentation to the National Academies' Committee on Science, Engineering and Public Policy. http://docs. nrdc.org/nuclear/files/nuc_08100901A.pdf.

O'Halpin, E. 1987. 'Financing British intelligence: The evidence up to 1945'. In Roberston, K. G. (ed.) *British and American Approaches to Intelligence.* Basingstoke, Hants.: Macmillan, pp. 187–217.

O'Sullivan, M. and Graham, M. 2010. 'Moving forward by looking backward: Business history and management studies', *Journal of Management Studies* **47**: 775–90.

Oswick, C., Fleming, P. and Hanlon G. 2011. 'From borrowing to blending: Rethinking the processes of organizational theory building', *Academy of Management Review* **36**: 318–37.

Page, G. (ed.) 2002. *We Kept the Secret. Now It Can Be Told – Some Memories of Pembroke V Wrens.* Wymondham, Norfolk: G. R. Reeve Ltd.

Page, G. (ed.) 2003. *They Listened in Secret. More Memories of the Wrens.* Wymondham, Norfolk: G. R. Reeve Ltd.

Page, S. E. 2007. *The Difference: How the Power of Diversity Creates Better Groups, Firms, Schools and Societies.* Princeton, NJ: Princeton University Press.

Parker, M. 2000. *Organizational Culture and Identity.* London: Sage.

Pascale, R. and Athos, A. 1982. *The Art of Japanese Management.* London: Penguin.

Paterson, M. 2007. *Voices of the Codebreakers.* Cincinnati, OH: David and Charles.

Pearson, J. 2011. *Neil Webster's Cribs for Victory. The Untold Story of Bletchley Park's Secret Room.* Clifton-upon-Teme, Worcs.: Polperro Heritage Press.

Perrow, C. 1986. *Complex Organizations: A Critical Essay.* 3rd edn. New York: Random House.

Peters, T. and Waterman, R. 1982. *In Search of Excellence.* New York: Harper and Row.

Pettigrew, A. 1985. *The Awakening Giant. Continuity and Change in ICI.* Oxford: Blackwell.

Pfeffer, J. and Salancik, G. 1978. *The External Control of Organizations: A Resource Dependence Perspective.* New York: Harper and Row.

Pitsis, T., Clegg, S., Marosszeky, M. and Rura-Polley, T. 2003. 'Constructing the Olympic dream: Managing innovation through the future perfect', *Organization Science* **14**: 574–90.

Popp, A. 2008. 'Business history', in Clegg, S. and Bailey, J. (eds.), *International Encyclopedia of Organization Studies, Vol. 1.* London: Sage, pp. 122–8.

Porter, B. 2010. 'Thank God for traitors', [Review of Aldrich (2010).] *London Review of Books* **32**: 20–2.

Pugh, D. and Hickson, D. 1976. *Organisation Structure in Its Context: The Aston Programme.* London: Saxon House.

Raisch, S., Birkinshaw, J., Probst, G. and Tushman, M. 2009. 'Organizational ambidexterity: Balancing exploitation and exploration for sustained performance', *Organization Science* **20**: 685–95.

Ratcliff, R. 2006. *Delusions of Intelligence. Enigma, Ultra and the End of Secure Ciphers*. New York: Cambridge University Press.

Reed, M. 1992. *The Sociology of Organizations. Themes, Perspectives and Prospects*. Hemel Hempstead, Herts.: Harvester Wheatsheaf.

Rehn, A. 2008. 'On meta-ideology and moralization – a prolegomena to a critique of management studies', *Organization* **15**: 598–609.

Rhodes, R. 1986. *The Making of the Atomic Bomb*. New York: Simon and Schuster.

Robbins, S. 1990. *Organization Theory: Structure, Design and Applications*. 3rd edn. Englewood Cliffs, NJ: Prentice-Hall International.

Roberts, J. 1984. 'The moral character of management practice', *Journal of Management Studies* **21**: 287–302.

Rose, S. 2003. *Which People's War? National Identity and Citizenship in Wartime Britain 1939–1945*. Oxford: Oxford University Press.

Rowlinson, M. and Hassard, J. 1993. 'The invention of corporate culture: A history of the histories of Cadbury', *Human Relations*, **46**: 299–326.

Samuel, R. (ed.) 1981. *People's History and Socialist Theory*. London: Routledge and Kegan Paul.

Sandbrook, D. 2010. *State of Emergency. The Way We Were: Britain 1970–74*. London: Allen Lane.

Schein, E. 1997. *Organizational Culture and Leadership*. 2nd edn (in paperback). San Francisco, CA: Jossey-Bass.

Sebag-Montefiore, H. 2000. *Enigma. The Battle for the Code*. London: Weidenfeld and Nicolson.

Selznick, P. 1949. *TVA and the Grass Roots*. Berkeley, CA: University of California Press.

Shenhav, Y. 1999. *Manufacturing Rationality*. Oxford: Oxford University Press.

Sheridan, D. (ed.) 1990. *Wartime Women. A Mass Observation Anthology 1937–45*. London: William Heinemann.

Simmel, G. 1906. 'The sociology of secrecy and of secret societies', *American Journal of Sociology* **11**: 441–98.

Simpson, E. 2010. 'Bayes at Bletchley Park', *Significance* **7**: 76–80.

Simpson, E. 2011. 'Solving JN-25 at Bletchley Park: 1943–5' in Erskine, R. and Smith, M. (eds) *The Bletchley Park Codebreakers*, pp. 127–46. London: Biteback. [Note: This book is a reissue of Smith and Erskine (2001) with the addition of this chapter.]

Smircich, L. 1983. 'Concepts of culture and organizational analysis', *Administrative Science Quarterly* **28**: 339–58.

Smith, H. (ed.) 1986. *War and Social Change. British Society in the Second World War*. Manchester: Manchester University Press.

Smith, M. 1998. *Station X*. Basingstoke, Hants.: Macmillan.

Smith, M. 2001. 'The Government Code and Cypher School and the first Cold War' in Smith, M. and Erskine, R. (eds.), *Action This Day*. London: Bantam, pp. 15–40.

Smith, M. 2004. 'Bletchley Park and the Holocaust', in Scott, L. and Jackson, P. (eds.), *Understanding Intelligence in the Twenty-First Century. Journeys in the Shadows*. London: Routledge, pp. 111–21.

Smith, M. and Erskine, R. (eds.) 2001. *Action This day*. London: Bantam.

Snow, C. P. 1947. *The Light and the Dark*. London: Faber and Faber.

Snow, C. P. 1962. *Science and Government. The Godkin Lectures at Harvard University, 1960. With a New Appendix*. New York and Cambridge, MA: New American Library/Harvard University Press.

Snow, P. 1982. *Stranger and Brother. A Portrait of C. P. Snow*. London: Macmillan.

Starbuck, W. H. 1992. 'Learning by knowledge-intensive firms', *Journal of Management Studies* **29**: 713–40.

Starbuck, W. H. 2003. 'Shouldn't organization theory emerge from adolescence?', *Organization* **10**: 439–52.

Steiner, G. 1983. 'Machines and the man', *Sunday Times* (London) 23 October, p. 42. [Review of Hodges (1982).]

Stiernstedt, F. and Jakobsson, P. 2009. '"Total decentring, total community": The Googleplex and informational culture', paper presented at the Annual Meeting of the International Communication Association, Marriott, Chicago IL. www. allacademic.com/meta/p298151_index.html.

Strati, A. 2000. *Theory and Method in Organization Studies: Paradigms and Choices*. London: Sage.

Strati, A. 2008. 'Organizational structure', in Clegg, S. and Bailey, J. (eds.), *International Encyclopedia of Organization Studies Vol. III*. Thousand Oaks, CA: Sage, pp. 1185–8.

Streeck, W. 2009. *Re-forming Capitalism*. Oxford: Oxford University Press.

Stripp, A. 1993. 'The Enigma machine. Its mechanism and use', in Hinsley, H. and Stripp, A. (eds.), *Codebreakers. The Inside Story of Bletchley Park*. Oxford: Oxford University Press, pp. 83–8.

Stodgill, R. M. 1974. *Handbook of Leadership: A Survey of Theory and Research*. New York: Free Press.

Suddaby, R., Hardy, C. and Huy, Q. N. 2011. 'Where are the new theories of organization?', *Academy of Management Review* **36**: 236–46.

Sugarman, M. 2008. 'Breaking the codes: Jewish personnel at Bletchley Park'. www. bletchleypark.org.uk/resources/file.rhtm/595696/breaking+the+codes+jewish +personnel+at+bletchley+park.pdf.

Summerfield, P. 1998. *Reconstructing Women's Wartime Lives*. Manchester: Manchester University Press.

Summerfield, P. and Peniston-Bird, C. 2007. *Contesting Home Defence: Men, Women and the Home Guard in Britain in the Second World War.* Manchester: Manchester University Press.

Taunt, D. 1993. 'Hut 6: 1941–1945', in Hinsley, H. and Stripp, A. (eds.), *Codebreakers. The Inside Story of Bletchley Park*. Oxford: Oxford University Press, pp. 100–12.

Taylor, S. 2007. 'The role of intelligence in national security', in Collins, A. (ed.), *Contemporary Security Studies*. Oxford: Oxford University Press, pp. 248–69.

Taylor. J. 2005. *Bletchley Park's Secret Sisters. Psychological Warfare in World War II.* Dunstable, Beds.: The Book Castle.

Taylor. J. 2009. *Bletchley and District at War. People and Places*. Copt Hewick, Yorks.: Book Castle Publishing.

Taylor, S., Bell, E. and Cooke, B. 2009. 'Business history and the historiographical operation'. *Management and Organization History*, 4: 151–66.

Thirsk, J. 2001. 'Traffic analysis: A log-reader's tale', in Smith, M. and Erskine, R. (eds.), *Action This Day*. London: Bantam, pp. 264–77.

Thirsk, J. 2008. *Bletchley Park. An Inmate's Story*. Bromley, Kent: Galago Books.

Thompson, P. 2000. *The Voice of the Past: Oral History*. 3rd edn. Oxford: Oxford University Press.

Tosh, J. 2006. *The Pursuit of History*. 4th edn (with Lang, S.). Harlow, Essex: Pearson Education.

Toms, S. and Wilson, J. 2010. 'In defence of business history: A reply to Taylor, Bell and Cooke', *Management and Organizational History* 5: 109–20.

Trice, H. M. 1993. *Occupational Subcultures in the Workplace*. Ithaca, NY: ILR Press.

Tsoukas, H. and Chia, R. 2002. 'On organizational becoming: Rethinking organizational change', *Organization Science* 13: 567–82.

Tsoukas, H and Knudsen, C. 2003. 'Introduction', in Tsoukas, H. and Knudsen, C. (eds.), *The Oxford Handbook of Organization Theory*. Oxford: Oxford University Press, pp. 1–36.

Uhi-Bien, M. 2006. 'Relational leadership theory: Exploring the social processes of leadership and organizing', *Leadership Quarterly* 17: 654–76.

Ulbricht, F. 1999. 'Enigma-Uhr', *Cryptologia* 23: 193–205.

Usdiken, B., Kipping, M. and Engwall, L. 2011. 'Historical perspectives on organizational stability and change: Introduction to the special issue', *Management and Organizational History* 6: 3–12.

Watkins, G. 2006. *Cracking the Luftwaffe codes. The Secrets of Bletchley Park.* London: Greenhill Books.

Watson, B. 1993. 'How the Bletchley Park buildings took shape', in Hinsley, H. and Stripp, A. (eds.), *Codebreakers. The Inside Story of Bletchley Park.* Oxford: Oxford University Press, pp. 306–10.

Watson, T. 1994. *In Search of Management.* London: Routledge.

Watson, T. 2011. 'Ethnography, reality and truth: The vital need for studies of "how things work" in organizations and management', *Journal of Management Studies* **48**: 202–17.

Weeks, J. 2003. *Unpopular Culture: The Ritual of Complaint in a British Bank.* Chicago, IL: University of Chicago Press.

Weick, K. 1979. *The Social Psychology of Organizing.* 2nd edn. New York: McGraw-Hill.

Weick, K. 1993. 'Organizational redesign as improvisation', in Huber, G. P. and Glick, W. H. (eds.), *Organizational Change and Redesign: Ideas and Insights for Improving Performance.* New York: Oxford University Press, pp. 346–79.

Weick, K. 1996. 'Drop your tools: An allegory for organizational studies', *Administrative Science Quarterly* **41**: 301–13.

Weick, K. 1998. 'Improvisation as a mindset for organizational analysis', *Organization Science* **9**: 543–55.

Weick, K. 2001. *Making Sense of the Organization.* Oxford: Blackwell.

Weick, K. and Roberts, J. 1993. 'Collective mind in organizations: Heedful interrelating on flight decks', *Administrative Science Quarterly* **38**: 357–81.

Welchman, G. 1982. *The Hut Six Story.* London: Penguin.

Whipp, R. and Carter, P. 1986. *Innovation and the Auto Industry. Product, Process and Work Organization.* London: Frances Pinter (Publishers) Ltd.

White, H. 1987. *The Content of the Form.* Baltimore, MD: Johns Hopkins University Press.

Wilkinson, P. 1986. *Facets of a Life.* Private publication available at King's College Archive Centre, Cambridge, The Papers of Lancelot Patrick Wilkinson KCAC/PP/LPW.

Wilkinson, P. 1993. 'Italian Naval decrypts', in Hinsley, H. and Stripp, A. (eds.), *Codebreakers. The Inside Story of Bletchley Park.* Oxford: Oxford University Press, pp. 61–7.

Willmott, H. 2011. '"Institutional work" for what? Problems and prospects of institutional theory', *Journal of Management Inquiry* **20**: 67–72.

Winterbotham, F. 1974. *The Ultra Secret.* London: Weidenfield and Nicholson.

Wright, A. 2007. *Glut: Mastering Information through the Ages.* Washington, DC: Joseph Henry Press.

Wylie, S. 2001. 'Breaking Tunny and the birth of Colossus', in Smith, M. and Erskine, R. (eds.), *Action This Day*. London: Bantam, pp. 317–41.

Zald, M. 1993. 'Organization studies as a scientific and humanistic enterprise: Toward a reconceptualization of the foundations of the field', *Organization Science*, 4: 513–28.

Zucker, L. G. 1986. 'Production of trust: Institutional sources of economic structure, 1840–1920', *Research in Organizational Behavior* 8: 53–111.

Index

Cullingham, Flying Officer Reginald 'Cully' 232
cultural identities 147
cultural studies 250
culture 258–259
  British wartime 108–109, 114–121, 258
  'dons and debs' 108, 132–135
  organizational 12–13, 107–110, 132, 138–139, 140, 165–167, 258–259
  Oxbridge 113–114, 137–139, 140, 223, 258
  structural accounts of 145–146, 153
  see also sub-cultures
Curtis, Major C. R. 66–68
Czarniawska, Barbara 250, 266–269, 271

Dad's Army 116–117
Daily Telegraph crossword winners 136
Dakin, Alex 179
Dalton, Melville 15
Davidson, Major-General Francis Henry Norman, Director of Military Intelligence (DMI) 60–61
Davies, P. 4, 94–95
D-Day landings, indoctrination and 159–160
de Grey, Nigel 1, 55, 58–60, 144, 161
  on age 162–163
  on billeting 155
  on conflicts 68
  on cover stories 141
  disputes with MI8 81, 83
  on handling of intelligence 79, 80
  and removal of Denniston 104
  management skills 210
  on intellect of staff 152–153
  meetings 197
  on organization 54
  on recruitment 136
  recruitment of 132
'debs' stereotypes 133–134
decoding (organization) 10–11, 251–254, 265
de-familiarization 6–7, 15–16, 266–267
de-naturalization 267
Denniston, Alastair 24, 33, 40, 52, 56, 89, 151, 229
  criticisms of 48, 64, 78, 210
  dispute with 90–91
  on finance 53
  Hut 3 conflicts 66–67
  lack of confidence in 91–92, 101–102
  rejection of TA operations 82–83

replacement as head of BP 89–90, 95, 100, 161
  personality 101–102
  and recruitment 180, 181
  recruitment of 132
  retirement 96
  success against Enigma 93
'Dilly's Girls' 134
discontent 191–197 see also morale
Dollis Hill 154, 176, 234
Dönitz, Admiral Karl 215
'Dr. Wynn Williams' section' 174
Drucker, Peter, 190
Dunkirk
  cultural image of 118
  spirit 116

Eachus, Joseph 52
Eastcote out station 151
emendation 198
Enigma (1995) (novel) 3, 170, 210
Enigma 34–36, 63, 252, 263
  GAF modifications 201–202
  keys 34–35, 79, 84, 196, 222–223
  and signals intelligence 79–89
  staff knowledge of 125, 131, 159–160
  Uhr 223–224
  see also Air Enigma; Army Enigma; Intelligence Enigma; Naval Enigma; Railway Enigma
environmental conditions
enwisement (indoctrination) 123–124, 125, 131, 159–161, 233
Erskine, R. 133, 142, 231
ethnicity 164
Ettinghausen, Walter 172
Etzioni, A. 7
European Group for Organization Studies 42
Evans, D. 38
Eytan, W. 164, 179

Far East Combined Bureau (FECB) 229
Filby, William 179–180
Fish 35, 125, 171, 252
Fletcher, Harold 210
Foreign Office (FO) 52–53
Foss, Hugh 230
Fox-Mail, Joyce 133
Freeborn, Frederick 186, 232–233

Printed in the United States
By Bookmasters